Land Warmed by a Song

An Original Screenplay

By Temur Chkuaseli

Rustaveli Publishing LLC
Chicago, IL 2019

Land Warmed by a Song

Published by Rustaveli Publishing LLC
Chicago, Illinois

ISBN-13: 978-1-7339582-0-2
ISBN-10: 1-7339582-0-7

Translated from Georgian by Maia Gvitidze
Book cover design by Tamaz Varvaridze
Cover Photos from Irakli Makharadze's collection

www.rustavelipublishing.com

PRAISE FOR *LAND WARMED BY A SONG*

"According to the author, The Land Warmed by Song is a script, but it reads like an exciting little novel to any reader. Only a writer can so skillfully string many dramatic stories, which developed around a sweet Georgian family and unfortunately ended tragically. The action takes place in Europe and Georgia during WWI and WWII.

The hero of the first one is the father and of the second – the son. Their biographies are very similar – they were both war prisoners, and both escaped their deaths due to the Georgian song. However, after safely returning home, they were persecuted by the Bolsheviks. Such historical facts are not uncommon for us" -

Natia Megrelishvili
Art historian/critic

"It is a wonderful, expressly visual and, at the same time, universal story that can serve as the basis for a very interesting, impressive feature film.
The Land Warmed by Song encompasses an entire epoch. The story about the song that saves the main characters from imminent death becomes the main concept of the book: the art will save humanity.

Although the story has a precise geographic location, it is not a local story. It is interesting for citizens of any country, for people of any age. It's a human story" -

Giorgi Ovashvili
Georgian film director

Table of Contents

Part One

***

France. A noisy street in the heart of Paris... A typical Parisian café... An older man is sitting at the window seat, with a cup of coffee on the table in front of him. There are several old faded sheets of paper lying on the table in a disorderly manner; his glasses are placed on one of the sheets of paper. The man sips his coffee, puts the cap back on the table and starts talking to us (the audience).

- Hello. I am Albert Beberak, I am Jewish. I live in Lyon, France. My father told me that our family had moved here from Georgia. My father's surname was Beberashvili, as it sounds in Georgian. As for me, I was born here, and I became Albert Beberak.

When I was born Adolph Hitler had already written: “Mein Kampf” - a theoretical foundation of physical destruction of millions of Jews and me among them. As soon as Nazi Germany occupied France, the persecution of local Jewish families began, but then I was too small to actually realize the fear of death. Only later my father told me that a perpetual fear – the fear of death - was in the air round the clock.
Pause. Albert Beberak takes a sheet of paper from the table, looks at it, puts on his glasses, and only after that he continues:
- But, one day, while being held hostage to the anticipation of death, this paper was delivered to our door. It is a very short message, so I allow myself to read it to the end.
“Mr. Pinas Beberashvili! I, the undersigned Joseph Eligulashvili, president of the Community of Mosaic Georgians in France, certify that, according to the decision of the Occupation Authorities, Mosaic Georgians are not considered Jewish.
Consequently, any measures administered against the Jewish community are not to be taken against them as they are referred to as the citizens of France of Georgian origin.
The list of the members of the community has been submitted to the Occupation Authorities. You and your family are entered in the list under the number 28.
Therefore, the Occupation Authorities consider you as Aryan ...
Paris, the 25th day of February 1942."

- It seems almost inconceivable that anyone could think of and succeed in misleading the Nazis to believe that we are simply Mosaic confessors, and specimens of Georgian “race” - pure-blooded Georgians. Or, after all, who managed to find the time and the courage to jeopardize their own existence in times of universal reign of chaos and why?!

Later, when I started to realize a lot of things in this world, naturally, I began to search for the answers to these questions. It turned out that our family, along with those of hundreds of others’, had been rescued by Georgians, Moreover, by the Georgians, who were themselves fleeing the Communist Regime.

Georgian emigrants to France had come up with the idea to save us. The idea was executed. That is how I first heard the name of probably not a world-famous person but the one who is the most valuable and dearest for me - Michael Kedia, a Georgian, the man, whose fervency literally grabbed the lives of 100 Georgian families of Jewish origin living in France out of the clutches of IMPENDING death, and as if that was not enough for one person, he saved the lives of 99 Juguti families - descendants of Persian and Turkestan Jews - in the same way. Unfortunately, it is impossible to list the individuals saved by him, but we do know that there were quite a lot of such cases as well.

Thanks to Mikhail Kedia, we also managed to ESCHEW[1] THE HUMILIATION OF wearing a yellow Star of David.

---

[1] deliberately avoid using; abstain from. synonyms: abandon, avoid, renounce

So, the Georgians, with the help of Mikhail Kedia saved the lives of their Jewish compatriots, and as far as I remember, this is an unprecedented event in the whole of Europe and maybe in the whole world...
He looks down at the table and continues:
- There are many other similarly interesting documents here. They came to me from my father's personal archive. They came and stirred up my sentiments. There are a couple of letters of gratitude to Mikhail Kedia. One of them is signed by Chief Rabbi of Paris, but... The point is that not only these faded sheets of paper should keep the memory of Mikhail Kedia's contribution and commitment. I strongly believe that he deserves more than that.
Sixty-seven years have elapsed. Sixty-seven years ago, these humble sheets of paper were priceless. Sixty-seven years later I learn that the events described in these papers were made into the film "Land Warmed by a Song." I also learned that the film featured the strange fate of some Georgian prisoners of war as well as the developments narrated in these faded sheets of paper.
I was so excited. I was looking forward to this film being shown in France, and here it is...
He turns his face to the window and through the window, across the street, we can see a cinema house and a billboard advertising the film and featuring the characters of the film and the title of the film "Land Warmed by a Song" written in large letters.
Albert Beberak LOOKS AT HIS WATCH, then collects the sheets of paper scattered on the table, puts them in a case placed against the leg of the table on the floor, stands up and says:
- I am going to see this film. The next film show starts soon ... I invite all of you to come and see the film...

He puts his hand in the jacket pocket, takes out some coins, puts them on the table and walks out of the café. Through the shop window we watch him crossing the street and disappearing behind a large glass door of the cinema.
A crowded cinema hall… the face of Albert Beberak can be distinguished in the crowd. The light goes out and after a second the film starts.

***

A coniferous[2] forest covering the slope of the Alps… It is a summer morning. In the background of birds singing, we can hear people talking. There is a small field among the trees of the forest, where we can see seven young men. Five of them are sitting leaned against tree trunks on the ground. One of the young men is standing his back pressed against a tree trunk and one of them is sitting on a dead tree branch, brought down by high winds or heavy snow, twirling dry needles on the branch between his fingers. Everyone seems tired with sleepless red eyes. The young man sitting on a tree branch says:
Gigi: If only I could find a dry leaf somewhere…
Dachi: why do you need a dry leaf, Gigi? I'd understand if you wished to find dried fruit here…
Gigi: Why? I would crumble it and wrap it in a paper, like tobacco. I tried doing this with needles, but it tasted awful… bitter… pah!

---

[2] vegetation composed primarily of cone-bearing needle-leaved or scale-leaved evergreen trees, found in areas that have long winters and moderate to high annual precipitation. The northern Eurasian **coniferous forest** is called the taiga

Thoma: My dad was fond of cutting tobacco leaves. Though, to tell you the truth, I don't quite know whether he loved doing this or not. I know that he used to cut tobacco leaves; I loved watching him doing this. First, he whetted a knife; rubbing it earnestly against a whetstone, slowly… like this… he would put tobacco leaves twisted together… on a plank placed on his lap… and go… The knife was so sharp… a Georgian knife, with crosses engraved on the bone handle. And the odor around... I have never smoked tobacco, but I'm crazy about its odor. I could smell it for hours. Dad kept the tobacco in a wooden box in the attic. All I wanted was to take the lid off the box and stick my nose in the pile of tobacco leaves, but I would not dare, I was afraid ... I was afraid of being caught by Dad; he would think I smoked ... and I was afraid. Though, Friday was a market day. There was a separate row for tobacco. So, I used to go there, I could stand there all day and smell tobacco.

Batsi: For God's sake, stop talking about tobacco! We've already devoured all the snacks we had. Evening is not a problem and we'll manage to survive till tomorrow morning, but what shall we do after that?!

Thoma: Don't panic. We aren't going to be starved to death. We are in the woods after all… we might find a bird's nest or berries. There are thousands of things we can think of. If only the Germans stopped chasing us, and then I know what I'll do.

Batsi: What will you do? Will you heap up charcoal and let us have a barbeque? (Laughing)

Ushba: Come on… where's barbeque? But Thoma is right… we should search for birds' nests.

Thoma: yeah, birds… You see they remind me of my dad…

Jango: Why? Did he finish cutting tobacco leaves and switched to birds' nests?

Thoma: Let me finish, Jango, tobacco has nothing to do with it! My dad met a German archeologist in Guria[3]; he was staying at someone's house in Ozurgeti[4]. Dad knew German well, he taught me to speak the language.
Batsi: Where did he learn German, in Guria?
Thoma: Where? He was a prisoner of war in Germany, just like us, but it was during the first war, the war that was before this one. It was there that he learned German.
Jango: Ok, go on, you were talking about birds…
Thoma: Well, do you remember the toy I gave to Maria? for her son… With the image of a cage on one side and the image of a bluebird on the other… A German man gave this toy to my dad… for me. It was the only toy I had in my childhood… I loved it… You know… I used to carry it with me everywhere… in my pocket… until I gave it to Maria.
Beso: It was a really great thing. A cage was on one side, a bluebird - on the other, and when you spun it, you would see the bluebird in the cage. I've got no idea why we saw it this way! Weren't the images on different sides?
Jango: Before a Rachian[5] understands why it happens so, the bluebird will pierce the cardboard with its beak and really enter into the cage.
Young people start laughing. Jango continues.

---

[3] A province in the western Georgia

[4] A village in Guria, a province

[5] A province in the western Georgia

Jango: But why did you recall that bird and the cage, Thoma? It seems to me that you wanted to say something, didn't you? We all do remember that toy; we used to play with it when Beso went to sleep. But why now…

Thoma: Why? I don't know… Maybe our life is like that of the bluebird…

Dachi: Will it fly away like a bird?

Thoma: No, I wanted to say that our life is an illusion like that toy. You live in peace and quiet, then, someone like Hitler comes up with some insane ideas, grabs hold of the strings of your life and spins them so rapidly… that you find yourself in a cage right away. He spins and spins them and bam! You're in a cage! He spins again and bams! Cage… we are 5 thousand kilometers away from our homes… What the hell are we doing here?! Did anybody ask us whether we wanted to be here or not? What are we after? What are we looking for?

Jango: We are looking for birds' nests, right now; we'll see what we are going to look for next…

Thoma: Even now, we are planning something, and the cage might be waiting for us nearby.

Jango: Bam! And Cage? Do you say?

Young people laugh again.

Thoma: Thank God, we can all find reasons to laugh… OK, let's do something: I'll go up the hill. I have noticed a tall tree. I'll try to climb the tree and see if I can find something in the surroundings, some building maybe. I'll be back soon. Try to have a nap. We have been walking all night…

Dachi: If you want to conquer a height, you don't have to go far. You can climb Ushba…

Young people start laughing again.

Ushba: Don't you want me to go with you, Thoma? Maybe you need my help when climbing the tree.

Thoma: No, I don't, Ushba, you need a rest. I'll be back soon. Don't worry; everything's going to be all right.

Thoma starts walking towards the trees and disappears behind them. The boys fall asleep.

Thoma walks down the hill between the trees. He seems full of vim and vigor with a HOPEFUL EXPRESSION ON HIS FACE. When he approaches the field, where he left his friends, all of a sudden, he stops dead in his tracks and we can see his big sad eyes out on stalks. We can hear music, Thoma tries to hide behind a tree trunk, but we can still see his eyes wide-opened.

***

World War I… The Eastern front… Russian soldiers are sheltered in the trenches. Gunfire… German aircraft flies over the trenches at a very low altitude. Then something resembling white mist spreads over the ground and towards the trenches. Desperate shouts and shouts of warning in Russian. "Газ! Газ!"[6] can be heard.

Soldiers creep out of their trenches en masse[7] along the entire front line and run to escape the cloud of poisonous gas but in vain, the wind blows in their direction and the cloud of poisonous gas moves fast towards them.

Opening credits start running on the screen on top of the above scene, which continuous till the end of the opening credits.

A virile[8] young man is in a trench. There is no one around. The man watches white fog approaching him, then he takes something resembling a large handkerchief out of his pocket, looks around, his eyes rest on a soldier's body lying face down. He goes near the body, turns him over and feels his pulse. Unfortunately, the soldier shows no sign of being alive; he moves his hand over the dead person's eyes to close them and then turns his head to look back at the field. The white fog is almost above the trench. He bents down dip his handkerchief in a pool of blood, puts the handkerchief to his nose and mouth and lies face down in the trench. We see the white fog filling the trench and engulfing everything: the trench, the young man and the field itself.

---

[6] Gas! Gas!

[7] A stroke made with an inclined cue, imparting swerve to the ball.

[8] (of a man) having strength, energy, and a strong sex drive. Synonyms: manly, masculine

Opening credits still run along with the screen.
The same field and the same trench… German soldiers march towards the trench in pairs along the almost entire front line. Two of them stop at the very point of the trench where the two soldiers are lying – one of them alive and the other dead. One of the German soldiers points his shotgun at the soldiers lying in the trench and shouts in German:
- Stand up and come out of the trench…

Neither of the soldiers reacts to his command. But suddenly, one of them, lying face down in the trench starts coughing. German soldier jumps in the trench and turns the one coughing, exposing his face covered in blood, and we see his eyes wide open and glowing like the eyes of a frightened animal in the darkness. At this time opening credits stop running along the screen and we hear:
- Look, Luther! Russians have sent vampires to fight us in this war.

***

An ad hoc POW (prisoner-of-war) camp set up near the railway station in the eastern part of Berlin. A caption on the screen: 'Berlin, 1915'
Lots of ragged, exhausted, dirty prisoners of war with faces deprived of any emotions lie directly on the ground. They are mostly Russians of Slavic appearance. German love of order can be seen and found nowhere in the camp. Barbed-wire fences and armed German soldiers dressed in the military uniforms of World War I can are seen around.

A commandant's room... The commandant is sitting at the table and talking to a guest. The guest is about 40 years old dressed in civilian clothes.

Commandant: I was told about your visit yesterday at the headquarters. A great plan, you need neither expedition nor unnecessary expenses. You can work without leaving Berlin. So, it seems someone can still benefit from this war.

Both men smile.

Commandant: Half of Russia is here, come and work. (Looks at his watch and continues) We can start in twenty minutes... they will be arranged by then.

Guest: Yeah, but, you see, we don't know what the contingent is like out there... So, it happens sometimes that you fail to find a normal singer in a group of 1000 people...

Commandant: You don't say so... it's hard to believe, there are so many people out there! What you have to do is only to give them a chance to escape the place and all of them will start singing, no matter whether they can or not.

Guest: They all might start singing, but the matter of fact is how. I'm only interested in traditional songs... old, authentic and undefiled. That's difficult to find.

Commandant: Let's see. Maybe you are lucky to find one... would you like a coffee ... or something more serious?

Guest: Thank you, only coffee, please. I wish I found something more serious among the prisoners.

We see the prisoners at the prison camp following the command of a German soldier who can speak a little Russian. He is the one who gives commands with a strong typical German accent. His strong and loud voice can be heard through a megaphone. The prisoners are being arranged in groups.

- 50 people per group. Stand in a row of ten, five in length... on both sides of the field. Fast! Fast! (Sometimes he also gives the command in German) Schnell! Schnell!
The commandant and his guest finish drinking their coffee. There is a knock on the door.
Commandant: Come in!
An adjutant enters.
Adjutant: Everything is ready, Sir.
Commandant: very good, we are coming. Where is the interpreter?
Adjutant: The interpreter is waiting for you in the field, sir.
Commandant: OK, let's go.
The commandant stands up. The guest stands up too and is about to follow the commandant with a cup of coffee in his hand. Then suddenly he stops, looks at the cup, smiles, turns around, puts his cup on the table and follows the commandant.
The commandant, his guest, and the adjutant walked out of a mediocre single-storied building. The commandant casts a brief look at the field.
Commandant: Look, there are so many of them there. It will take a long time to examine them ... shall we use a megaphone to instruct them and only those who know something will have to stay? And ... we'll instruct the rest to leave... this will make our task easier...

Guest: No, this will be a waste of time. They'll get confused. I prefer them to stay where they stand, and I'll talk to each group separately. I'll look in their eyes and immediately find out whether any of them is worth being listened to.

Commandant: As you wish. I guess you even plan to make some of them sing right here. I'll gladly listen to them and have a little bit of fun; you see I am so tired of this ugly monotony. (Turning to the adjutant) Where is the interpreter?!

The interpreter is standing just behind the commandant. He quickly steps forward and says:

- Here I am, sir.

Commandant: OK, let's start then.

The commandant, his guest, the adjutant, and the interpreter approach the first group of prisoners. They stop in front of the group which is mostly comprised of the prisoners of Slavic appearance.

Commandant: Listen carefully. This person is Mr. Werner Pere, a famous musician, a Berlin University professor. He is interested in traditional Russian songs ... (he stops and looks at the interpreter. The interpreter starts interpreting. The commandant turns to the guest) Russian songs, and if I'm not mistaken, you mentioned Cossack folk songs as well, didn't you?

Guest: Yes, Cossack songs as well… if anybody knows one…

The interpreter finishes interpreting his words and looks back at the commandant.

Commandant: Russian folk songs and Cossack songs as well... Those who know one raise your hands and we will speak to each separately. That's all for now...

The interpreter interprets these words as well. A close-up view of the faces… Nobody utters a word, and nobody raises their hands. There is a kind of tension around. The commandant's and the professor's faces show signs of impatience.

Professor: They might be frightened! (He turns to the interpreter) Tell them that we are going to take with us those who express the willingness to cooperate with us, i.e. those who know a folk song or even a verse of a song, and that they will enjoy better living conditions.

The interpreter interprets everything immediately, but in vain. Not a single person shows any interest in what they hear. After waiting for a while, the commandant throws up his hands and says:

Commandant: I think we are wasting our time with them. Can't you see the faces of these Russians? I'm not even sure they understand what we say to them.

The commandant, his guest, the adjutant and the interpreter move to the next group of prisoners and the commandant starts again.

Commandant: Listen carefully. This person is a famous musician and a scientist, a Berlin University professor. He is interested in Russian songs and Cossack songs as well... folk songs, in short. Raise your hands if you know and can sing such songs. We will let you leave this camp… of course, after an appropriate examination…

The interpreter interprets his words. There is silence for a while among the members of this group as well. Then a prisoner - a typical Russian man - raises his hand and asks:

Prisoner: - А гармонь дадите?[9]

Everyone looks at the interpreter. He immediately says in German.

- He is asking for an accordion…

Professor: Tell him an accordion will wait. Let's first listen to him singing to find out how good he is at singing and we'll see what's next.

---

[9] Would you give me an accordion?

The interpreter interprets his words and the Russian prisoner immediately steps forward, he opens wide his arms in a way characteristic of Russian dance, stamps his feet and says in a singing voice:

Prisoner: Эх, мама родная, была, не была[10]... (First, he imitates playing the accordion with his hands as well as with his voice and then suddenly starts singing a Russian Chastushka[11] in terribly unpleasant, almost shouting voice):

Мы с миленьком целовались
Целых сорок пять минут!
Только встали и оделись,
Наши жены – тут как тут!

The Germans watch the performance for a little while with smiles on their faces. Even the prisoners watch this stupidity and smile. Eventually the professor throws his hands up in despair and heads towards the next group of prisoners. The commandant says with a strict tone:

- Stop it!

The interpreter repeats his wards in Russian with even stricter tone and the team follows the professor.

The team approaches the next group of prisoners. The man we saw lying in a trench, with a blood-soaked handkerchief at the beginning of the film, is among the group of prisoners. His face is no longer covered in blood, but he stands out among the rest of the group members by his looks, together with the two prisoners standing next to him.

The commandant starts again:

- Listen attentively! This gentleman is famous...

---

[10] Come hell or high water

[11] A traditional type of short Russian or Ukrainian folk humorous song with high beat frequency

Suddenly a prisoner interrupts him. This is the very man who looks so different from the other group members.
Prisoner: You don't have to bother and repeat everything, we've been listening to you and we know well what you are looking for. I have a question if you allow me to ask you.
The commandant looking quite surprised turns his face to the interpreter.
Interpreter: He says they have heard everything and know...
Commandant: What do they know? Do they know how to sing?
Interpreter: He didn't say. He only wants to know if he is allowed to ask you a question.
Commandant: He is allowed if it has something to do with songs.
Interpreter: If your question is about songs, you are allowed to ask it…
Prisoner: Of course, it is about songs… Is a professor interested in only Russian songs?
After this question asked by the prisoner, the following dialogue takes place between the prisoner and the professor, with the help of the interpreter.
Professor: Do you mean that you can sing some other songs?!
Prisoner: Not other songs… we sing our own songs, we aren't Russian.
Professor: Who are you, who else do you mean?
Prisoner: Me and the guys standing beside me. We are Georgian.
Professor: Georgian? It's interesting. I have heard about you, more precisely, about your songs. Mr. Bucher wrote about you in his famous work "The Music of the Nations of the World". A whole chapter of the book is dedicated to your songs. Have you heard about Mr. Bucher?

Prisoner: No, never...
Professor: But he is so inspired ... I can assure you that he doesn't speak about the music of any nation with the admiration and enthusiasm he displays while speaking about Georgian folk music... or maybe it only seems to me? Well, let's leave alone Mr. Bucher. However, he writes that the songs of the East and West Georgia differ considerably, and the polyphony of West Georgian folk songs is so distinguished. Don't you know anything about it either?!
Prisoner: Of course, the man is absolutely right.
Professor: And where are you from, which part of Georgia?
Prisoner: We... all three of us are from West Georgia.
Professor: And you claim that you can sing polyphonic songs? Or at least one?
The professor can't hide his excitement in anticipation of a positive response and while the interpreter translates his words he turns to the commandant:
Professor: If this Georgian man is telling the truth, it means that we have found a treasure chest full of gold.
Prisoner: I don't quite understand the meaning of this word. How do you say? Yes, polyphony. If you explain to me what you mean, I will try to answer.
Professor: What does polyphony mean? I'll explain it to you. Polyphony is a Greek word and means "many sounds". Music is polyphonic when more than one tones sound simultaneous. The word implies an additional nuance when we talk about the song, but this time let's stop talking about it and let me ask you again: will you really sing different tones?
Prisoner: Now we understand. Yes, Professor. After all, there are three of us here and, naturally, we will sing in three voices. Well, otherwise what's the point?

Professor: Behold! I've got one more question. Mr. Bucher mentions the name of a Georgian person in his work, the person who helped him. His surname is Berdzenov. Do you have such a surname in Georgia?
Prisoner: You probably mean Berdzenishvili; the surname of my neighbors. They live in the region I am from as well as this young man (he points to a prisoner standing next to him).
Professor: can you tell me how many songs you know?
Prisoner: Personally, I know a lot of songs. I can't say exactly how many, because I have never counted them. Anyway, we need a little time to practice a song. You see we have never sung together.
Professor: OK, I do understand.
The commandant joins in the conversation.
Commandant: So, you need time?! Are you planning anything and try to gain time? I warn you, beware! This rally could end badly… badly for you.
Prisoner: Why badly? You asked, and I answered. That's it. What on earth might we be planning? You can see very well, we are prisoners of war and do you really think we have any choice?
Professor: I do agree with you. But ... you know what, will you still sing something, even one verse... just to find out whether it is worth trying.
Prisoner: Do you mean singing here, right now? No! I did not say we would sing here, I said, I could sing.
Commandant: Why, what's the problem? If you are thirsty, tell us, and they will give you water if you are hungry, and you probably are, they will give you something to eat... but only after you sing.

Prisoner: No, it has nothing to do with being thirsty or even hungry. We will certainly endure hunger... But, Professor, you noted a minute ago that West Georgian songs are particularly complex, didn't you? We all, the three of us come from different villages. We have never met one another before; we only saw one another here and how can we sing so carelessly? This would mean being disrespectful not only towards you but towards the song itself. We need time, a little time...
Professor: How much time? A week? A month? Or a year? (A hint of sarcasm can be detected in professor's voice)
The prisoner turns to the man standing beside him and talks to them in Georgian. Only fragments from their conversation can be heard: - Which one, the short?! Yes, that's easy ... Of course, ... Yes, yes ... One is enough. Then he turns again to the interpreter and says in Russian.
Prisoner: One!
Professor: One what? One week or one month?
Prisoner: One hour.
The professor and the commandant look at each other. Then both of them smile.
Commandant: Only an hour?
Prisoner: Yes, sir. One hour is enough for what you need. We will prepare a song in an hour and if you like it, we can decide then what to do next.
Commandant: Everything is so crystal clear now. So, we'll give you two hours. Follow the interpreter right now. They'll give you something to eat and ... (he looks at the professor) maybe a glass of schnapps for each... to reward them beforehand... what would you say?!
Professor: Why not? If they want to... They'll feel encouraged.

Commandant (to the interpreter): take them to my room, then go to the chef and tell him to make three sandwiches for them.
Interpreter: And what about schnapps?
Commandant: Yes, schnapps as well... a tot of schnapps for each of them... Yes, and find out if there is a smoker among them and... there is an ashtray on the table there. OK, go... remember, the timer is on. Professor and I will go to the town and will be back in two hours.
Georgian prisoners follow the interpreter. Professor together with the commandant walks towards the gates. The rest of the prisoners are ordered to be dismissed.

***

The Commandant's room... The interpreter enters the room and leads the prisoners in the room.
Interpreter: Get organized and start. I'll go and fetch the things I've been ordered. Don't touch anything... or it's going to be your swansong. (The interpreter leaves the room)
First prisoner: I did expect everything, brothers, except that. Would they really find our songs interesting?
Second prisoner: We'll see... in two hours. Anyway, we are given a chance and we don't have to miss it, don't you agree with me?
Third prisoner: You're right, it's worth trying. If we are lucky enough to escape this place, we won't be starved to death after all.
First prisoner: OK, we don't have much time either, and we can't afford wasting it on small talks. Let's first decide who is going to sing which voice, and then let's choose something easy to sing and practice it a little.

Third prisoner: Didn't we agree on a short Mravalzhamieri?[12] I'll sing higher.
First prisoner: Will you? Then I'll sing the lead and Kalistrate has to sing bass.
Kalistrate: Ok, let it be bass. To be honest, I wanted to sing bass. Theopile, let's start, let's find out if we can make it.
Theopile is about to start singing, but he stops shortly after singing several notes because the interpreter enters the room together with another soldier, who puts the commandant's gifts on the table.
Interpreter: Our commandant is so generous... Remember that you owe him. I've brought a tot of schnapps for each of you. If any of you don't want it, tell me now and I'll immediately take it back. (There is a smile on his face. The commandant is gone, and he seems to feel a little bit encouraged. He is the one who controls the situation at the given moment.) Ok, why don't you say anything? (He takes a pack of cigarettes out of his pocket and puts it on the table.) There are several cigarettes and matches in this pack; you may take a puff.
Theopile: You just leave everything here and...we will take care of them.
Kalistrate (in Georgian): They've given each of us a thimble of schnapps, bastards! I hoped to be encouraged a little; I am really lily-livered about all these.
Interpreter: Tell him to speak Russian in my presence. Now I'm going to leave you. As for him, he will stay and wait for you outside and listen to you as well.

---

[12] A traditional Georgian feast song

The interpreter grins and leaves the room. The soldier follows him and closes the door behind him. The three young men gather around the table. There is a plate with sliced sandwiches on it and another one with three tiny glasses full of schnapps on the table. The young men take the glasses and clink them before making a short toast speech.
- May God have mercy on us all... May God help us to return to our families safe and sound! Amen! Amen!
The young men empty their glasses and start eating sandwiches.

***

The professor and the commandant are having dinner at a café. There is a bottle of wine on the table. The commandant looks through the glass full of wine to the light and says:
Commandant: This wine is feculent like Europe. (He sips the wine and continues) It tastes not bad... But as to Europe, it's gone mad, I think. A prince was shot in Sarajevo and Europe is wounded. Our once pragmatic and old Continent is like a demolished ant colony. Everyone is confused.
Professor: Judging according to the number of prisoners of war, things aren't going bad in the front.

Commandant: You don't say so. Germany is being overwhelmed by the number of prisoners of war; especially by the prisoners from the Eastern Front. The lives of people are worth nothing to the Russian government. They treat them as cannon fodder. There is a continuous flow of prisoners of war, though in no way is this reflected on the front line; the ranks there being filled on a daily basis. Fighting with the British and French has turned into a tradition for us. We have got a lot in common, but as for the Russians... It's hard to understand them. They seem to be doomed to eternal torment by our Heavenly Father. They withstand everything and obey everyone.

Professor: Historically it has always been the case. Recently I read a book by an English traveler; his surname is Spencer. He traveled to the Caucasus in the 30-es of the last century. It turns out that he was there when the Russian soldiers were building a road from the North Caucasus southward, towards the country the Georgians are from – the young men we left in your room. Spencer describes some astonishing facts: A number of soldiers were assigned to guard the posts at cannons with burning wicks in their hands, while others equipped with only pickaxes and shovels were busy building the road. All of a sudden, the brave highlanders would descend from the mountains of the Caucasus, kill everyone, and the very next day the ranks would be filled anew. And so, on endlessly. Can you imagine? They managed to build the road and today nobody cares about how many thousands of lives the endeavor took.

Commandant: Do Georgians belong to the Caucasian race?

Professor: Yes, they do. Georgia is situated in the South Caucasus. Spencer, as well as German botanist Robert Koch, provides us with so many interesting facts about the country and the people, but the facts that interest me the most are entered into the book by Bucher. This is the book I mentioned not long ago. By the way, while talking to that young Georgian I didn't tell him that Bucher had never listened to a Georgian song and unlike Spencer and Koch had never been to Georgia. As if it is not enough, he had only met one Georgian man, I've already mentioned his name – Berdzenov, who presumably was studying at a German University when Bucher wrote his book. The book was published in 1899. He might have been studying at our university in Berlin. When I happen to be there I have to search the archives. This way or that, Bucher was a great old man. He sounds so convincing when talking about the phenomenon of Georgian songs as if he had spent half of his life there in Georgia. He dedicated a whole chapter of his book to Georgia and Georgian songs. Just imagine he included several Georgian song notes in his book.

Commandant: Yea, but how did he manage this? If there were lyrics included, that would be understandable, but notes…

Professor: Berdzenov might have helped him by singing some tones, or he might have brought the notes from Georgia. Otherwise, it's unimaginable.

Commandant: He might have had someone else helping him besides Berdzenov.

Professor: I'm not sure. By the way, approximately a decade ago Pate's firm managed to record several Georgian songs in Georgia. They say the records are stored in London, but, unfortunately, I have never listened to the records. So, if we are lucky today... If those Georgians do not make us listen to something stupid like that Russian did... OK, let's wait and see!
Commandant: somehow, I think we are going to listen to something special. That Georgian guy looks like a normal person. I mean the guy that talked to us. Didn't you notice the way he responded? With dignity: "I did not say we would sing here, I said, I could sing." These kinds of people are the ones who can be trusted, I think.
Professor: Let's see. May God hear you! I also have a feeling that I'm standing at the threshold of a great discovery. One step forward and ... do we have to wait long? (He looks at his watch) Ah, it's time to go. If we are fortunate today, I will take the three of them to my farm. They'll have to live there, work and rehearse. They will have to work for free, but they won't die of starvation. Shall we go?
Commandant: Of course. To be honest I'm a little nervous.
Professor: Oh, don't ask me. (He looks around the hall, in hope to catch a glimpse of a waiter, and then he turns to his companion) Let me pay for you.
Commandant: No, you are my guest today. If the Georgians prove themselves worthy, then it'll be your turn. (The commandant puts money on the table and both men walk out of the cafe).

***

We return to the commandant's room. The table is cleared. The men speak with each other.

Gregory: We did it! This song is ready, but if we are fortunate enough to escape this place, then we'll have to work hard. I personally know ten songs, not more. My dad used to say to me: "Let me teach you the songs my boy, till I'm alive. Maybe one day you'll use them somehow." So, you see, his words came true! I would never have imagined that one day I would be captured and demanded to sing?

Theopile: You know ten songs; I can sing thirty, or more; maybe Kalistrate knows some as well so that will do. The point is whether we will manage to escape this place so easily.

This time the door opens. The commandant, professor, and interpreter come into the room. The young men immediately stand up and line up against the wall. The commandant sits down at his desk; the professor takes his sit on a chair standing nearby; the interpreter is still standing.

Commandant: How are things going?

Interpreter: As you instructed, Mr. Commandant, sandwiches and a glass of schnapps for each.

Commandant: very good. Then ask if they are ready. And ask them how they prefer to sing, tell them they can sit while singing.

The interpreter translates his words.

Theopile: No, we'd rather stand while singing.

The interpreter translates his words.

First, the commandant looks at the professor; waits until the latter shows readiness by nodding his head and says:

Commandant: of course, they may start.

Theopile starts singing. Gregory and Kalistrate join him soon. They are singing short Mravalzhamieri. They start off modestly, but with every other note, they gain strength, courage, and confidence. Against the background of the young men singing we have close-up views of the faces in turns: faces of the singers, the face of the commandant, the face of the professor. Everyone seems to be excited. The young men go on singing; the song reaches the climax and slowly moves towards the end. Then all three singers' voices traditionally merge in unison and this pure unison gradually disappears.

Silence permeates through the room. The professor is sitting with his head downcast and says nothing. The commandant is looking at him waiting for his reaction. Silence gradually becomes inconvenient. The young men are standing at the wall and look confused. Theopile breaks the silence and speaks up in Russian, his voice betraying his disappointment.

Theopile: I guess we have to go…

On hearing his words, the professor raises his head and looks at the interpreter.

Interpreter: They are asking for permission to go.

Professor: (in a wondering manner) Where to?

The interpreter shrugs his shoulders.

Professor: (stands up and utters one single word while trying to hide his emotions) Bravo! (Then he smiles and repeats) Bravo! (The commandant leaves his seat with a smile; the professor turns to him and says) I think they have no idea what a treasure they keep in their throats. (Then he again turns to the young men and says) That's it, starting from now you have to forget this cursed war. Tomorrow we'll start another war on another front.

* * *

Top views of Germany... A caption appears on the screen: “Two years later”
We see a lone rider from above, riding an ambling horse on a plateau covered with bright green grass. We are approaching the rider to see that the rider is a woman of an extremely charming appearance.
The rider approaches a huge gate. A beautiful detached house can be seen in the yard beyond the gate. Without getting down off her horse, she knocks on the gate with the handle of the whip. Shortly after a middle-aged man comes out of the smaller gate next to the huge gate and welcomes her joyfully and in a respectful manner.
Alfred: Fräulein Lola, I am so happy to see you, when did you come back?
Lola: Hello, Alfred, you are the same you haven't changed at all. Is my brother at home? I miss him so much... I came back last night.
Alfred: just a moment! Fräulein Lola... I'll open the gate right now. (He disappears behind the gate and immediately sticks his head through the gate and says), Yes, Mr. Werner is at home. He is upstairs working in his study. I'll open the gate, and then I'll go upstairs and tell him you are here.
Lola: No, Alfred, there is no need to warn him. I'll go and see him myself... You just take the horse... It must be thirsty and bring it to water. (Lola gently strokes the horse's neck)
Alfred opens the gate; Fräulein Lola enters the yard and gets off the horse; she gives the bridle to Alfred and heads towards the house. She stops in the midway and turns to Alfred.

Lola: Wait a minute, Alfred, I have to take something. (She walks towards the horse reaches up to a leather bag hanging on the saddle, takes a wrapped thing out of it, continues her way towards the house and disappears behind the door)

Werner Pere is in a room resembling a library; he is sitting on a swivel chair with his back turned to the grand piano; there is a sheet music book lying open on the small table in front of him and he is writing something in this book. He puts down the pencil on the table; stretches his right hand to the keyboard of the grand piano and plays an accord characteristic to Georgian songs several times. He smiles, starts writing again, and says to himself:
Werner: My God, what a wonderful way to think creatively…
At this very moment, the door opens, and Fräulein Lola enters the room. Werner jumps up from his chair with joy as soon as he sees Lola coming into the room.
Werner: Lola... When? how? It's so unexpected… (Werner approaches his sister with his arms wide open and they hug each other in sheer joy) How could you do this to me? Why didn't you tell me you were coming? Did anybody meet you at the station?
Lola: Yes, the Red Cross. I wanted it to be a surprise for you.
Werner: You really managed that. I am so happy ... I prepared at least a thousand questions to ask you but now I saw you and I'm afraid I don't remember any. Just imagine, I can't even recall one.
Lola: Don't worry, you'll recall everything. If you want, I will remind you… something surely concerning polyphony of African tribes...

Werner: Believe it or not, you are right... That was my key question. Have you got anything for me? I mean information.

Lola: Yes, I've got something for you. Look, isn't it beautiful? It's an authentic African mask, made of black wood, it's handcrafted.

Werner: That's a very nice thing! I really like it, thank you. (Werner kisses her on the cheek several times), and I will ask Alfred to hang it up somewhere.

Lola looks around the room, then keeping her gaze fixed on one of the walls, goes to the wall and brings the mask close to it. There is a rifle with a rifle scope hanging on the wall.

Lola: I think, it's better to hang it here. Look, it looks nice? It changed the appearance of the whole wall. However, you've got to move this rifle somewhere. The mask made the wall look nicer.

Werner: But what about polyphony? Don't you remember how I'd been asking you before you went?

Lola: I do remember, Werner. I haven't forgotten. There are so many different tribes in Africa, one cannot even count them, a lot of them, but not all of them sing polyphonic songs. I was told that the Zulu tribe does, and one more, I don't quite remember the name of that tribe. Pygmies are said to have something like polyphony. Have you ever heard of Pygmies? They are unusually short, and they use poisoned arrows while hunting for birds. They try to imitate birds in their songs. But I have not seen any of those people: neither Pygmies nor Zulu or the tribe, I cannot recall the name of. I worked in another region. They're too unhappy to feel disposed to sing, people are dying of hunger there. So, just be satisfied with this mask.

With these words, Fräulein Lola walks towards the window and looks through it to see three strangers in the yard. She asks:

Lola: Werner, who are these people? They don't look like locals.
Werner: I'll tell you later, but first… do you mean I have to give up on my dream of African polyphony? I need it so badly. I can't finish the book without it.

Lola: You'll have to travel to African polyphony yourself. As for me, I can take up the role of your guide if you want me... Who are they, Werner? They don't look like Germans, Do they?
Werner: Why should they look like Germans? They are Georgians.
Lola: Who, Georgians? But what on earth are these Georgians doing in our yard? My God! Where from, Werner?!
Werner: They are prisoners of war, Lola. We are at war, have you forgotten that as well?
Lola: No, I do remember, but where are they from?
Werner: Where from? From Georgia, of course, Lola! Their country is a part of the Russian Empire.
Lola: I have been asking exactly that. I meant Russia... I understand that they are prisoners of war, but what are they doing here? Did you set up a camp for prisoners of war here in our yard in my absence?! (Lola laughs. Werner laughs, too)
Werner: That's true for these three men. They have been living here with us for two years. They are so distinguished. Well, guess, why I moved them here from a POW camp?
Lola: That's not hard to guess, Werner. They probably sing, and...

Werner: You are absolutely right, but if we put it so simply and say that they sing, it would perhaps mean underestimating what they do in reality. You have to listen to them to guess what I mean. Didn't I tell you they are unique? (Werner goes to the window, looks through it at the yard and continues) We can say that your brother has been very lucky; I found the most precious treasure virtually without leaving home. We have already recorded 36 songs. Look at this guy, who is standing near a horse, a tall one. He knows a lot of songs. He knows and remembers all the voices of polyphony, and he is the one who teaches the rest. I write their songs sheet music. I have to admit, that's pretty hard work. Can you imagine, Lola, they can't read music, and they have never heard of the word polyphony, let alone the counterpoint, but they deal with both so ingeniously, in a masterly way, even Bach himself would have appreciated their work if he had listened to them. It's already more than a year I have been working on their songs, but I do not have enough material to complete my monograph. I have to go to Georgia. So, Africa can wait. I wish this cursed war would end soon...
Lola: Yes, but how did you manage to find them?!
Werner: Quite by accident. There are thousands of Russian prisoners of war in Berlin. I thought, maybe I could come across something interesting from Russian folklore. I was looking for Russian folklore and found Georgian. Singing songs is one thing and being such decent is quite another. They are good at almost everything: they look after horses, cows, our vineyard, our garden etc. They even prepare delicious cheese using the technology known only to them. You're going to stay for dinner, aren't you? So, you've got a great chance to taste it; it tastes like Italian mozzarella but is much tastier.

Lola: I hope you pay for them.
Werner: No, I'm afraid not. They are prisoners of war, so it's quite enough to offer them some meals and other necessary things. You should taste their cheese. I usually have dinner with them. We drink some wine as well. You have to listen to their stories they are such interesting people.
Lola: I was not going to stay for dinner, but what you say sounds so intriguing! I just can't wait to meet them and talk to them.
Werner: Go downstairs and talk with them, who say you shouldn't?
Lola: Do they speak German?
Werner: Of course, they do. They are really talented people. It took them a couple of months to learn the language.
Outside we see a black blood-horse approaching Theopile. It stops in front of him. The horse stretches out its neck to reach his face with its nose and sniffs Theopile's face... Theopile smiles and gently strokes the horse's neck. Then he approaches the horse and presses his face against its head. The horse holds its head downcast and they stay still in this position for a while. Fräulein Lola can't take her eyes off the scene; she watches the man passionately caressing the horse's mane, whispering something in its ear, kissing its forehead from time to time. Then he takes something out of his pocket and brings it to the horse's mouth. The horse starts crunching the tidbit and nodding its head up and down, as if in a sign of gratitude.

Fräulein Lola is closely watching the scene and can't take her eyes off the young man and the horse. Werner is standing next to her and he also overlooks the yard. All of a sudden, her eyes glitter with anxiety. She quickly goes to the wall where the rifle scope is hanging, takes it off the wall, goes back to the window, brings the rifle against her eye like a proven sniper and aims it at Theopile's face. Werner is a bit surprised; he cannot understand what is happening to his sister.

Lola: Do not worry, Werner; I'm not going to pull the trigger... I want to have a close look at your Georgian guests.

And so, she does: first she sees a sad eye of the horse; then she moves the scope slightly aside to see the Theopile's face. She stays in this position for a long time her eyes fixed on his face in an attempt to read his emotions as he gently caresses the horse's neck and whispers in its ear. She can see his eyes full of sorrow. Then, all of a sudden, she moves the rifle off her eye and says:

Lola: I've changed my mind, Werner, I can't stay for dinner. Sorry, you have to forgive me, brother.

Werner: As you like it, dear ... I can't make you stay. I thought you'd like to listen to them.

Lola: Another time, Werner ... another time! Now I have to ask you something, you know, don't even try to refuse, or... I'll run back to Africa...

Werner: Ok, what do you want, Lola?

Lola: I had a look at my yard this morning and I'm afraid it doesn't look pretty at all. You should see it yourself! The entire yard looks horrible... covered in weeds. I was thinking of hiring someone to look after the place. What if you let me take one of your Georgian guests to help me, for a week or two? I'll send him back as soon as everything is in order. This could give you a short break... a break from writing notes...

Werner: Ok, I'll let you take one of them with you! I think Kalistrate would be of great help to you. A wonderful name, isn't it? Kalistrate! He is quite hardworking and an excellent cook. I'll make a list of things you need, and the rest is up to him.
Lola: Show me, which one of them is Kalistrate, is he the one caressing the horse?
Werner: No, the one is Theopile! The man over there... standing farther away is Kalistrate.
Lola: No, Werner. I don't want him. If you want to make me happy, let me get what I want, and I want the one caressing the horse.
Werner: Theo? (Werner glances askance at his sister) Now it's clear, Lola! I always thought we had the same taste.
Lola: What do you mean? What is clear? I guess what you mean, but, I'm afraid you're wrong, dear. He was just the first one here to attract my attention, and that's all... (She touches her brother's nose with her finger) ... DON'T PLAY TRICKS on ME.
Werner: O, my God, do you mean me?! Ok... Ok... take whoever you want with you. Come, let's go down and I'll tell him to get ready. And you'll meet the three of them.
They walk out of the room and go downstairs. They continue their dialogue on their way to the yard.
Werner: Anyway, how long do you plan to take him away?!
Lola: I do not know. I'll see. I may even decide not to send him back... (She LAUGHS OUT LOUD) Don't be afraid, as soon as my yard is in order, I'll send him back to you. Would you tell me if he can ride a horse?

Werner (laughing): Can he ride a horse? I think he was brought up on a horse. His father was a famous rider. Together with his friends, he won the race in America defeating Indian Jockeys in horseracing. So, when you get him into bed, ask him to tell you his stories; they will certainly interest you.

Lola: Werner, stop it! (She flourishes the whip she is still holding at him)

Werner: Sorry, sorry! The words JUST SLIPPED out of MY MOUTH... (He laughs and steps back to AVOID a WHIP STRIKE)

As soon as they appear in the yard, Theo, Gregory and Kalistrate immediately stop working and look at the young woman with their eyes filled with curiosity. Werner starts speaking loudly for everybody to hear:

Werner: I want to introduce you to my younger sister. She was a member of the Red Cross mission in Africa for two years, you know, I've told several times... Now, she wants to go to your country, Georgia. (He smiles and continues) So, when she learned that you were Georgian she was very glad and ... Now she's right here, let me introduce you to her.

Young men approach Werner and Lola.

Theopile: Do you really want to go to Georgia, Madam? If it's so, we recommend waiting for a little. You should come to our country when we return there. It will be a great pleasure for us to welcome you and host your stay there.

Lola: You don't have to listen to my brother, he's joking. I've barely arrived from Africa and I'm no longer willing to go anywhere. At least not right now. But I have to admit that I'm really glad to meet you. Werner is fascinated with you, I dare say.

Gregory: Why, Madam? On the contrary, we are fascinated with your brother. But one thing is clear, he literary tortures us makes us sing all the time here. (He laughs) We have never ever sung so much.
Werner: So, I've decided to take a break and let you rest for a while. My sister has to take care of her yard. She needs some help. I think no one can do it better than you. Theo, would you move to her house for a few days. You'll get the yard in order a little and come back in a couple of days. What would you say?
Theopile: What should I say, of course, I'm ready to help her, though...
Werner: though… what, is there anything you worry about?
Theopile: No, nothing to worry about? Just ... maybe we shall go there together… I mean the three of us, or at least two, we'll do everything more quickly.
Werner: No, no. I need Gregory and Kalistrate here. There is something to be done here as well, isn't it so? Besides, you're not going far from here. She lives almost next door. You can even visit us in the evenings. We will have supper together. So, go, get a horse. You'll ride there.
Fräulein Lola is listening to the dialogue attentively. She looks at her brother and at Theopile in turn. When Theo is about to leave, she stops him with her whip and says:
Lola: I want you to know that my brother has nothing to do with this. I asked him, it was my desire to take you with me. If you ask me why, I'll answer that I'm going to tell you later, but ... if you don't want to go with me, you can stay here and sing… just for my brother.
Theopile: (gives her an inquisitive look and then answers) If Werner wants me to go with you, I'll do exactly what he wants me to. I'll get ready right now. It'll take me only 5 minutes.

Theopile walks towards the stable; takes a saddle from the stable; equips the horse and looks at Lola. They all walk towards the gates, where Alfred is waiting to hold Lola's horse by a bridle. They mount their horses. The gate opens, and they ride through the gates.

The riders ride out of the fairly dense forest onto a green plateau. We hear the conversation between them.

Lola: Werner told me that you are a very good rider. Is that really so?

Theopile: What else did he tell you?

Lola: What else? OK, that your father was also an outstanding rider and that he outperformed Indians in America. Is riding your national tradition?

Theopile: Not only my dad. Almost everyone can ride in my country. The most prominent among them went not only in America but in England as well. They say the Queen of England watched their performance and enjoyed it so much that they invited all of them to her palace. By the way, the two of the riders were women. Our women learn to ride a horse when they are children. But one thing is disappointing, in America, as well as in England, our riders were mistaken for Cossacks for some reason.

Lola: I have to admit that initially, I thought you were Russian.

Theopile: I understand, and I'm not surprised at all. This is the case everywhere. I am not surprised, but I'm disappointed. There is a huge difference between us and the Russians... we are different as night and day. That's why there is no understanding between us; they don't understand us, and we don't understand them. You know, we have huge pottery containers to store wine in them. The containers filled with wine are buried to keep them protected from the summer heat. Heat ruins wine and the ground is most of the time cold and keeps it cool. When Russians entered our village and found wine buried in the ground, they thought Georgians did not want them to drink their wine and drank as much as they could, till losing their consciousness and spoiled the rest of the wine that they weren't able to drink. As if it was not enough, in the end, they filled up the containers cherished by us through centuries with earth. No one could make them believe that Georgians were not hiding wine from them and that was just a tradition of ours. If they had asked, nobody would have refused to give them wine. That's another tradition in my country, we offer wine to anyone.

Lola: My God, how awful! Real savagery, isn't it? Anyway, what do you think who was a better rider your dad or you?

Theopile: My dad of course… I can't ride as he could.

Lola: What was so special about him? Would you tell me?

Theo stops the horse. The Lady pulls the bridle and asks:

Lola: Why did you stop? Are you angry with me again?

Theopile: Are you really interested in what my dad and his friends did?

Lola: Of course, I am. Werner listened to you and was interested, as far as I know, so why shouldn't I.

Theopile: Ok. But I think I'd rather show you some things than tell you about them.

With these words, he darts off, riding the horse across the plateau and to the edge of it. Then he turns the horse, makes it stands up on its hind legs with the forelegs off the ground, shouts out loud, his voice sounding somehow strange and gallops his horse towards Lola, performing all the stunts Georgian riders do, on his way towards her. In the end, he hangs upside down off of the side of the horse; plugs a wildflower and stops his horse abruptly just in front of Lola. He bends low over the saddle and stretches his arm out presenting the flower to her.

Theopile: It's yours!

She is so excited by what she's seen that she takes the flower, but forgets to say, "thank you". Theo says:

Theopile: If you let me ride your horse as well I'll show you one more stunt.

Lola: My God! Do you mean you're going to perform one more?

Lola gracefully jumps off her horse and stretches her hand to give the bridle to him.

Lola: Here you are! But for God's sake, be careful…

Theo takes a brief look at her, and without uttering a word trots the horse away and takes the other one with him. Then standing upright atop the pair of horses, with one foot on each horse, trots back to the place where Lola is standing. When he approaches Lola, he moves to his horse, then gets off the horse and brings Lola's horseback to her.

Theopile: I've only told about all these to Werner, and you are the one who saw everything… So, you see, I do not sing just for your brother. (He smiles at the woman for the first time. Lola smiles back at him)

Lola: So, you are no longer angry with me, are you?
Theopile: No, I'm not…why should I… though…
Lola: Though… what?
Theopile: Though, I have something to tell you… but only after you keep your promise. You promised to tell me why you have chosen me.
Lola: A promise is a promise. I'll tell you, but later, maybe in the evening, at dinnertime, OK?
Theopile: As you wish. I'll tell you what I want then.
Lola: Let's go then. (She starts riding her horse and Theopile follows her)
An estate can be seen downhill, with a beautiful fence and an old-fashioned two-storied house. Theopile and Lola enter the back yard. Theopile looks around. His experienced eye immediately notices that the place actually needs to be taken care of: the grass in the yard needs to be mowed down, lawns – to be trimmed, trees and vines require pruning, several ornaments on the pavilion need to be repaired; a rain groove above the second-floor window is broken and so on.
Theopile: Yes, there is much to be done…
Lola: You're not discouraged, are you?!
Theopile: Not at all? We'll take care of everything… step by step… I'll start with the yard. I'm sure you have a scythe somewhere and a whetstone. I'll start right now. Till you find a scythe, I will take care of the horses I'll take them to graze in the backyard. Is it safe for them there?

Lola: Safe? Yes, it is! By the way, that pasture belongs to us, to me and my brother; the pasture and a part of the forest uphill. We own a vast area in Lotharingia[13] as well; I hope it isn't appropriated by the French ... I'll go upstairs and prepare a place for you. You can let the horses go but forget about a scythe for a time being. We're going to have dinner, first. Martha, my cook, hasn't come yet, but that's okay, I'll make it myself. Are you choosy? I hope you're not!

Theopile: Of course, I'm not, Fräulein Lola; being a prisoner of war I can't afford to be one!

Lola: You know what; let's agree on something from the start: I don't quite know what was going on at my brother's place, that's not my business, but while you are here with me, I want you to forget these words. You are not a prisoner of war, you're my guest. To tell you the truth, all the fuss about the yard was simply an excuse to help us build a relationship; I have a gardener and a cook, as I've told you. They'll both be here as soon as they learn I'm back. You can even forget about a scythe, a whetstone, a saw, a hammer and more importantly, you have to forget the word – "prisoner". I see life hasn't been extremely fair to you. I don't offer you a leisurely life here, but you deserve a little treat, don't you? So, I will go and prepare a place for you. And you let the horses go out and graze and come straight to the kitchen. Here, you have to enter this door; it's at the end of the corridor, on the left.

---

[13] It was a medieval successor kingdom of the Carolingian Empire Comprising the modern-day Netherlands, Belgium, Luxemburg, Germany and France

Theopile: Everything is clear, Madam, I am so grateful to you for your mercy and compassion, but, unfortunately, I can't accept your offer. I am a prisoner of war and will remain as such until this war ends. When Werner took us from the camp, the commandant relegated all responsibilities to your brother. Your brother trusted us. We gave him our word not to try to run away. Now you want to convince me that I'm given the freedom to choose? If I were to believe that, no one would be able to make me stay here. What makes me stay here is the very word you want me to forget – prisoner! But one day, when the war ends, I'll leave this place immediately. Thank you so much for your kindness. But unfortunately, our desires have to go through arduous trials most of the time… So, don't try to stop me, Madam, I'll let the horses out to graze ON PASTURE and I'll find a scythe myself, as while working it's easier for me to imagine that I'm already there!

He turns and leads the horses to the back gates holding them by the bridles. On his way to the back gates he hears Lola asking:

Lola: where?

Theopile stops; standing between the two horses only turns his head and says:

Theopile: In my motherland, of course. (he sounds sorrowful)

Theo continues his way to the backdoors. The woman stands still and can't take her eyes off the man walking away.

Lola (saying to herself): Oh my God, I think things are looking blue for you, Fräulein Lola. Everybody's fed up with this cursed war, and what you desire is for it to go on forever.

Theopile is standing near the main gate and is looking into the yard. He's holding a scythe in his hand; he crosses himself and starts mowing the grass. He mows so skillfully, in a gracious manner. He seems to be a master of what he is doing. A woman walks through the smaller gate. She is holding a large basket in her hand. Theo looks at the woman without stopping mowing and the woman greets him at the moment. Theopile nods his head and continues mowing the grass.

Lola is looking at Theopile through the second-floor window. There is a knock at the door. A woman's voice can be heard from outside.

Martha: Fräulein Lola, dinner is ready. Would you like to come downstairs?

Lola: (comes to the door opens it and says to Martha) All right, Martha, I'm coming.

Martha: Would you like me to tell your guest to come?!

Lola: There is no need, I'll tell him.

Martha moves away from the door. We see Theopile again. He stops working for a second, looks at the Sun, takes off his shirt, throws it on a hydrangea bush and goes on mowing. Lola comes out of the house and calls the man with a smile on her face:

Lola: Theo, it's enough for today. Come, have a shower, Martha's prepared dinner for us.

Theopile: Fräulein Lola, would you excuse me? Please, have dinner without me? I want to finish mowing before sunset, so let me join you later for supper maybe. And could Martha bring me some water?

Lola: As you like. I'll tell Martha not to clear the table. You can go to the kitchen at any time and have dinner ... (Lola is a bit irritated, then says to herself) A dogged Georgian ... (she enters the house and says to Martha) Martha, bring him a jar of water. Don't clear the table, leave it as it is. Somehow, I lost my appetite. When he enters the kitchen, call me ... (she is about to go, but stops) After you bring him water, bring me a glass of white wine; I'll be upstairs.

Martha: All right, Fräulein Lola.

Lola goes upstairs and starts looking at Theo from the window. She watches Martha bringing him a jar of water and a glass. Theo doesn't take the glass; he takes the jar full of water, raises it over his head and pours water straight over his face, quaffing water in large quantities and cooling himself off. Streams of water together with sweat drops start flowing down his strong masculine body. Lola looks at him through the window with a smile on her face.

The Sun descends towards the horizon. Theo swings the scythe he is holding several times and finishes mowing, unbends himself and the expression on his face radiates satisfaction as he looks at the mowed lawns. He walks towards the house, places the scythe against the wall and he is about to enter the house when he suddenly remembers his shirt hanging on a hydrangea bush. He hurriedly goes back, takes his shirt and enters the house through the door and into the hall; stops and looks around. Martha can be seen coming out of the kitchen.

Martha: Fräulein Lola asked me to show you the bathroom and your room as well. Which one first...?

Theopile: I'd rather go to the bathroom first... the room will wait.

Martha leads Theopile towards the bathroom. Theo goes into the bathroom and closes the door. He turns to see a new shirt lying on the chair. He takes it, brings it close to his face enjoying its smell. Then he has a shower.

We are in the Kitchen. Lola is sitting at the end of the table facing the entrance; she is sipping wine. The sound of steps can be heard shortly after. Theopile enters, his hair is still wet.

Lola: At last! Don't you have dinner in your country?

Theopile: Of course, we do. But we work far away from our houses in summer in my country, so dinner is generally brought to us directly to the place we work, not to waste time.

Lola: Aha! So, you wanted us to take the table to the yard? You could have told us and…

Theopile: No, I didn't mean that? I promise, tomorrow I won't behave the way I did today. But (passing his hand over his face) I have to go back to Werner; I forgot to take my shaving accessories.

Lola: Do not worry! I have a full kit of Werner's accessories here. I'll find them after dinner. Now, please, come and sit at the table ... the problem of shaving is solved. I'll light these candles right now. I would light a fire in the fireplace for more comfort if it were not so hot today.

Theopile takes his seat at the opposite end of the table and pours some wine into his glass. Martha is serving a plate of soup to both of them.

Lola: Martha, after you finish serving soup, you may go. Thank you for everything. I'll take care of the rest. I'll be waiting for you tomorrow, as usual.

Martha: But tomorrow is Sunday, Fräulein Lola. Do you want me to come? I can but only after I attend Morning Prayer in the church.

Lola: No, no! I'm sorry, Martha, I forgot that tomorrow is Sunday. You know, we did not pay attention to such things in Africa. There was always someone in need of our help there, every single day. So, see you on Monday...

Martha: (taking off the apron) Goodbye, Fräulein Lola. Goodbye, sir.

Martha walks out of the kitchen. Theopile takes a spoon in his hand, dips it into the soup and tastes the soup. Both are heaving the meal in silence for a while. Then Fräulein Lola breaks the silence. She raises her glass of wine and says:

Lola: To our meeting!

Theopile raises his glass of wine, smiles at Lola and empties his glass.

Lola: I see, you enjoy drinking wine.

Theopile: Maybe you're right! Wine is part and parcel of any occasion in my country. But you know... I'd rather listen to you than talk about wine. You promised to tell me something, didn't you?

Lola: Well, I'll tell you. But it seems to me that I have to start from the very beginning ... (she smiles) from Africa! So, you may put that plate away and here is some meat, help yourself and listen to me. You already know that I was a member of the Red Cross mission in Africa for two years. Our main task was to vaccinate people in the countries of Central Africa, but we had plenty of other things to do as well. One can hardly imagine the pain and suffering of so many people there. I experienced all these in the past two years and there were times when I thought I couldn't stand it anymore. But none of them had anything to do with a human spirit. There were only extreme poverty, hunger and people crippled by all kinds of accidents. I've seen people torn by lions or trampled by elephants or wild buffalos. Even chimpanzees sometimes kidnapped babies, dragged their prey high up into the trees and ate them alive in front of their unfortunate mothers, my God, how many atrocious things I've seen... so many people bitten by black mambas. The black mamba is an African snake, highly venomous and very fast. It slides through grass, like a military cruiser, with its head raised well off the ground. Woe to them who cross its path, it doesn't matter whether they are people or animals. So, that's what I experienced there in Africa, but what I've seen today… I mean you… do you remember stroking a horse this morning? I took Werner's rifle scope off the wall and aimed it at you (she smiles) I didn't mean to harm you. I wanted to get a closer look at your face… and your eyes.
Theopile: Really? And did you manage?
Lola does not answer this question. She stands up, walks around the table to get near Theopile, stands by him, wraps her arms around his shoulders and whispers:

Lola: Yes, I did! I saw such sorrow in your eyes, so much sorrow, that none of the troubles experienced in Africa can compare to it. That's because they mirror your soul ache. That was the point I decided... all of a sudden...

Theopile: what did you decide?

Lola: I decided... I don't quite know how to explain it...to ease your sorrow... or, say, share in your sorrow... You call it as you like ... And we women have a sole remedy for this. (SHE begins caressing of his face and neck. Theopile sits still for a while, but when her caressing intensifies, he stands up)

Theopile: Thank you so much, Fräulein Lola, for your decision to ease of share in my sorrow, but if your care is an expression of your sympathy, maybe it's not worth bothering.

Lola blushes. She walks quickly away towards the kitchen wall and stops by an old cupboard. After a short pause she says with her eyes cast down:

Lola: You know, it seems, it's not so easy to talk with you. You are not a simple person. You make people tell the naked truth.

Theopile: Wouldn't it be more natural if you told one?

Lola: So, you want the truth? Well, I'll tell you then. The truth is that recently I frankly wished the war would go on for a long time. Better it would never end. Perhaps you understand why. That is the truth. (She raises her head and looks at Theopile) Did you like it? I am a member of the Red Cross mission and wish for an endless war...

Theopile: Everything is clear, Fräulein Lola, But...

Lola: But? Again?

Theopile: Yeah, right! I'll try to explain it to you; now it's my turn. I promised to tell you something, didn't I? I'll put it in a couple of words. Your brother helped two of my friends and me as well and who knows, maybe, he's saved our lives. Besides, we managed to make friends with him during these two years. Anyway, I think so. So, would you tell me, Fräulein Lola, how can I be with… his sister... isn't it immoral? How can I look at *HIM IN THE EYE* tomorrow?

Lola looks astonished as if she was not ready for what she's just heard. She wants to say something, but she can't, she mumbles something and then suddenly bursts out laughing, she laughs heartily for quite a long time. Theopile looks rather gloomy. Lola tries to signal something to him using her body language. And then somehow, she manages to say:

Lola: Do not get angry with me ... please ... I'll try to calm down right now and explain it to you ... everything ... (She takes a breath and wiping TEARS from HER eyes with HER hand says) Oh my God, Theo, is that the only reason? Yes, but I'm no longer a child, neither Werner... That is, we do not interfere in each other's lives. We simply don't have the right! We do not judge each other's choices, we simply respect them. And not my brother but your talent helped you to survive. Therefore, you don't have to think that you owe Werner. It may sound harsh, but the truth is that he was thinking about his business when he took you from the camp not about you. Didn't I promise to tell you the truth? Well, that's what I'm doing right now. Do you really think that my brother worried a lot about the fate of several prisoners of war from one of the remote provinces of Russia? So, I have to state it again, you own talent saved your lives not Werner's humanity.

Theopile: I do understand what you mean, Fräulein Lola, but it was not here that I acquired this talent. I had had it until I found myself on the front line of the battlefield, filling my lungs with poisonous gas. Talent needs to be recognized as appreciated and valued, Fräulein... That's what your brother did. We shouldn't under-appreciate his merit, should we? As for your relationship with your brother, frankly speaking, what you've just told me still sounds a bit strange to me if not entirely unclear. I have been brought up in a country with absolutely different traditions! However, I try to accept everything as you say. I've learned that this kind of behavior is acceptable and is not considered immoral, but…

Lola: But? Again?... Why don't you forget this word?

Theopile: I will, I promise… But maybe you'll try to help me decide what to do to my traditions? It can be said, that I came here from a very different world. Therefore, please, help me answer a single question. I've heard that the period of a night at the poles is slightly longer than six months, i.e. they have SIX whole MONTHS of darkness there, is it so?

Lola: It is… So, what?

Theopile: So ... What do you think a rooster would do if you took it to the place where there is a six-month night? Would it crow or wait for six months to crow at the break of dawn?

Lola: I guess, besides horse riding, singing and mowing you might be fond of philosophy... (She laughs) As for the rooster, I can't say whether it would crow or not. Probably not... Anyway, you expect me to answer your question that way, don't you?

Theopile: I do. I think it wouldn't crow because roosters are born to herald the break of dawn. Therefore, according to all the rules and laws it should keep silent for six months; wait until morning and get ready for the main crowing ... (Expression on Theo's face changes; sorrow fills HIS FACE and he continues) I am like that rooster. I am waiting for the dawn. It has to come one day. And I'll crow then.

They are silent for a while. Lola looks thoughtful. Then she looks at Theopile with loving eyes.

Lola: But (She smiles and continues smiling) we are neither at the North nor South Pole, are we? Damn it, we are in the middle of Europe. Here, roosters crow at any time… in the morning and at night ... immoral roosters. (Still smiling slyly) Besides, Werner already knows everything? He even told me…

Theopile: What does he know?

Lola: He knows about you... He knows what's happened... Oh my God, what am I saying? I'm rattlebrained[14] right now. I wanted to say that ... he knows what might happen. He told me, we had the same tastes. He meant you.

Theopile: Did he? It's strange. I would have deserved a bullet through my head for anything like this in our country. (He looks thoughtful for a while, and then smiles and continues in a quiet and decisive tone) Though, I'm ready to do anything for you even take a bullet for you, Fräulein Lola. (He approaches Lola caresses her and they plunge deeper into the ocean of love)

---

[14] adjective. Empty-headed, stupid; foolish and noisy.

* * *

Time goes by. Theo still works in Fräulein Lola's yard. He planes boards, sawa logs. HE repaired the pavilion, fixed the rain groove above the second-floor window. We see him working in the garden as well, collecting apples fallen on the ground from the apple trees in a bucket, etc. a few times we also see the couple making love in bed, on the background of the view from the window showing the images of changing seasons: first it's autumn, then winter.

Then we see Theopile standing still next to a horse with his arms around the horse's neck, looking sad and thoughtful. We follow his imaginations to see Theo's homeland:

We see a very beautiful view from above: a river, a bond bridge, a green valley, two bull calves of golden color are grazing grass. Then they raise their heads at the same time and look together in the same direction as if someone has called them; we see a beautiful fenced yard and a wooden house looking over the valley. We hear a plaintive melody specially selected for this scene. Fräulein Lola approaches Theopile; she literary stands next to him, but Theopile can't notice her.

Lola: Theo, what's the matter with you, I think your mind is somewhere else!

Theopile: (Theopile COMES to his SENSES, smiles, and answers) Yeah! ... I was in my village we have pastures there uphill. In the summertime, cattle come to these pastures from a neighboring village. The cattle belong to a famous family of herdsmen; their surname is Kvaratskhelia. Do you know? In the event of coronation of Nicholas as the Emperor of Russia, Kvaratskhelia sent him 60 bull calves of exactly the same color and age as a gift. The bull calves were even of the same weight. Can you imagine? They were almost absolutely identical. Georgians sometimes like to distinguish themselves by incomprehensible generosity.

Lola: Really? Your herdsman hasn't been as lucky as one might think, you know? What did you say is his surname?

Theopile: Kvaratskhelia.

Lola: Yes, Kvaratskhelia. It's already six months the Emperor's been deposed from the THRONE.

Theopile: I know, Werner told us. The Emperor is deposed, but, apparently, the empire remains. It would have been better for us if it had happened JUST THE OPPOSITE way. The war is still going on!

Anyway, my father used to allow the Kvaratskhelias to use our pastures in the summer for free. And one day they gave us bull calves exactly of the kind they had sent to the Emperor. The bull calves were of the golden color. I used to look after them… before the war started. I used to take them out to graze on pasture and take them down to the river to wash them. I used to feed them goat milk. So, now, when I think about Georgia, I visualize them so clearly. Now they must be bulls but, in my imaginations, they are still calves. They used to graze at the river bank just in front of our yard. I would call them from far away, they would immediately stop grazing grass, raise their heads and start looking at me with their overly large and clever eyes. Their eyes were filled with love ... It's a shame I'm saying this... I miss my wife and my two boys so much... but whenever I think of Georgia, the same image comes to my mind: a river, a bond bridge, a green valley in front of a wooden house and bull calves raising their heads and looking at me as they used to do... And I'm so far away. (He stops speaking, starts stroking the horse's neck for a while and then turns to Lola) you wanted to say something, didn't you?

Lola: Yeah! Werner's invited us to have breakfast with them tomorrow morning. We have to start early in the morning...

Theopile: What's going on?

Lola: I don't know, He says it's going to be a surprise... Theo, what's your wife's name? You've never mentioned her.

Theopile: Melita… Her name's Melita!

* * *

Werner's dining room. Werner, Gregory, and Kalistrate are sitting near a festively laid table and talking. There is a fire burning in the fireplace. Kalistrate stands up goes to the fireplace, adds some pieces of wood to the burning fire, and says:

Kalistrate: What is going on, Werner, it seems to me we are going to enjoy our morning feast. Sometimes we also do so in Georgia, especially in the period of heavy snow; when we have nothing else to do.

Werner: Let's wait for Lola and Theopile to come and I'll tell you what's going on. In the meantime, shall we have a glass of wine before breakfast? French people do so before their meals. Moreover, wine is French. (Werner goes to the table; opens a bottle in a SINGLE, quick MOTION and smells the cork) It smells great. (He pours wine into glasses) Come on let's drink! (He presses his glass against his cheek) How do you Georgians like your wine, I mean temperature, cold or warm?

Kalistrate and Gregory start laughing in answer to his question. This timing noise is heard from outside. Werner pays attention to the noise.

Werner: I think they've come. (He is about to go out to meet them, but at that moment Lola and Theopile enter the room)

Their greeting is warm. Werner lights candles on the table and invites everyone:

Werner: Well, take your seats, please... you may choose your own places... (Werner takes the head seat at the end of the table. Alfredo enters carrying a bottle of champagne)

Lola: Werner, do you see what I see? Is it a bottle of champagne... for breakfast? What's going on? Do you have a bride hidden behind the curtains? If so, do not be shy, let us see her.

Werner: (pouring champagne into glasses) Calm down, dear. What I have to tell you, is more important than that. So, please, take these glasses first. (Then he stands up and takes one to the glasses and solemnly declares) Yesterday, March 3, 1918, Germany and Russia signed a peace treaty. Although the war is still going on, you guys are no longer prisoners of war. Congratulations.

Everyone sitting around the table stands up except Lola. The young men cannot hide excitement; even tears can be seen in their eyes. They cross themselves, hug and congratulate one another. Werner watches them and looks genuinely happy. As for Lola, a deep concern can be read on her face; TEARS WELL UP IN HER EYES, but she tries to curb her emotions.

Werner: Congratulations again! And now boys, you have to decide what to do next. You may return to your homeland or stay here, as you like. Of course, I don't mean my yard... I mean Germany. I promise I will prepare all the necessary documents in any case.

Lola springs out of her chair hastily leaves the room, enters the bathroom and locks the bathroom door behind her.

Werner: Lola, dear, what's happened? Look at your face! (He goes to the bathroom door) Lola, are you, all right?

Lola: Nothing, Werner... Don't pay attention to me... I'm a bit excited just like all of you... I'll be right back, don't worry

Werner: (comes back to the table) She'll be right back.

Lola: (comes back, takes her seat by the table and asks with a bitter smile on her face) Don't you want to sing?

Theopile, Gregory and Kalistrate start singing. Werner listens to them with his head buried in his hands. Lola can't take her eyes from Theopile. After they finish singing, Theo stands up, raises his glass and says:

Theopile: Fräulein Lola, Herr Werner, I want to say something... if you allow me (He looks at Gregory and Kalistrate) on behalf of everyone ... but I do not know how to express in words the gratitude that we, all three of us, feel towards your family (There is a short pause) What I can think of right now is a single simple phrase. Herr Werner, Fräulein Lola, we love you! I drink this toast to your health. Thank you for everything. (There is a short pause again and then he empties his glass. Gregory and Kalistrate stand up and drink a toast to Werner and Lola, saying short phrases, which are hardly heard in the noise)

Werner: You don't have to be so grateful. I think what I did for you is nothing compared to what you have given me.

Lola: I said exactly that, Werner, I told it to Theo. I told him that it was their talent that saved their lives and that they don't owe you.

Werner: You are absolutely right.

Lola: Are we going to go home, Theo?

Theopile: I think I'll stay here, Lola, I have to decide what to do next together with my friends.

Lola: You don't mean that you aren't going to accompany me, do you?

Theopile: Of course, I don't, I'll accompany you. Anyway, we can't run back to Georgia this night.

***

The same plateau, familiar figures of the riders… We hear the conversation.

Lola: Can you help me understand one thing Theo? You said you had to decide something together with your friends… What do you have to decide when you have already decided what to do?

Theopile: You are right, but I have to learn whether they think the way I do.

Lola: But is there anything that might make you change your mind?

Theopile: Lola, you know that I love you very much… I've told you that so many times. Besides my feeling towards you can't be simply called love. It is more than love; it's love and a kind of obligation simultaneously…

Lola: (She seems embarrassed) Please, I've asked you not to mention this word again. I wish you would quit harping on obligation. Love makes a person forget about obligations, Theo. And you keep on talking and thinking about some obscure obligations. I've asked you a very clear question… is there anything that might make you change your mind? And I want you to answer it in a clear and direct way.

Theopile goes into a dream. In his dream he sees the same images of his homeland, as before: the same river, the same bull calves, and the same wooden house, etc. the same melody can be heard. He wakes up from his dream and says:

Theopile: I think nothing. Nostalgia appears to be stronger than love ... and obligation. It doesn't even bother to ask me what I want. It feels as if I am bound by some invisible, unbreakable string and a mysterious power holding the other end of this string draws me to my homeland, and I fail to resist. So, I have to go.

Lola: All right. Everything is clear... and if you've mentioned obligations, I am obliged to DISCLOSE one thing to you - we will have a baby soon.

Theopile pulls the bridle like one THUNDERSTRUCK. HE PULLS IT SO STRONGLY THAT THE HORSE stands up on its hind legs.

Theopile: what did you say, Lola?

Lola: Did I say anything wrong? Theo, we've been together for more than six months now and ... I think we are both healthy people... Please, don't think that you are under any obligation... I simply want to ask you to do something for me - Please, do not leave me until our baby is born. I think the baby will make it easy for me to let you go...

Theopile approaches Lola on horseback, BENDS down and kisses her on the cheek. Tears well up in Lola's eyes…

***

We see a church with a courtyard, a German cemetery, a funeral ceremony. It is the end of summer, August. It is hot. A close-up view of an open grave; Werner, Theopile, Gregory, Kalistrate, Martha, and a few unfamiliar people apparently from the Red Cross and the University of Berlin are standing at the grave. Theopile and Werner are standing side by side. Their conversation can be heard against the background of a priest reading prayers and performing some funeral rites.

Werner: We are relatives now, Theo. MISFORTUNE has COME ON US, Lola has left us, but we both have her baby, she left him to us. (There is a TREMBLE in his VOICE; he hides his face in his handkerchief and whimpers)

Theopile: He is my son. I have to take care of him. I can't take a newborn baby on such a long journey! I have to wait a year and a half, at the very least; or perhaps, even two years... we'll see. I think I have to wait until he walks... My friends promised they won't leave me here alone. They'll also wait for me.

Werner: You're right, it would be better. Lola's House is yours now. It's up to you to decide where to live before going to Georgia; you may live there or stay at my house, with the baby. I'll hire a nanny for him.

Theopile: And what about boys?

Werner: It's up to them to decide, they may live wherever they want. Though, I'll be happy if you all decide to stay at my house. I got so used to you… We may even work together, sometimes.

Theopile: we'll see, Werner.

A caption on the screen: "Two years later"

We see the same church and the same cemetery, the same grave, but this time there is a gravestone there and the inscription on the gravestone reads: “Lola Pere 1893-1918”. Theopile and his two-year-old child – Thoma is standing at the grave. The child is very handsome, and he looks like his father. Gregory, Kalistrate, and Werner are standing not far away. A black car can be seen standing further.

Theopile: Thoma, let’s say good-bye to Mom. Take these flowers and place them near this stone. Do it, you are a good boy, my son.

The child first looks at his father, then takes the flowers with both hands and places them on his mother's grave. He looks at his father again, as if checking whether he’s done everything well or not. Theopile smiles. Then he bends down, takes Thoma into his arms and starts walking towards the car. Gregory, Kalistrate, and Werner go after him and get into the car. Werner is sitting behind the wheel of the car; he starts the car and says:

Werner: Your luggage is in the car. You have the documents and tickets with you. It will take us 40 minutes to get to the station in Berlin. First, you’ll arrive in Helsinki by train where you’ll change the train and arrive in St. Petersburg[15]. You know what to do next. I think I will come soon to your country – to independent Georgia.

They drive away in a car that disappears over the horizon.

* * *

[15] A Russian port city on the Baltic Sea.

A train carriage... Little Thoma lies asleep in the lower bed of the train compartment, he seems to be in a deep sleep; we see his face with slightly flushed cheeks and rosy lips. Theopile, Gregory and Kalistrate are standing outside the compartments, in front of the open door of the compartment and are looking through the window. Rapidly changing views of Georgia can be seen through the window. Two other men are standing nearby in the corridor. They look at the three men with curiosity from time to time.

Kalistrate: Shall we wake him up? He should look at the views of his motherland. (He says in Georgian) Thoma, wake up, boy; you've had enough sleep; look what's going outside! You're in your motherland!

Theopile: Don't wake him up, Kalistrate, let him sleep, he'll wake up by himself. And besides, do you think he understands Georgian?

Kalistrate: I think he understands a little.

Theopile: You mean, he understands when one says "hello" and "hi" in Georgian. I have to wait for a little and he'll learn Georgian. You know, the little ones learn languages quickly.

Gregory: You are right Theo. Kalistrate let him alone and enjoy the views. Look, I can't believe, we've finally arrived.

One of the two men standing nearby looks at them again, then turns to the other and says in a quiet voice:

Passenger I (Spiridon): I wonder what they are happy about. They might not know that Bolsheviks have come to power, that they hold the reins in their hands and the bastards have already exterminated half of Georgians.

Passenger II: Be careful, Spiridon! Be careful, or you risk putting your foot in it. And don't say then you haven't been warned. Do you know for sure who they are? Maybe they are happy about the very fact that Bolsheviks have come.

Passenger I (Spiridon): Do you really think so? (He looks at them again surveying the young man with an inquisitive look on his face) I don't. Have you ever seen a Bolshevik[16] enjoying the views of the mountains seen through a train window? How can they care about their native land or mountains when they are ready to betray or even kill their own mothers?
Passenger II: Yes, but we have to be on our guard, so calm down, please.
Views of the suburbs of a small provincial town can be seen through the window. The train slows down.
Theopile: I think we are arriving... it's time to wake up Thoma. (He enters the compartment bends down to wake up Thoma, but the child is already awake. He looks at his dad with his wide-open eyes and smiles. Theo says in German: Wake up, Thoma? And get up, quickly. I'll help you to put on your shoes. We have arrived.
The train slowly enters the station of a provincial town. It's noon. It is hot. There are a lot of different kinds of people on the platform. Some are in a hurry, while others, on the contrary, walk sluggishly and look at the people. Street vendors are everywhere shouting in front of the passers-by to sell their goods. Uniformed coachman can be seen here and there on the platform hunting for customers from the groups of newly-arrived passengers. There are much bustle and fuss. The train brakes hiss and screech and the train finally stops. Train conductors are the first to get off the train and they are followed by passengers, among them we can see the familiar faces of Theopile, Gregory, Kalistrate, and Thoma, walking together and carrying some luggage. Behind them we see the two men from the train.

---

[16] A member of the majority faction of the Russian Social Democratic Party, which was renamed the Communist Party after seizing power in the October Revolution of 1917.

Kalistrate: Theo, stay here with Gregory and Thoma. I'll go and find a coachman. If they see, we are with a child they'll charge us a higher price. So, wait for me here, I'll arrange everything and come back soon.
A coachman approaches them.
Coachman: If you need a coach, I am here to serve you. How many of you are there and where do you want to go?
Kalistrate: Give me a short pause, my friend, I have no time to get acquainted with a coachman, I've got to have a look at the coach and horses first. (He walks away and into the station building)

Theopile, Gregory and Thoma are standing on the platform. The train makes a deafening noise and starts moving quietly, slowly leaving the platform. The people on the platform watch the train with its half-empty carriages leaving the place. The last carriage leaving the platform is like a theater curtain opening at the beginning of a performance. The "stage" looks like this: there is a luggage carriage on the third track from the platform; a wooden plank is placed in an inclined position at the open-door carriage entrance serving as STAIRS leading to the carriage. Someone walks up on the wooden plank and enters the carriage. We see a lot of people inside the carriage. There are a lot of men on the ground as well, surrounded by a few others wearing Cheka[17] uniforms. The men surrounded by Chekists are mainly dressed in Chokhas[18] and can be distinguished by their looks; they are all handsome, tall and respectful. One of the Chekists is calling the names on the roll. Another Chekist standing next to him appears to be the chief - one, who is in charge of everything that's going on. The Chekist calls the first name:

Chekist: Kereselidze Jason!

Jason Kereselidze proudly steps forward, leaving the group of detainees, calmly walks up the wooden plank and enters the carriage.

Chekist: Lortkipanidze George! Iashvili Avtandil! Tsereteli Vakhtang! Matchavariani Konstantin! Tsereteli Samson!

---

[17] (Russian acronym ЧК – чрезвычáйная комиссия - Extraordinary Commission) the state secret-police organization in the Soviet Union

[18] A traditional male dress of the peoples of the Caucasus

The difference between those, who enter the carriage after their names are called and those who are wearing Cheka uniforms is clearly visible and not only THEIR APPEARANCE but something else makes them stand out. Theopile and Gregory are watching the scene with astonishment as well as Thoma, who has put his arms around his father's leg. The two elderly men from the train are standing nearby; they look shocked while watching the scene. Theopile turns to them:

Theopile: Excuse me, gentlemen, could you explain to me what's going on? I am a little confused; I haven't been here for ages? (He points to the people waiting their turn to enter the carriage) Did they do anything wrong?

Passenger I (Spiridon): Where have you been, man, what kind of place was it? Did you fell from the sky? What might be going on? Can't you see the nobles - honest and decent people - are detained and taken by Chekists? It's not the first time! (There is a tremble in his voice) They aren't criminals, they have done nothing wrong, man, absolutely nothing ... but for Bolsheviks it doesn't matter what you've done, they can arrest you just because you walk on land or breathe air!... if you are decent and honest, that's a crime today. If you are noble, that's it, you are their enemy and you are doomed.

Theopile: But ... Is it possible? Where do they take them? What do they do to them? Even prisoners of war weren't treated this way... there is not a place in the world where such things happen...

Passenger I (Spiridon): I'll tell you something, man, you look like those they're hunting for, and I advise you to leave this place as soon as possible. Or... they might notice you, suspect something and move you from one carriage right to the other. They've got neither mind nor conscience to stop them. Go, man, go! Take this child and go away.

Theopile doesn't respond. He is standing paralyzed and looking at the carriage. There are fewer and fewer people in the group of detainees waiting their turn to get on the carriage. Actually, there are only three waiting for their names to be called by the Chekist[19].

Chekist: Abashidze Geidar! Anjaparidze Arsene! Ioseliani Rostom!

The person whose name is called last is Rostom Ioseliani, an extremely charming man with grey hair. His appearance is so distinguished that even Chekists can't take their eyes off him and look at him as if they feel pity for him. This time the Chekist who has been calling the names on roll turns to the chief and says:

Chekist: That's all, Aslan, all of them are on board.

Chief: How many of them do we have onboard?

Chekist: That's ninety... (He says before looking at the list, then he looks at the list and adds) six… Ninet- six of them!

Chief: Not a big game, but that will do. We'll catch others too, they can't go far! Go ahead, close the door and roll in the platform. Go! Quickly! I am hungry…

Chekist: Aslan, there are people standing on the platform... Do you want them to witness this?

The Chekist called Aslan turns his head a little and looks at the platform. He looks through everyone standing there, among them Theopile; first, he simply looks at him and moves his eyes to another man, but then suddenly he looks at him again and stares at him for a long time. Theopile is looking straight into his eyes. At last the Chekist turns back to the compartment full of detainees and says to a person standing next to him:

---

[19] In a narrower meaning is an agent of the Cheka (ChK), in a broader meaning is an agent of Cheka and its descendants NKVD, KGB, FSB, Lubyanka (see Lubyanka Building). It may relate to: Cheka, first of a succession of Soviet state security organizations.

Chief: Let them stand there and watch. I want them to watch this and memorize. All should piss their pants from fear when they hear our name. Go ahead and do it... F...k them all...

Several uniformed men push an open platform that rolls slowly towards the carriage; there is a machine-gun on the platform, a machine-gunner and his assistant, who is holding an **ammunition belt** with both hands. As soon as the platform is aligned with the carriage, the machine gun starts firing at the carriage, slowly moving ahead. Sounds of **crashing** wood and creepy groaning are heard. The bullets fired from the machine-gun have pierced the wall of the carriage at a man's height and down. The Chekist slowly rolls the platform along the carriage and when they reach the end of the carriage they go around to the other side of the platform and start pushing it in the opposite direction. The machine gun starts firing at the carriage again. Blood starts leaking from the carriage and then flows in streams. During firing the people standing on the platform react adequately, but on seeing so much blood all their reactions gather in a simultaneous groan. Theopile covers Thoma's eyes with his hands. Drops of sweat are running down his face in streams. One of the two men standing next to him, Spiridon, starts yelling loudly and mourning bitterly:
Passenger I (Spiridon): Woe is me, my sons! Woe is me, my brothers! Woe to your unfortunate mothers! What the bastards have done to you! Why did they kill you?! What for?!
Passenger II: (The other is trying to silence him) hush! Spiridon, hush! They might hear you and if so we are doomed...
Kalistrate rushes to the platform; he looks terrified.
Kalistrate: What's going on, Theo, who's been shooting here? Has another war started?

Theopile: Worse! Let's go! Let's get out of this place!
Kalistrate: OK, let's go. I was coming here to tell you that a coach is waiting for us. But I was scared to death... what was going on, wouldn't you tell me?
Theopile: Let's go! Let's go, Kalistrate, I'll tell you everything on our way home, but Let's get out of this place immediately.

***

Crossroads... One road curves to the right, leading to the bridge, the other goes straight ahead. A coach appears from afar. The coachman is sitting on the coach-box and Gregory is sitting next to him. Kalistrate and Theopile are sitting inside the coach in the back seat and Thoma is sitting on his father's lap.
Kalistrate: Stop at the crossing, man. I have to get off here, Theo. I'll walk to my house from here; it's not far; I only have to get over the bridge. The man will take you both to your houses. That's what we agreed on.
Theopile: Listen, maybe you'll come with us? What would you say, Kalistrate. You have been away so long; one more day won't make a big difference? Both of you will stay with me tonight, you and Gregory, we'll celebrate our peaceful return to our homeland. Besides, you'll meet my family.
Kalistrate: No, I can't, Theo. You've just said that I had been away long. I just can't wait to step in my yard... Let me go, I'll look around a little, and then, one day, Gregory and I will visit you.
Theopile: All right then. Wait, I will get off to say good-bye. Gregory, what are you waiting for? Get off, or are you tired of each other and don't even want to say good-bye?
Gregory: It's true! I'm so tired of him; I don't even want to see him... (With these words he gets off the coach)

Theopile seats his son in a coach back seat and gets off the coach to say good-bye to Kalistrate.

Theopile: Well, you know, as soon as you "look around" as you say, take this old man and come and visit me. You know what you mean to me! You waited for me for two long years. You've done more than a brother can do for his brother. (He hugs Kalistrate and they stay in this position for quite a while. Then Gregory hugs Kalistrate. The coachman is looking at this scene of saying good-bye from his seat in the coach-box and smiles. Then he says smiling again, pretending to be scolding them)

Coachman: What's up, men? Why do you take so long to say good-bye? Come on get on the coach and wave him good-bye or we won't be able to get to the place until dark.

Theopile: The coachman is right. Gregory, let him go and get on the coach… Thoma says he is hungry…

Kalistrate goes to the coach, hugs Thoma and kisses him. Theopile and Gregory get on the coach and the coach starts moving.

* * *

There is an old pomegranate tree on a hill. Theopile and Thoma are standing by the tree. The father and the son are looking at a coach going down the road. Then Theopile takes Thoma in his arms, takes his luggage in his hand and takes a few steps forward to look at the view from the hill. He smiles. We see a very beautiful landscape below; exactly the one Theopile used to see when he was away from home. A green valley, a country road that leads to the gates of a nice fenced yard, a small river, a bond bridge, a RIVER BATHING PLACE full of boys splashing and having fun in it; an elegant wooden house in the yard and two golden bulls grazing grass slowly.
Theopile's face shines with joy on seeing the landscape he's missed so much. He puts his luggage down, holds Thoma tight against his chest with his both hands and whispers in German:
Theopile: Look at all these, Thoma... Your eyes should hold the memory of this beauty, my son. I had this image before my eyes for six long years spent in Germany and it helped me come back home. MAY God BLESS YOU and PROTECT YOU from being ever forced to leave this place, but, who knows, if it still happens, you should bear this image in your mind, never let it escape your memory… nowhere and never ... because ... because ... this is your homeland, Thoma... (He takes the luggage in his hand again and walks down the narrow path)

As they approach the river bathing place, the noise made by the boys having fun in the river can be clearly heard. Some of them are swimming, while others are jumping from a cliff and diving into the water, others are lying on a sandy bank of the river. Not far away a bond bridge can be seen. Two young men are walking over the bridge, one follows the other; they are looking at the boys having fun in the river and are smiling. Suddenly they see Theopile and Thoma and start looking and inspecting them.

Manuchar: Who's that man?

Sisona: I wonder… he might be our dad, Manuchar… His MANNER of walking is like that of our dad's…

Manuchar: No, brother, it's impossible. Can't you see he's holding a child in his hands?

Sisona: (He NARROWS HIS EYES in an attempt to focus) He's our dad, Manuchar, I swear he's our dad… My God… move, Manuchar, move, he's our dad, I say!

Manuchar: Yes, Sisona, You're right... he's our dad. You go first... Move ahead, I've gone weak at my knees...

Manuchar lets Sisona walk ahead of him and follow him. They hurry to the river bank. The bond bridge swings as they run over it. The bridge is about to be torn, but both boys manage to run over it safely and sound and they run to the place where their father is standing with a child in his hands. Theopile sees the boys and lets the child to stand on the ground, puts down the luggage and hugs both boys at the same time. Neither of them is able to utter a word, their eyes are full of tears. Finally, Manuchar speaks up, but his speech is not fluent, he speaks separate words and phrases.

Manuchar: Dad... Where... How... The war is over... So long... And you?... Mom? Does she know? Maybe not... I'll run... Dad... Tell her... No, no... Sisona will go... He'll tell her... No, not him... You go... go alone... We'll come later... Who's this child, Dad?

Sisona: Yes, Manuchar is right... Go there alone, we'll hide and come later... Who's this child, Dad? (He looks at Thoma) He looks like Manuchar and me. (Sisona throws his father a questioning look)

Theopile: Ok, you win! I'll go there alone... together with Thoma. His name's Thoma, welcome him. He's your youngest brother, Thoma Darchia. He's a good boy, but he can't speak Georgian yet.

Manuchar: Really? What language does he speak then?

Theopile: German! He speaks German. He hasn't learned Georgian yet, but he'll learn it when you speak to him.

Manuchar and Sisona SQUAT down to the child and look at him with a smile on their faces.

Sisona: He's a good boy indeed! Is your name Thoma? Hello Thoma! (Sisona extends his right hand to Thoma) Come on let's shake hands. (Thoma smiles back at him and after a short pause shakes his hand with Sisona. Everyone looks happy and they start walking towards their house)

Manuchar: Dad, there are our bulls grazing grass at the gates, do you remember them? They were calves when you left home, I wonder if they recognize you.

Theopile: We'll see, let's get near first. You're asking me whether I remember them, they would come in my dreams. I would call them from afar and they would immediately stop grazing grass, would raise their heads and fix their big eyes on me. I'll do so now. I'll call from afar, let's see whether they recognize me or not.

Sisona: You're right Dad. You don't have to get near them either, in case they don't recognize you. They don't get on with strangers. They only obey Manuchar and me. Even Mom finds it difficult to make them do anything. We won't go any further, Melita will see us and that will be the end of our plans.

Manuchar and Sisona turn off the road and hide behind a huge tree standing nearby. Theopile and Thoma continue their way towards the gates. There is two big golden bulls grazing grass near the gates. The golden RAYS of the SETTING SUNSHINE over their sleek horns. Theo stops and watches them for a while with a smile on his face. Then he calls them as before:

Theopile: Attila! Ocean!

The bulls immediately stop grazing, raise their heads and look at Theopile. One of them stretches its neck and bellows as if expressing joy.

Theopile: Come here Attila! Come here Ocean!

On hearing these calls both bulls start trotting towards Theopile. Theopile puts Thoma down on the ground and stands in front of him, protecting him by covering him with his body and is waiting for the bulls to approach him. The bulls approach him and try to lick his hands. Theopile strokes their necks. His eyes are full of tears. He kisses one of them on the forehead, then the other. Then he scratches them both on the forehead. Bulls occasionally bellow with their nostrils flared as if expressing satisfaction. Sisona sticks his head out from behind the lime-tree and looks at his father.

Manuchar: What's going on Sisona?

Sisona: You wouldn't believe; they recognized him… It's simply amazing… after so many years…

Manuchar: I knew... What are they doing?

Sisona: They're licking his hands, I think. (Suddenly Sisona hides behind the tree trunk) Manuchar! Mom has come out of the house; she is in the yard walking to the gates.

A woman walks upright towards the gates. She is tall and slender with a beautiful face, but she seems to be burdened with the sorrow of parting with the loved one. She is wearing black clothes and a black HEADDRESS, FROM WHICH her black hair with a FEW sparse of GREY can be seen. Her face looks slightly tired but that can't hide her amazing charm. Invisible melancholy is in her big black eyes. As she walks towards the gates, her face puts on an expression of surprise when she notices a stranger standing by the bulls. She opens the gate, walks through them and stops.

Theopile notices Melita. He raises his head, straightens himself and smiles at her. Melita's expression reveals the surprise for a brief moment as if she's stepped on a thorn, and then she struggles to utter a single word, but she finds it difficult to speak, she moves her lips and we guess that she wants to say: Theo...

They stand still for a while, staring at each other. Then Melita finds the courage to move forward, takes off her apron in a single swift move and throws it on the ground; then she takes off her headdress and throws it on the ground as well. She lifts HER HEAD and TOSSES HER HAIR BACK over HER shoulders, takes a step towards Theopile and overcome with EMOTIONAL EXHAUSTION, she faints and FALLS to the GROUND. Theopile immediately comes running up to Melita, kneels down and they hug each other.

Theopile: Melita, you'll never know how much I've been missing you.

Melita: Theo... My... Theo...

They keep on repeating these words speaking simultaneously. They remain in this position until a cough is heard; they look up to see Manuchar, Sisona, and Thoma. Theopile smiles, he looks very happy. He stands up and helps Melita to stand up. Then he takes Thoma by the hand and makes him stand in front of Melita:

Theopile: Melita! This is Thoma. He is an orphan ... his mother died. You have to look after him...

Melita throws Theopile a questioning look, and then she bends down towards Thoma and looks at him for a while. Then she takes Thoma by the hand and they start walking towards the gates. Thoma follows her without any protest. They enter through the gates. Theopile, Manuchar, and Sisona are standing and watching them walking towards the house. Theopile calls out for Melita and Thoma to hear him:

Theopile: Melita, he doesn't speak Georgian...

Melita walks unhurriedly towards the house holding Thoma by the hand.

***

Gurian kitchen... There is a poorly laid low table on the porch of the house. A hearth can be seen from an open door. The fire is burning in the hearth and there is an earthenware frying-pan over the fire in the hearth. A sooty chain suspends from the smoke hole and the hook at the end of the chain holds a black cauldron with bubbling millet in it. Melita is busy making dishes. There is an earthware pot full of cornbread dough near the fire. Suddenly heat dried dough noisily cracks in two or three places and streams of vapor start coming out of it with a specific noise. Melita takes the earthware pot with her hands covered with her apron and puts it on the hearth surface. There are Theopile, Manuchar, Sisona, Makharbeli – Theopile's neighbor and Batlome – Theopile's friend sitting around the low table. Thoma is sitting next to his father on a small stump.

Theopile: Melita, are you going to bring us anything else, or do we have to finish?
Melita: (Melita answers him from the kitchen) Just a minute, Theo, the duck is ready and millet as well. I'm bringing them.

Makharbeli: I want to raise a toast to Theopile. We're all so happy you are back, Theopile, I mean not only your family but the whole village especially your neighbors and friends. We were brought up to love one another; our parents taught us to respect one another; we've always relied on one another and thanks to God, we will always be there for one another. Your sons are good boys, Theopile; they did their best to make your absence more bearable and less painful for your family. In case they had failed we would definitely have stood by them, been there for them. But now, you're back and everything is much better, Theopile. We've all been missing you so much. Let's thank God for your safe and sound return to your homeland. Let's raise our glasses and drink to that!

The men raise their glasses and drink the toast. Theopile raises his glass to thank them all. Melita comes out of the kitchen, holding a cauldron with her both hands and puts it in the middle of the table.

Batlome: Long life to you, Theopile, my friend. I was on cloud nine when I heard you'd come back. My son saw you when you came; He was swimming in the river; he came rushing to me, shouting: "Dad, Dad, Uncle Theopile has returned from the war". At first, I thought my son must have mistaken someone else for you. So many years have passed since the war ended and ... it's now 6 years since you went away, isn't it?

Theopile: Yes, it is.

Batlome: So, that's why I was not sure, but how could I have stayed there at home and not check what was going on? I thought I would go and look around to find out whether it was true. May all your wishes come true as it was the case with me! And may the Lord bless you and your family as you made me feel so happy! You have your sons standing by you and here's Thoma, a great boy! So, may God bless you and your family with all the happiness and protect you from all the troubles. Let's live in peace and let's love and respect one another 'till the end of our days. (He drinks the glass to the end; puts the glass on the table; turns to Theopile and says) Where did you stop? The Germans walked in front of you and asked who could sing. You were saying this, weren't you?

Theopile: Exactly, but they were interested in Russian songs.

Batlome: Why Russian and why not Georgian?

Theopile: Because… do you think, Batlome, anyone in Germany, maybe with a few exceptions, knows that we - Georgian people are a different nation and Georgia is a different country? That's not the case believe me. For Germans all the prisoners of war in the camp were Russians and of course, they would look for Russian songs there, wouldn't they?

Makharbeli: But how did they learn that you were not Russian?

Theopile: I told them. I told them I could sing but not Russian but Georgian songs. Luckily, the man had heard about Georgia and Georgian songs as well. He was a professor at the University of Berlin, Werner Pere, after that we got on well with each other. We lived in his house all this time.

Manuchar: What did you do Dad? Did you sing alone?

Theopile: How could I sing alone? There were two Georgians with me in the camp; one was from Ozurgeti, Gregory Megrelishvili and the other from Senaki, Kalistrate Kankava. They gave us two hours to prepare a song. The two men both were very good at singing... we were so lucky.

Sisona: Then, Dad? So, what happened afterward?

Theopile: Afterwards, they liked our song and let us - the three of us - move to the professor's house. We were working there in his yard - he had a huge one there - and singing songs. Meanwhile the war was over. We were about to leave, but we couldn't because of him (Theopile strokes Thoma's head) - Thoma! His mother died while giving birth to him. We couldn't travel such a long way with a newborn baby. We had to wait two more years. My friends didn't want to leave me there alone... and now I'm here with you. (Theopile smiles)

Batlome: Which song did you sing, Theopile, when you sang there for the first time?

Theopile: We sang short Mravalzhamieri.

Batlome: This one? (He starts singing a tune)

Theopile: Exactly! Kankava sang higher and the man from Ozurgeti sang bass... No, no, on the contrary, Kalistrate sang bass.

Makharbeli: Ok, but did you sing well? A silly question to ask, if you hadn't, I wouldn't be holding this glass now! Frankly speaking I would like to sing one right now, but... Batlome is of no help and what about your sons? Which of them can help us?

Theopile: Wait a while. Kallisto is coming. He'll be here in a minute. He let me know he'd close the shop and come running right away. Let's wait for him and sing together when he comes. I've been missing you and singing together with you.

Batlome: (looks in the direction of the wooden house) Speak of the devil and he doth appear; Kallisto's come.

Kallisto appears from a corner of the wooden house. He is holding a large pack of something in his hand. Theopile stands up, meets his friend and when he is about to hug him, Kallisto stops him with his hand.

Kallisto: Wait a minute... Batlome, stand up and take this. Where is Melita? Give it to her. I've brought something from my shop...

Melita: (coming out of the kitchen) That's so kind of you, Kallisto, but you didn't have to bother bringing all these, we have plenty of everything...

Kallisto: I do know, Melita, but ... don't mention it? The shop is mine, at least until the Communists confiscate it. (He gives the pack to Melita and turns to Theopile) What's going on, man? I was planning to go to Germany to see you. If you don't believe me you may ask Batlome, I was going to Germany tomorrow and you arrived just in time. Come Theo; let me hug you. (They hug each other and tap each other's backs with their open palms) What's going on, Theo? We've been missing you so much? I haven't heard of anyone who fails to find his way back home for six years!

Makharbeli: Stop it now, Kallisto! Leave him alone! The man survived the war and do you want to smother him with your hug? Come, sit down here, take this glass, have a drink and let's do something... I just can't wait.

Kallisto stops hugging Theopile and turns to Thoma doing his best to hide his tears that fill his eyes.

Kallisto: Who is this young man? I've been told his name is Thoma... Is it so? Hallo, Thoma. (Kallisto holds out his right hand. Thoma immediately taps his hand against Kallisto's hand very hard) Look, how strong this little guy is! I wanted to shake hands with you I didn't want you to break my arm! (Kallistro stokes Thoma's head smiling down at him, and then he takes his seat on a stump, takes a glass and asks) Did you say, Makharbel, that you can't wait? Start then! What are you waiting for?
Makharbeli: Which one do you want me to start, Kallisto?
Kallisto: Which one? Let's sing the one about Theopile's grandfather - a great man; Theopile named one of his sons after him... Sisona is his namesake...
Makharbeli: you mean a song about Sisona Darchia? May God bless you. Manuchar, give me that Chonguri[20], please.
Manuchar takes the Chonguri placed against the kitchen wall and gives it to Makharbeli. Makharbeli takes the Chonguri and strums up and down the strings several times to tune the Chonguri and then starts playing it, screws up his eyes and starts singing. Theopile and Kallisto join him immediately. Melta can be seen through the door, she is standing still, holding a plate with boiled chicken on it. The dish is still hot, giving off steam. Melita can't move. She is standing behind the door and listening to the men singing. Her eyes twinkle like chips of coal. She brings the plate close to her chest. We have a close-up view of her face lit with delight and see her face blurred by the steam drifting up from the plate.

---

[20] A four-stringed musical instrument widespread in the western part of Georgia

Kallisto: (After finishing singing raises his glass and says thoughtfully) They say the nobles were shot dead today in Zestaponi, they were herded and packed into a carriage like cattle and… shot dead with a machine-gun, the bastards. And the nobles were all the best, outstanding men… Can anybody tell me what's going on?
Theopile: I witnessed this mass killing, Kallisto. It was quite by accident... (Theopile frowns) Our train had just entered the station. It happened right in front of my eyes. First blood leaked from the carriage and then flew in streams. I would never have thought I would be horrified by anything after the war? What's really happening here? Is it the end of the world?
Batlome: What's happening, Theopile... how to say, I don't know ... hard times came upon us. A half of Guria found their shelter in the forests and the second half is chasing after them. Gogia Ghlonti has a group of his own and Lasaia[21] Mantskava[22] – another group. They chase after Chekists and kill them wherever they find them, but no one is able to put them to rout. You kill one and they are sending three. When you were coming back home by train, didn't you go through Russia? Did you see how huge it is? And there is a handful of us there; so, we'll all die in fight with them, but should we? All our efforts will be to no avail. Is there a way out? I would sacrifice my life if anyone told me where a way out of this stalemate is.
Kallisto: That's enough, Batlome, stop complaining now. What good is it? Our friend has just come home and we grieve him instead of trying to make him feel happy.

---

[21] A name of a man

[22] Last name

Batlome: I was not the one who started talking about this. Was it me who said that the nobles were shot dead in Zestaponi?
Kallisto: No, it wasn't you, it was me. But I said it was enough, didn't I? Now listen to me, OK? (Kallisto starts singing a new song. Theopile and Makharbeli join him. We hear only the beginning of the song and the episode ends with this song)

***

We see the same river. There are a lot of boys in the river; only their heads can be seen on the surface of the water; they are all looking up at a cliff. There is a caption on the screen "Nine Years Later". One of the boys, his head turned towards the cliff, says:
A boy: Are you scared, Thoma? Take a STEP BACK, then rush forward and jump!
Thoma is standing at the edge of the cliff. He is about 11 or 12 years old, a very good-looking boy. He is smiling and looking down at the river. The bathing place full of boys' wet heads seems dangerously remote to him, but he takes some steps back then rushes forward crying:
Thoma: I'm coming! (He plummets into the water with a loud splash and then comes out of the water looking happy)
At the same time, two men dressed in Chekists' uniforms step onto the bond bridge. They are carrying firearms and heading towards the center of the village. They hear the boys making noise and look in the direction of bathing place. Not far from the bathing place, there are two bulls standing in the shallow water and drinking water greedily. The bulls attract the Chekists' attention.
Chekist I (Borya): Zorbeg, do you see the bulls? We need them. I wonder who their owner might be. Let's ask Oboladze.

Chekist II (Zorbeg): Why on earth! We don't need to ask Oboladze. What the hell we are doing here? I don't care whose bulls they are. No one dares to refuse us to give what we ask for. Come on let's call those suckers. (Zorbeg calls loudly) Boy, look here... Yes, I'm calling you. Come here.

One of the boys treads[23] along the river noisily towards the bridge, stops under the bridge, where the Chekists are standing and looks up at them with his eyes WIDE OPEN.

Chekist II (Zorbeg): Whose are those bulls over there? Do you know?

The boy: They belong to Thoma's father. Thoma is here with us. Do you want me to call him?

Chekist II (Zorbeg): Yes, tell him to come.

The boy goes running and calling Thoma. He runs to the bathing place and says something to Thoma, pointing to the bridge. Now Thoma comes running to the place where the two Chekists are standing.

Thoma: Here I am. He (points to the boy) told me you wanted to ask me something.

Chekist II (Zorbeg): Are those bulls yours, boy?

Thoma: Those bulls? Yes, they are my father's bulls.

Chekist II (Zorbeg): Who is your father?

Thoma: My father is Theopile Darchia...

Chekist II (Zorbeg): Very good! I mean your bulls are very good and maybe you have a cart as well? A good cart... I mean.

Thoma: Yes, we do, we have a cart as well...

---

[23] walk in a specified way.

Chekist II (Zorbeg): (His voice gets stricter all of a sudden) Then go, pull the bulls out of the water. Run to your father and tell him to come to the Cheka yard in half an hour... and to bring the cart with him. We have to transport some arms to Ozurgeti. We will return the cart tomorrow. Go ahead and do as I say. (In order to sound more convincing, while speaking he touches his Mauser several times) We'll go now, and you tell your father to let sleeping dogs lie... In half an hour...
The Chekists go over the bridge. Thoma looks at the bulls first and then runs home.

***

The residence of the head of Gurian Chekists, a so-called extraordinary chargé d'affaires Aslan Oboladze... is located in an open area. Trees have been purposefully cut down in the territory surrounding the residence, making it nearly impossible for anyone to APPROACH the yard UNNOTICED. The fence around is very high and has a big wooden gate made of thick planks. The yard together with the house once belonged to a local nobleman Gugunava. Now a bigger house serves as an office; Aslan Oboladze lives in a smaller one; the stable is made into barracks and the cattle-shed into a prison. The two Chekists we saw on the bridge are now standing by the wooden gates. One of them takes a watch out of his pocket, opens it and looks at it.
Chekist II (Zorbeg): Where is that son of a bitch?! If he doesn't appear in five minutes, I'll go there and I'll make away with him right in his yard...
Chekist I (Borya): Calm down, Zorbeg. He's coming. Don't you hear a SQUEAK OF cartwheels? It's very near now, just behind the tree we didn't cut.

The cart arrives. Theopile is sitting in it. He looks relaxed and is smoking a pipe. The Chekists open the gates. There is a pile of arms ready to be transported: rifles, wooden boxes full of ammunition and a machine gun. Theopile jumps off the cart lead the bulls through the gates and parks the cart comfortably by the pile of arms. He greets the Chakists coldly and asks somehow indifferently:

Theopile: Is that all or do you have to add anything to this pile?

Chekist I (Borya): No, that's all what we have to take.

They start loading the cart with the arms. Theopile is the one who does almost everything. He puts the arms and ammunitions in the cart so that the weight is evenly distributed between the two bulls.

Aslan Oboladze is standing at the window and watches Theopile through the break in the curtains. Aslan Oboladze is the very person who supervised the execution of the nobles at the station. He addresses a person standing just behind him:

Aslan Oboladze: Lazare, come and have a look at this person! Who is he?

Lazare looks through the break in the curtains to see Theopile.

Lazare: He is Theopile Darchia; he lives on the other side of the river.

Aslan Oboladze: I have never heard the name... Theopile Darchia, but I think I have seen him somewhere before. I can't quite recall where exactly, but I'm sure I have seen him... Look! His bulls are just perfect...

Theopile finishes loading the cart and turns to the two Chekists:

Theopile: What are you going to do? Will you come and sit in the cart or will you follow it on foot?

Chekist I (Borya): Does it really matter to you?

Theopile: It does. If you decide to get in the cart, I will have to redistribute the load evenly…

Chekist I (Borya): We'll get in the cart. You don't think that we are going to walk all the way to Ozurgeti, do you? We'll put some hay on these guns and hit the hay.

The Chekists put some hay on top of the arms in the cart. Theopile leads the bulls through the gates and out of the yard; one of the Chekists closes the gates and then both Chekists get in the cart. Theopile takes a front-seat and says:

Theopile: Go ahead, Attila, Ocean…

The bulls take to the road. A boy climbs down the tree standing nearby. He clings to the lowest branch of the tree, jumps down on the ground and runs away.

***

We are in Theopile's yard. Makharbeli – Theopile's neighbor, Manuchar, Sisona, and Melita are standing at the door of the wooden house and discussing the latest developments. The gates open and Thoma is coming through the gates.

Makharbeli: Here he is... They sent Thoma to tell Theopile to go there, didn't they?

Melita: Yes, Thoma delivered the message saying they would be waiting for him in half an hour...

Makharbeli: I was told there were two of them there, Thoma. Is it so?

Thoma: It is. There were two of them there.

Makharbeli: There were two of them on the bridge, but who knows how many of them joined them afterward...

Thoma: No one. I secretly followed Dad. Nobody saw me. Then I climbed the tree and watched them from there. The tree is a bit far from the gates, but I saw everything that was going on in there. The same two men I had seen on the bridge accompanied Dad. They put some hay in the cart and both lie down on that hay.

Makharbeli: So, it seems that they were not lying when they said that Gogia Ghlonti and Lasa Mantskava left for Turkey together with their squads. Otherwise neither a pair of Chekists would dare to wander at night nor would they dare to take arms to Ozurgeti. I think they had hidden their arms in the homes of their agents in different villages; they never knew where and when they would need them. I was not quite sure before but now I see Oboladze feel relieved. He is no longer as aggressive as he used to be. He is now a so-called extraordinary Chargé d'affaires, they have forged a title and given him the right and power to do whatever he thinks of. Give a bastard a power and one should know what might happen! Power can be intoxicating, my son. Oboladze, that dirty bastard brought misery and desolation to so many people in Guria. If he doesn't like a person, he aims the muzzle at his forehead and that's all; nobody would judge him. Anyway, as only two men accompanied him, believe me, Melita, everything will be fine; he'll deliver the arms to Ozurgeti and come back tomorrow afternoon. Wait a little while.

Melita: May God hear your words, Makharbel. He went there to save the boys from danger; but you know him, if anything goes wrong there, he won't give in... That's what I'm afraid of... I don't want him to make the ultimate sacrifice.

Makharbeli: But Melita, you've forgotten that we're talking about Theopile. Do you know anybody wiser than him? Not in our region, I suppose. Do you really think he will surrender to these two bastards? So, don't worry, go into the house and calm down. We have to wait for him; anyway, we don't have any other options.

Sisona: We do have one, Uncle Makharbel; Manuchar and I can saddle our horses and follow them, take a short-cut road and catch them up. And if we manage to find a short cut through the Rukhumela gorge, we will get ahead of them and meet them there. Isn't it so, Manuchar?

Manuchar: It is. And besides, there are only two of them there, even if there were a dozen of them, it wouldn't be a problem. We'll disarm them and let them go.

Makharbeli: And then? Have you thought what you are supposed to do afterward? You wouldn't return home and find shelter in the woods; that's just what Gogia Glonti did! Stop talking nonsense. Let us wait a while. It is never late to take up arms and wage war... we can do this when the time comes...

***

It's night. A bright moon lights the sky. A cart is going along the road, making a squeaking noise. Two Chekists are lying in the cart and speaking in a low voice. Theopile is lying near the coach-box and sleeping. The bulls are making their way on their own.

Chekist II (Zorbeg): In short, Oboladze is furious. He had been chasing Ghlonti and Mantskava for such a long time and both men found their shelter in Turkey. Besides, they say they had left a message threatening they would be back soon and slit Oboladze's throat, wouldn't even bother to waste a bullet on him.

Chekist I (Borya): I agree with you. He hasn't been in a particularly good mood recently, but he tries not to show it. He must be happy that they have gone. He couldn't go a day without thinking about them. He hadn't even had a good night's sleep till they went to Turkey. Ghlonti and Mantskava haunted him even in his dreams. He failed to cope with them and now he tries to make scapegoats of us. Can't you see how he treats us? He raises his voice whenever he speaks to us... yelling at us all the time… (He looks at Theopile) Look at this bastard! He is sleeping like a log. Does he think he has clairvoyant bulls? How can they make their way on their own?

Chekist II (Zorbeg): Wake him up and tell him to lead his bulls… They're his not mine…

Chekist I (Borya): Let him sleep for a while. He might refuse to turn to the river; the river is swollen, and he might say he can't cross it. Therefore, let him sleep and when we come to the point I'll make the bulls turn. He'll be obliged to face the fact and will have no option but to cross the river. This way we will get there at least two hours earlier…

Chekist II (Zorbeg): Refuse you say? Is it at his pleasure to decide what to do? We have our Mausers here in case he refuses, don't we? When he feels the cold muzzle on his forehead, he'll be as pliant as a bamboo.

***

Manuchar, Sisona, Makharbel, and Kallisto are sitting on a balcony of Theopile's house. Thoma is standing nearby and feverishly listening to each of them speaking one by one. Melita is not with them.

Manuchar: Uncle Makharbel, Uncle Kallisto, we have already decided what to do! Sisona and I will set off at dawn. If we meet him on our way to Ozurgeti, we'll come back together. If not, we'll have to ride to Ozurgeti and try to find out what has happened to him. Who knows maybe misfortune has fallen upon us!

Kallisto: It's not a problem, Manuchar, but maybe you have to believe us, we are older and more experienced. Don't you think about Melita? Now all of her worries are about Theopile, and you're going to make her worries triple. As if one is not enough to worry about! I ask you to stay at home until yesterday afternoon. If he is not back till then, Makharbel and I will join you. I think Batlome will come with us as well. And we know one or two daredevils there and we can turn to them for help.

***

It's night again. A bright moon lights the sky and the road on which the cart is being pulled by the bulls making their way slowly along the road. Theopile is sleeping and the two Chekists are talking.

Chekist II (Zorbeg): Did you see the rifle they delivered yesterday? It has a rifle scope attached to it.

Chekist I (Borya): Really? Has it already been delivered? I knew that they had ordered it but I haven't seen it.

Chekist II (Zorbeg): It's so beautiful you can't take your eyes off it. It's made in Germany... I even held it in my hands. It's so gorgeous I wanted to kiss it, you know?

Chekist I (Borya): Don't you know what he needs it for?

Chekist II (Zorbeg): Who do you mean, Oboladze? Don't give me away; I think he needs the rifle for that German man who's come to Ozurgeti. Have you heard of him? A ubiquitous fellow; he is constantly on the move, twenty-four hours a day; he's never in one place long.

Chekist I (Borya): Yes, but what does Oboladze have against him? Has he had enough of Georgian blood and now wants to taste that of a German?

Chekist II (Zorbeg): I have no idea what does Oboladze wants... who knows? Who can tell what thoughts could occur to him? I was commissioned to besiege the German. I'd been after him for a month or so, besides I was instructed to remain invisible to him. Oh! I wish you know the distance he covered in a month! I was absolutely exhausted. I don't know why, but he was prone to walk along the riverbanks. He would start at dawn and follow the riverside upstream all the way to the Riverhead. He would often stop, stand still a while as if stiffened and observe surroundings. Neither woods nor prickly hedge or weather could stop him – the bastard. He was dressed in canvas clothes, protecting him from thorns and burdocks. As for me, I used to bleed in the evening because of scratches on my skin. I have trekked the banks of Supsa[24], Natanebi, Rioni[25] and Pichori, Bzhuzhi and Gubazeuli[26] with him.

Chekist I (Borya): Why does he do this? Is he insane? Walking up and down the riverbanks... He should have a reason for this...

Chekist II (Zorbeg): I don't know. I couldn't explain it. I even asked Oboladze, but...

---

[24] A Black Sea port village in western Georgia.

[25] The Rioni or Rion River is the main river of western Georgia. It originates in the Caucasus Mountains, in the region of Racha and flows west to the Black Sea

[26] A river in western region of Georgia

Chekist I (Borya): And what did he tell you?

Chekist II (Zorbeg): He told me it was not my business... that my duty was to follow him wherever he went and told me to mind my own business. I was lucky that they delegated the duty to someone else. It was such a burden for me... I nearly died.

Chekist I (Borya): Who did they make happy? Is he one of us?

Chekist II (Zorbeg): No, a woman arrived from Tbilisi; she speaks German... She is pretending to be his personal interpreter. They are planning something against this German, believe me. He says he is an archeologist. Have you heard of them? They dig ground and look for some old things... So, don't be surprised if they make him dig ground ahead of time, dig his own grave. When Oboladze makes up his mind, no one is ever able to make him change it.

Chekist I (Borya): hush! Don't talk so much. He might not be sleeping and what if he hears everything we talk about? We should be more careful.

Chekist II (Zorbeg): You mean what if he hears us?! What's the problem? Let him... Do you think he would go, find the German and warn him about all these? Do you think he is in the mood for caring for a German? Even if he suddenly feels like committing a heroic deed or sacrificing his life for a higher cause, he will not do it for two reasons!

Chekist I (Borya): What's the second reason?

Chekist II (Zorbeg): And do you know what the first reason is?

Chekist I (Borya): No, I don't. But you can tell me in short. Come on what are you waiting for?

Chekist II (Zorbeg): Ok, first of all, he must be aware of what awaits him in this case… a bullet in his head… from Oboladze. Besides, how are they supposed to communicate at all if they don't speak the same language? That man doesn't understand Georgian and this one doesn't speak German. As for the interpreter, I've told you that she is our agent. So, if he isn't asleep and if he hears what we talk about, he'd better pretend to be asleep.

Chekist I (Borya): Look here, I think we've just passed by the crossing. We had to turn there… (He sits up and looks closely at the road) Yes, we definitely passed by it! We have to stop these bulls. (He jumps off the cart; goes ahead the bulls; stops them; catches hold of the rope wrapped over the yoke and try to make them turn, but he fails, because the bulls don't obey him. They stand stubbornly and don't move. The second Chekist jumps off the cart)

Chekist II (Zorbeg): What's up Borya, can't you make them turn?

Chekist I (Borya): No, I can't. I just can't make them move. One of them turned its head so abruptly… nearly caught me on its horn... F...k … stop laughing… come and try yourself.

Chekist II (Zorbeg): Let them alone. We won't manage to make them turn. They must be obeyed only their owners. We have to wake him up.

Theopile: I'm not sleeping. Tell me what's going on! (Theopile is standing and looking at them)

Chekist II (Zorbeg): What do you think is going on?! We had to turn there and we can't move these bulls. They are as stubborn as a mule. Get off that cart; don't just stand idly there... Get off and make these crazy bulls move... Do what I tell you... immediately, if you don't want us to...

Theopile: Easy, man. What's all that buzz about? I'm not a coward. I'm here with you trying to help you not because I was scared... You'd better leave those bulls alone. Didn't I tell you they would find their way on their own? They know that they have to go straight ahead to get to Ozurgeti; they won't turn if I don't tell them to do so.

Chekist I (Borya): What are you waiting for, then? Get off and make them turn. We have to take a short-cut road.

Theopile: No way! It has been raining heavily for the last two days in the mountains. The river is swollen, and we can't cross it. The bridge is very old and made of narrow wooden planks. I don't think it can bear the load of the cart full of arms. Even if it could, how would the bulls go over it? Look at their hooves; they are fully covered in clay mud; and besides, those narrow wooden planks of the bridge must be wet; they may easily lose their foothold there or get their legs trapped between the planks and break their legs. What if one of them breaks its leg? How are we going to get to Ozurgeti then?

Zorgeb draws his rifle and says in a strict tone:

Chekist II (Zorbeg): Did you finish? Now listen to me carefully. Get off that cart, immediately! Make your bulls take a short-cut road, or I'll have to bury your dead body here together with your bulls...

Theopile doesn't even move. He stands there eyeing the author of these words for a while; then he turns his look to the second Chekist and then looks at the first one again.

Chekist I (Borya): Just look at him, Zorbeg, he's eyeing us so evilly (He draws his rifle, aims it at Theopile and says through clenched teeth) Don't you hear us?

Theopile jumps off the cart. The two Chekists step back instinctively. Theopile seems to have made a decision. He approaches the bulls saying:

Theopile: Don't get so furious, put those toys away. I have seen worse when I was out on the battlefield. Ok, men, you won, let's take a short-cut road... But remember if something happens to these bulls you only have yourselves to blame...

The Chekists look at each other in amazement.

Chekist I (Borya): Did I hear him right? Has he just threatened us, Zorbeg?

Chekist II (Zorbeg): Leave him alone! We have to get to Ozurgeti... first.

***

Theopile's house. Melita is in her room; she is in her bed, lying on a bedsheet, her knees bent and slightly folded in towards her chest; she is dressed in her casual clothes; a shawl covers her legs. She is reading a book, with old faded pages. A faint light of a kerosene lamp illuminates the room. She gets up, puts the open book on a chair that is standing by the bed; turns the wick of the kerosene lamp down, takes it in her hand and tiptoes to the room next to hers. Thoma is lying in his bed asleep. Melita looks down at him, covers him up with his blanket and goes to the small room, where she puts the kerosene lamp on an old-fashioned chest-of-drawers. There is a Virgin Mary icon on the chest-of-drawers. Melita lights a candle looks at the Virgin Mary icon with her hands held out in supplication and starts praying in a very low voice:

Melita: Virgin Mary, I humbly beseech Thee, look with favor upon my family, have mercy upon my Theo, deliver him out of all troubles. If he has committed an unforgivable sin, let me repent of his sins, Virgin Mary, lay penance on me ... Let me do penance for him, take my life and take my soul to Heaven when I die. As Theo has already suffered a lot, Virgin Mary; Therefore, I implore Thee, don't make Thoma an orphan and me a widow, and don't leave us alone in this sinful world. Have mercy and pity upon your son Theo, light his path on his road and bring him back to me safe and sound. Teach him the only true way and lead him in a straight path, don't ever let him expose himself and his family to danger. I pray you, Virgin Mary...

***

The cart is near the dangerous bridge. Theopile is standing in front of his bulls and is looking at the bridge as if examining it. He looks worried. The Chekists are standing behind the cart, waiting for further developments.

Theopile: So, we have to unload the cart and carry the arms over the bridge. After that, I will try to lead the bulls over it.

Zorbeg: Don't touch the arms. We'll take them over the bridge. Take care of your bulls... It is definitely not a bridge but a monstrosity!

They start unloading the cart and carrying the arms across the bridge. They slip on their way over the bridge a couple of times. When they have carried all the arms across the bridge, they shout at Theopile from across the river:

Chekist I (Borya): We've carried everything and now it's your turn.

Theopile: And this machine gun? What are you going to do with it? I'd rather you took this machine gun than arms.

Chekist II (Zorbeg): Let's leave it in the cart... I think the bridge can bear the weight of this single machine gun.

Theopile doesn't answer anything. He goes to the cart, rolls the machine gun to the back of the cart, then approaches the cart from behind, takes it in his arms and carries it across the bridge, puts it next to the pile of arms, and goes back to the place where he left his bulls. The Chekists look at him. One of them says:

Chekist I (Borya): Did you see that? He is as strong as an ox. I DON'T ENVY those who dare to put up with him!

Theopile goes to one of the bulls, strokes and kisses its forehead. Then he turns to the other and strokes it as well. Then he catches hold of the yoke, stands facing them and says:

Theopile: Attila, Ocean**...** keep your chins up, the bridge has very large fissures, and it's wet, you should be very careful. Do you hear me, Attila? First, you have to examine well the place where you have to step with your hooves and only then put your leg there. You have to do the same, Ocean. You understand me, don't you? Let's move, I rely on you, you know. So, follow me slowly... Slowly, I said. Slowly, Attila, slowly, don't try to go ahead of Ocean... Don't hurry... Now you are a good boy. You are both my good boys!

Bulls step on the bridge and start moving slowly as if they have understood everything, what Theopile told them, we see them stepping on the ground and moving ahead only after examining it by their hooves. At one point one of the bulls - Ocean slips and the other one - Attila, as if sensing something is going wrong, stops abruptly, even holds its leg in the air until Ocean regains balance and finds solid ground to step on.

Finally, they reach the end of the bridge safely. The Chekists standing at the bank of the river look surprised. They have been watching them crossing the bridge with their jaws dropped open and when they see that everything is over one of them says:

Chekist I (Borya): Zorbeg, I don't believe my eyes. No one will ever believe me if I tell them what I have just seen. I'm happy I was not alone. You have to confirm my words when I tell this, OK? Have you ever seen anything like this?

Chekist II (Zorbeg): No, I haven't. I'm just shocked. Did you see how they were examining the ground before stepping on it? Do you think they understood what the man was telling them?

Chekist I (Borya): Believe it or not... the bulls have pulled the cart over the bridge. (He turns to Theopile and says in a reconciliatory manner) Bravo, man, you have to be proud of your bulls. You saved them from breaking their legs, but you have to remember that they have just saved your life. You owe them your life... Leave these arms alone. We'll take care of them. You may have a rest for a while.

The two Chekists start loading the cart with the arms.

***

It is night. Theopile's cart is standing in front of a gate. Moonlight falls on a pretty house standing on flatland in the middle of a neat yard. A well with its windlass can be seen near the gate. Theopile'e cart is empty and the Chekists are no longer accompanying him.

Theopile gets off the cart and goes to the gate. He starts calling in a low voice as if trying not to disturb others.

Theopile: Is anybody out there?

He waits for a while and calls again.

Theopile: Gregory!

A noise of a door being open with a squeak can be heard in the yard that is followed by a man calling.

Gregory: Who is it?

Theopile: It's me - Theopile Darchia. Would you let me in?

Gregory: Theo, is that really you, man? You've chosen the right time to visit me – midnight!

He is hurrying to the gate with these words. He comes to Theopile, looks at him with his face lit up and says:

Gregory: I can't believe my eyes! Is it really you! But I guess you've lost the sense of time.

After these words, he hugs his friend and looks at the bulls.

Gregory: Fair enough, man, you can visit me any time, but why don't you leave these bulls alone? By the way, they are just great. Which of the two is Attila?

Theopile: That one... with bigger horns.

Gregory: Wait a minute. I'll open the gate and you lead them in. Untie them; they'll find somewhere to lie. Something must have happened... let's get in and you have to tell me everything in detail.

Theopile: Your door needs to be lubricated. It squeaks. The whole village must have heard you getting out. There is a buffalo horn in the cart. I keep a lubricant there. Remind me in the morning and I'll lubricate your door.

Gregory: Yes, if you are in the mood of doing anything in the morning. Let's first get ourselves properly lubricated… with wine... Chkhaveri[27]. Where would you like to have it in the kitchen or in the dining room?

Theopile: No way, Gregory, I am exhausted. Not because I traveled but because of the stress I've been through. I'll tell you about it later. But first tell me where I can lay my head. Please, don't wake up your family and I don't want anything; so, don't bother yourself.

Gregory: Listen to me, Theo; you might have lost your marbles because of the stress. Natela is already awake, as well as the hen which is to be boiled and the cheese in the cheese vat that is to be made into Khachapuri[28]. You have to tell me how Thoma is! So, you want to lay your head somewhere? No way, man!

***

Theopile and Gregory are in the kitchen. They are sitting by a small table. There is a kerosene lamp on the table.

---

[27] Pink semi-sweet wine

[28] A traditional Georgian dish of cheese-filled bread

Theopile: They've become so swollen-headed... I didn't want them to invade my house and frighten my family. I mean Thoma and Melita... As for my elder sons, they'd rather keep out of Manuchar's and Sisona's way.

Gregory: So, they are evildoers, aren't they?

Theopile: They are evil-minded and how one can expect them to do any good? Do you know how I guessed they've become swollen-headed? I had hidden my gun in the cart, in case I would need it. And they didn't even look at me, not to mention the cart. They are not afraid of men like me and that's why they behaved that way.

Gregory: All is well that ends well! If I happen to meet those Chekists I'll thank them for giving me the opportunity to host you. Now you have to tell me how Thoma is. It's almost two years since I saw him last. As I remember I visited you together with Kalistrate two years ago.

Theophile: Exactly, two years have elapsed... Thoma is fine. He's going to be a brave man. He's so small and rolls haystacks better than we do. When the Chekists told me, I had to owe my life to my bulls they gave me some sugarplums... just threw a box of them in the cart, did me a favor in their own way. The box is in the cart now. I'm going to give you half of its content for your kids and give Thoma the remaining half.

Gregory: I'm not going to take Thoma's sugarplums; I'll get some if I want. You know what? I'll ask my kids to collect some pears for Thoma in the morning and I'll send him some peaches as well, crispy peaches. But you shouldn't forget to tell him that Uncle Gregory has sent them. Don't even dare to confuse our names and tell him that Kalistrate has sent them.

Both men laugh.

Gregory: By the way, don't you want to see Kalistrate, Theo? Let's plan when to visit him.

Theopile: Ok, let's visit him in the winter, after Christmas... when he has had Megrelian Kupati[29] cured in smoke... OK, let's drink one more glass of wine and have a rest. It's a fact that I'm tired as if it is not enough I have kept you up so late.

Gregory: You don't say so! This is the first time such a thing is happening to us. Would anyone dare come to the gate and step in the house as dusk falls?! If nobody comes into your home, nobody opens your squeaky door, and nobody needs your help then what the hell are you doing here on this earth! You might as well be dead... So, if you are tired and want to take a rest, you are welcome, but you don't have to apologize...

Theopile smiles, Gregory smiles back at him.

Theopile: Gregory, until we leave this table I want to ask you something. They say a German man is here in Ozurgeti. Have you caught a glimpse of him? I want to meet him...

Gregory: A German man? I haven't heard of him, Theo. But we'll have no problem collecting information about him. Let's go to the market place tomorrow morning and we'll learn everything straight off. Besides, tomorrow is Saturday. Gurians will give you a detailed account of what's going on even in Africa.

---

[29] A type of Georgian sausage made from pork

Theopile: Let's go, but we have to go there early in the morning because the German, they say, is an early bird; he leaves home at dawn. We have to be there before he leaves.

Gregory: What's the matter? Is everything all right?

Theopile: I'm not quite sure… I think Oboladze is plotting something against him. They've invited a specialist in the German language from Tbilisi to spy on him. She pretends to be his interpreter; and yesterday they received a rifle scope; like the one that was hanging on the wall at Werner's, do you remember? The Chekists were talking about all these on our way here. They thought I was asleep and didn't hear their conversation. They said Oboladze had ordered that rifle for the German. He must be planning to kill him by shooting at him from afar… to leave no trace.

Gregory: You don't say so! Theo, we need to act promptly; that bastard might kill him.

Theopile: That's why I want to find him, Gregory, I want to warn him. Let's go together to find him, but only I will speak to him. I don't want you to show up there. It's risky. Besides we have to arrange everything so that the woman does not suspect anything… or else we will have to say good-bye to our families.

Gregory: Do you mean death, Theo? Neither German gas nor bullets made you think about death, and you want to say you're afraid of Oboladze?

Theopile: So, you think I meant death when I said we would have to say good-bye to our families, don't you? No, Gregory, I meant that they would start persecuting you and you would be obliged to find a shelter in the woods. That's what I meant. As for Oboladze, he must himself be afraid of the outlaws.

Gregory: And he was. 60 armed men used to guard him every night when he was supposed to be sleeping but he couldn't sleep until Gogia Ghlonti and Lasaia Mantskava were here. Now, I heard, he's relieved a little... Let's drink to tomorrow as tomorrow's another day. May God wake us up to meet the beautiful dawn and may God bring us peace at dusk.

Gregory empties his glass.

Theopile: Let's drink to tomorrow, Gregory, and to the day after tomorrow. And may God help us to have the toasts ready to be raised to all the days ahead.

Theopile empties his glass.

***

A crowded market square of a provincial town in Guria - full of people, carts, horses, cattle, and poultry. It is Saturday and the beginning of a day full of the hustle and bustle. We see Gregory and Theopile. Gregory stops near a bicycle parked in front of a chemist's that seems to have drawn the attention of several passers-by.

Gregory: Theo, look... Do you recognize it? You used to ride one... Lola and you.

Theopile: Yes, exactly the same kind of bicycle, but this one is newer. Frankly speaking, I could do with a ride right now. Whose is it, I wonder?

Gregory: That's a good question, Theo. I'll bet my life that it belongs to a German we are looking for. He must be at the chemist's. Let's go inside and check.

Theopile: Wait a minute, if he is inside he won't be alone; the woman must be with him. Do you think that the chemist speaks German? He needs an interpreter.

Gregory: But one doesn't need an interpreter at a chemist's... Tell them "spirit" they'll give you spirit. Tell them this they'll give you this... I mean the name of a medicine, you know. If you need medicine for your headache, you only have to put your hand on your head. This way, look! If you need medicine for your backache... this way... for the pain in your hand... this way...for the pain in your leg... this way, and so on. Do you need an interpreter to communicate this sort of thing?

Theopile looks at Gregory with a smile the latter twirling and twisting his body, and then he says:

Theopile: If he happens to be using your method, Gregory, he should know how to dance at least Khorumi[30]. Just think about what might happen if he puts his hand in the wrong place!

---

[30] A Georgian war dance inspired by military traditions

Both men laugh.

Gregory: I won't bother thinking about this... It's the chemist's problem.

A middle-aged man walks out of the chemist's shop. He stands out so much among the locals because of his appearance and the clothes he is wearing that there is no room for doubt that he is the one Gregory and Theopile are looking for. He is accompanied by a strict looking woman. Theopile and Gregory immediately turn their attention back to the bicycle, as if it is the first time they have seen such a thing and try to look very interested.

The man (Tobias Koch) who is walking out of the chemist's shop looks at them and turns to the woman accompanying him and says in Germans:

Tobias Koch: These men seem like they have never seen a bicycle before. Please, ask them if they know what it is.

The woman (Clara) turns to Theopile and Gregory and starts:

Clara: This gentleman is interested in... (She stops because Theopile interrupts her, turns to the man and says in German)

Theopile: Unfortunately, you are wrong, sir. I stopped by this bicycle because it is just the type I had a few years ago. It's very durable.

Tobias looks astonished.

Tobias Koch: You speak fluent German... almost without an accent. Where did you learn it?

Theopile: I lived in Germany for six years. A six-year period is more than enough to learn a language; if you want to learn one, of course. I haven't spoken German since I returned to my homeland and I was so glad when I heard you speaking the language. If you are not in a hurry, I'd be happy if you spared a few minutes for us to talk. God knows when I am going to have such an opportunity. But I see, it's impossible, you are with a woman here... So, sorry, I'm not going to bother you any longer. We have to go, I think.

Theopile turns and is ready to walk away but Tobias stops him and says:

Tobias Koch: Wait a minute. Clara is my interpreter. You might guess how difficult I would have found it here without one. But now I will ask her to leave us. I think ten or fifteen minutes will be enough if you don't mind.

Theopile nods in agreement. Tobias turns to the woman.

Tobias Koch: Fräulein Clara, you may go for a 15-minute walk; the weather is fine. I'll sit down there perhaps under that plane-tree with this gentleman and I'll be waiting for you in about 15 minutes.

Clara nods approval but looks irritated.

Clara: That's all right, Herr Tobias. I can come back earlier or if you would like I can stay here with you in case you need my help.

Tobias Koch: No, no, Fräulein Clara... after a quarter of an hour. It's Ok.

Clara nods approval again and walks away. She looks back several times as she walks. Theopile and Tobias head for an empty bench on one side of the lane of plane-trees. Before they go, Theopile turns to Gregory and says:

Theopile: Gregory, maybe you would like to walk a little; you won't understand our conversation and you may go for a walk with Clara.

Gregory smiles and walks in the same direction as Clara walked seconds ago.

As soon as Theopile and Tobias sit down on the bench Theopile starts speaking in a changed - a bit stricter and business-like tone.

Theopile: Listen to me, Herr Tobias, we have a lot to discuss and we don't have much time. I have been looking for you, I have to inform you about something, but first could you explain to me in a couple of words who you are, why you are here and what your plans for the future are. But in short please, as I've told you we don't have much time.

Tobias Koch: Well, it turns out that everything that you have said so far was a masquerade?!

Theopile: Exactly!

Tobias Koch: But, why on earth? What is it all about?

Theopile: I am here to explain it to you. I'll tell you everything, as I've told you… but only after you answer my questions. I have to apologize for my strict tone, but time is running out and… Please, try not to pay much attention to it.

Tobias Koch: I won't... You know, it's easy to answer your first question – I'm Tobias Koch. I'm a doctor. Besides, I graduated from the University of Jena; I studied history there; more precisely Oriental studies and archaeology. As for your second question, that is why I am here, I do not know how to answer it, as I tend to avoid disclosing the true reason for my visit here. When I'm asked about it I try to divert attention away from the point. I have a lot of sham answers ready. Say, I like your country and people I have read a lot about your country and I came to learn more about it ... If you ask me why I behave this way, I will answer: because whenever I try to disclose my true reason for coming here, people just keep giving me a misgiving look... it's true that they've never said it directly, however, they might have thought I was a bit insane, or even worse, a German spy. One of the two... but, now I feel somehow that I have to tell you the truth.

Theopile: I'm all ears.

Tobias Koch: I don't quite know what to start with. Schliemann! Have you ever heard this surname?

Theopile: Do you mean Heinrich Schliemann an archaeologist?

Tobias Koch: My God, I can't believe my ears! So, you've really heard about him!

Theopile: Your reaction is quite understandable but as unbelievable as it might sound to you, I have heard of Schliemann, I know his biography and about his famous excavations at Troy. I know that he planned to launch excavations in historical territory of ancient Colchis[31] to prove that the myth of the Argonauts[32] is based on real facts, but he failed to get the Russian Emperor's consent to carry out his plan. Do you mean that your presence here has anything to do with Schliemann?!

Tobias Koch: That's right… you've come home!

Theopile: Yes, but Schliemann… if I'm not mistaken, died at least 40 years ago when you probably weren't yet born.

Tobias Koch: You are absolutely right. He died in 1890; I was born 8 years later. But his idea was not buried together with him. His idea is alive. My father worked with him. He was Schliemann's, right-hand man.

Tobias looks askance at Theopile and asks:

Tobias Koch: I am amazed; you are so thoroughly informed. Maybe you have heard about Koch as well?

Theopile: No, I have never heard the name until you mentioned it.

---

[31] In pre-Hellenistic Greco-Roman geography, Colchis was an exonym for the Georgian polity of Egrisi located on the coast of the Black Sea, centered in present-day western Georgia

[32] A band of heroes in Greek mythology, who in the years before the Trojan War, around 1300 BC, accompanied Jason to Colchis in his quest to find the Golden Fleece.

Tobias Koch: That's fine, or I was starting to think you were spying on me! As I see, you are all fond of such surprises here. A man followed me for a whole month. Finally, he gave up. Perhaps he got tired.

Theopile: You might be surprised again but I know about it as well. I happened to overhear some men talking about it last night. To put your mind at ease, I'll tell you in short how I learned about all these; I mean about Schliemann and his excavations. I learned about all these while living in Germany. There was a very nice woman there - Lola Pere; we lived together. She used to tell me interesting things like this in the evenings. Did I satisfy your curiosity, or would you like me to continue?

Tobias Koch: O, my God, Now I understand everything. First, I thought they had prepared you to talk to me…

The chemist's shop... People walk in and out… Clara is standing by the window greedily looking in the direction of the plane-trees lane. She keeps her eyes glued to Theopile and Tobias. Gregory is sheltered in a quiet place, sitting on a stump across the street and looking at the window of the chemist's shop.

The lane of plane-trees...

Theopile: So, you want to follow in Schliemann's and your father's footsteps and find the ruins of the Palace of Aeëtes - the legendary king of Colchis, don't you?

Tobias Koch: I do… It's my dearest dream! If I manage to make it true, I'll be the happiest man in the world!

Theopile: And most famous, I presume! It explains your obsession with river banks. Ancient cities were built close to rivers, weren't they? - At strategically convenient places.

Tobias Koch: How did you learn about this? That I explore river banks?

Theopile: I've already told you that I happened to overhear two men talking about it last night. They were Chekists. They thought I was fast asleep. You have to admit that God has mercy on you, Mr. Koch. You've guessed it correctly, that true reason for your coming here raises everyone's suspicion, but I see you can't realize what danger awaits you ahead. You are literally being hunted. They even procured a rifle with a rifle scope two days ago and I think they have already hired a sniper. They know your routes back to front, thanks to your interpreter, by the way. I see you're shocked, aren't you?! There's nothing you can do! Alas! Fräulein Clara is one of them; she's been sent here to spy on you. Believe me, she must be spying on you right now, standing somewhere near and watching us. Just think, didn't the person you mentioned a minute ago disappear after she appeared? So, that's why my friend and I improvised the show. How did you call it? Masquerade ... We wanted that Chekist woman to have no reason to suspect us. You're left with no time to get anything done Mr. Koch. Not even a few days, your very next trip to a riverbank can in fact turn out to be the final one and fatal. So, you have to forget about Aeëtes Palace and archaeology in general, at least for the time being. Forget about laurel wreaths, archaeological achievements and personal satisfaction. Get away from this place as fast as possible. Think of a reason that won't invoke Fräulein Chekist's suspicion and go, go back to your homeland. Guests do not appeal to Communists and Chekists.

Tobias Koch looks genuinely astonished at hearing this information. He even finds it difficult to continue the conversation. He is obviously scared. Then somehow, he manages to pull himself together and says:

Tobias Koch: My God! I can do nothing but thank you! But why?... I mean, why you are doing this. Aren't you putting yourself in danger for my sake? That is for the sake of a total stranger?! Why did you do this?

Theopile: We don't have time to discuss this Herr Tobias. Look, who is coming back, Fräulein Chekist.

Clara is walking towards them with a fake smile on her face. Gregory can be seen walking towards them. Theopile manages to say a couple of sentences until Clara approaches them.

Theopile: I think I am obliged to do so.

Then he goes on as if saying to himself rather than seeking to be heard:

Theopile: Because of obligation and… because of love. I was once told that love makes a person forget about obligations, but it turns out to be not quite true…

Clara approaches them saying:

Clara: I hope I'm not late!

Tobias Koch: No, of course not, Fräulein Clara. Everything is OK. We've just finished our conversation.

Theopile: That's right, but until you go, shall I ask you to do me a favor? It's not a very big deal, but I need a sheet of paper and a pencil for this.

Tobias Koch: Just a minute, I have my pockets stuffed with paper and pencils. Here you are.

Tobias gives Theopile a sheet of paper and a pencil. Theopile puts the sheet of paper on the bench and writes a couple of words on it. Then he gives the paper to Clara, saying:

Theopile: You know, madam. I speak a little German, but I find it difficult to write German properly. If you don't mind, would you please have a look at what I wrote here to correct me if I made any mistake? I 'm going to give it to our guest and I don't want to be ashamed.

Theopile gives Clara the sheet of paper. Clara takes it and starts reading aloud the name of a settlement in Germany and the name and surname of Lola Pere. Then looks at Theopile and says:

Clara: Everything is correct. But I don't quite understand what it is all for.

Theopile answers in German for Tobias to understand.

Theopile: This is a small settlement in Germany, near Berlin. Mr. Koch, what I want to ask you is that: there is a grave of Ms. Lola Pere in the churchyard. It's on the right, near the fence at the entrance to the yard. If it isn't a problem for you, would you go to her grave and bring some flowers when you get back to your homeland. We've had such a nice conversation, that you would probably not turn down my request. So, let me give you this sheet of paper...

Tobias takes the sheet of paper. First, he looks at it, and then he folds it neatly, puts it in his pocket and says:

Tobias Koch: I know that place. Certainly, I'll go there, when I get back to Germany. I remember there are beautiful houses and yards there, but ... I do not quite know whether to ask you or not about the woman. You once might have been very close to each other.

Theopile: I'll tell you. That's not a big secret. She was the mother of my youngest son. She died during childbirth.

Tobias Koch: Please, accept my sincere condolences. And does your son live in Germany?

Theopile: No. he doesn't. I had had to wait two long years until he started to walk. Then we came back to our homeland together. He has his second mother here. He is being raised by her.

Tobias looks as if he has made up his mind about something.

Tobias Koch: You have to wait for a minute. Let me go to my house and I'll be right back. It's very near; it's just across the road.

Tobias Koch hurries across the road.

Gregory: You talked his ear off and the man ran away, is it so, Theo?

Clara: He is always in a rush - running around like a blue-arced[33] fly and nobody has found out what he wants and what he is looking for. Nonetheless, it's none of my business. It's OK as long as they pay me (She adds and looks aside).

Tobias Koch is rushing back carrying something in his hand. When he approaches the others, he raises his hand for them to see what he is holding in his hand. It is around a cardboard plate with straps on both sides. There is the image of a cage on one side of the plate and the image of a bluebird on the other.

Tobias Koch: Look, there is a cage on one side and a blue bird - on the other. But when you spin it with these straps, like this... you see the bluebird in the cage. This used to be my favorite toy when I was a child. My father gave it to me; he told me Schliemann also loved looking at it being spun. I kept it with me all the time, but today I want to present it to your son. What's his name?

Theopile: His name is Thoma... But you say it's very precious to you. It's not just a toy but a commemorative gift – a relic... especially so if Schliemann once had it in his hand...

Tobias Koch: No matter, now I want Thoma to hold it in his hands. Take it. It will remind you of our meeting.

Theopile takes the toy. Clara looks confused. She can't make it out how the two men managed to make friends in such a short period of time.

---

[33] is someone who had been running around, doing everything , being realy busy (Urban Dictionary)

Theopile: Thank you very much. I'm sure Thoma will like it. Now it's time to go. Good-bye, Mr. Koch. (Then he says in Georgian) Good-buy Madam. Let's go, Gregory.

They walk along and out of the plane-tree lane.

***

A flat stretch of land by the river... A shallow water area ... Clearwater gurgles down over pebbles. The river flows in braided streams at some places, forming tiny islands in between the streams. There are some goats on one of these islands browsing the bush plants. A row of white ducks waddling towards the river can be seen not far away. Further the rays of setting sun are beginning to blanket the tops of some dark blue mountains, some of them crowned with white clouds. A bird of prey is gliding slowly high up in the blue sky observing the surroundings.

Two bulls – Attila and Ocean - are grazing fresh grass at the riverside. Nearby at the side of the path, a cart is waiting for them. Right between the two bulls Theopile is lying straight on the ground his arms wide open; he is looking at the bird of prey gliding high in the sky. The noise of approaching horses can be heard first from afar, encroaching on the place and disrupting the silence that has reigned there. When they come closer we can see the riders; they are Manuchar and Sisona. They seem to be looking for their father.

Sisona: I can see a cart and bulls, Manuchar, but where is Dad? Can you see him anywhere?

Manuchar: No. I can't... but he must be somewhere near. He might be in the river and that's why we can't see him from here... or he might be lying in the cart...

Sisona: I wish you were right...

They catch a glimpse of Theopile standing up in the field between the grazing bulls. He is looking at his sons and is smiling. As soon as the boys see him, the same word slips off their tongues:

Manuchar: Dad!

Sisona: Dad!

The riders slow down their horses and turn towards the field. The boys jump off their horses when they approach their father. The father and the sons look at one another without uttering a word and through this all-embracing silence they communicate love and respect they feel towards one another. At last Theopile speaks up:

Theopile: You must have been worried, but Attila and Ocean were hungry; they have had enough now; you can yoke them now, let's go home. They'll ruminate on their way home. Do you remember which side each should be yoked?

Sisona: You have told us so many times, Dad. We do remember: Attila is to be yoked on the left side and Ocean – on the right.

Theopile: That's right! Then do it... I'll look at the sky until you finish your job.

He lies down on the ground.

* * *

It is morning. A rooster flies up on the fence and crows very loudly. Sisona comes out of the wooden house and stops on the balcony rubbing his eyes with his fists. Manuchar is in the yard. He is holding two pitchforks in his hands. He puts the pitchforks leaned against the sidewall of the stairs and says to Sisona:

Manuchar: Has Thoma already woken up? We have to hurry up or else we'll be late. If we don't finish building haystacks until noon it will get hot and we'll find it difficult to work in the field.

Sisona: Thoma is already behind the house, in the cattle-shed. Mom is milking the cow there and he's standing there waiting with a glass in his hand. Imagine what Melita might be feeling. The calf is waiting on one side and Thoma on the other. Has Dad already gone?

Manuchar: Yes, he has. He took the bulls down to the river and horses as well. And he said he had something else to do and would be back by the time the haystacks were ready to roll. So, we have to build haystacks and he will join us in rolling them.

Sisona: What else did he say?

Manuchar: What else? He said Sisona should carry Thoma on his shoulders right to the pastures...

Sisona: Only Thoma or foodstuff as well?

Manuchar: Only Thoma, He said we didn't have to worry about food, he would take care of it.

Sisona: Now it sounds to be true. I see those pitchforks, but where are the ropes?

Manuchar: I was just going to find some. Tell Thoma to leave the cow alone and let's go.

Sisona walks across the balcony to the other side of it, leans over the guardrail and calls:

Sisona: Thoma! Thoma! Where are you? Leave that cow alone, we have to go now.

We see Thoma coming with a thick white milk mustache on his upper lip. He comes to the balcony and starts going up the stairs to meet Sisona there on the stairs.

Sisona: Just look at yourself... Come here...

Thoma goes to his brother with a smile on his face and stops just in front of him.

Thoma: What do you want?

Sisona: What do I want? (Sisona cleans Thoma's lips with his fingers and says) I see you want the poor calf to die of starvation; you've launched a milk-drinking competing with it; haven't you?

Thoma: No, Sisona. Mom let me drink only a glass of milk, she said I couldn't drink more, or I would have a diarrhea. Do we have to go now? Where is Manuchar?

Manuchar: I'm here! Take these ropes. You have to carry them and let's go. (Then he turns to Sisona and says) Give them to me! (He points to the pitchforks leaned against the sidewall of the stairs)

Sisona gives him both pitchforks.

Manuchar: Do you want me to carry both pitchforks? Keep one for you. Look at Thoma, how many ropes he is carrying! (Then he turns to Thoma) Thoma, did you tell Mom we are off?

Thoma: Why did I have to? She already knows we have to go...

Manuchar: She does, but we have to tell her it's a kind of "must". (He turns towards the house and says in a very loud voice) Mom, we're leaving... Thoma said he would like a bottle of wine. Tell Dad to fetch a bottle with the food. He says a meal without wine is like a day without sunshine!

Thoma: leave off! Mom is not going to believe you!

We see Melita carefully pouring milk from one bucket into the other which is covered with a piece of gauze. On hearing Manu char's words, she smiles and says to herself:

Melita: My sweet boy!

* * *

There are four haystacks standing neatly in a row up a steep and mowed slope. Three of them are big and approximately of a similar size. The fourth one is smaller. Sunshine is beating down directly on the slope. Manuchar, Sisona, and Thoma are sitting on dry hay in the shade of one of the haystacks.

Sisona: Where has Dad gone so long? If he had come earlier, we would already have rolled down these haystacks. Thoma tell me what do you prefer drinking milk or rolling haystacks?

Thoma: Milk!

Boys laugh and Sisona continues:

Sisona: Ok, let me ask you this way then: milk or Dad?

Thoma: A silly question!

Sisona: Why? What if you hadn't seen Dad for a long time and he stood over there, and there was a glass of milk that you hadn't drunk for ages, which direction would you run first?

Thoma: I've told you it is a silly question to ask! You'd better ask me what I love more you or milk. Aren't you interested what I will answer?

Sisona: OK, tell me. Consider I've already asked you.

Thoma: No, not this way... First you have to ask me and I'll answer then.

Sisona: Ok, what do you love more Manuchar and me or milk?

Thoma pretends to be thinking. Then he smiles, takes the toy a German doctor or archaeologist has sent to him out of his pocket, first looks at the side of it where cage is depicted, then at the side where bird is depicted and says decisively:

Thoma: Dad!

Manuchar and Sisona start laughing. Then suddenly Manuchar looks thoughtful and says:

Manuchar: We all love Dad, Thoma... but (He looks up at the sun and continues) I wonder where he has gone so long? He said he would be back by noon and it's already evening. Where might he be? It's not like him at all! It's all right with us but he would never have left Thoma without dinner. If he had been busy, he would have sent someone else to bring us dinner, Mom or Uncle Makharbel. I have no idea what to think.

Sisona: Don't worry Manuchar. He is sure to come soon. Let's do something now. He told us not to roll the haystacks down, but as long as he is late, let's roll these haystacks down and catch them there, on the road; all the same, we have to carry them in a cart.

Thoma unexpectedly says in reply to Sisona's words, leaving the elder brothers surprised.

Thoma: Sisona, it's your fault...

Sisona: Why Thoma, what am I to be blamed for?

Thoma: I say, it's your fault that Dad is not coming! You didn't have to say that... "What if you hadn't seen Dad for a long time." I have learned through my experience that when someone says, "what if this or that happened". it happens the way they say. I remember it was a sunny day and someone said: "what if it rained" and it rained actually. The other day boys said, "what if a snake bit you" and do you know what happened? We nearly stepped on a snake! Can't you see how it goes? He is not coming! You didn't have to say that... "What if you hadn't seen Dad for a long time". I didn't like that... He is not coming...

Thoma is about to cry. His eyes are full of tears.

Manuchar and Sisona listen carefully to Thoma's affectionate monologue and seem to be surprised. Then Manuchar tries to help Thoma calm down:

Manuchar: Calm down Thoma! What's up, man? Who knows what could have happened? He might have cut his hand while cutting tobacco; or a dog might have overturned the basket with a dinner Melita had made for us and Dad might not want to come without food, Or Melita might have over-cooked the dinner...

Manuchar strokes Thoma's head, but this makes Thoma feel even sadder.

Thoma: I don't want anything, Manuchar... neither dinner nor milk. I will never ever drink milk I swear! If only he comes now... Dad!

Now Sisona is trying to calm him down.

Sisona: Stop it Thoma... I didn't know you had such an apprehension... If I had known I wouldn't have said that, believe me. Just calm down! Let's roll these haystacks down. We will learn everything when we get home.

The brothers stand up; Manuchar ties the three haystacks with ropes: two larger haystacks and a smaller one for Thoma. Then the three of them tie the ropes of their haystacks and start running down the slope towards the road at the bottom of the slope, rolling the haystacks with them at a high speed. We see the rolling haystacks from above, watch them becoming smaller as they roll down away from us. Then the haystacks reach the road at the bottom of the slope, stop and we now see three figures emerging from the haystacks: two of the figures are bigger and the third is smaller, they head down. The scene is spectacular.

***

A view from Theopile's yard... We see the brothers approaching the yard. They come to the gates and now we have a view from the outside of the yard. Makharbel is standing in front of the house at the bottom of the stairs and is smoking tobacco. Batlome is sitting at the stair and hewing a stick with a pruning knife unconsciously. Manuchar, Sisona and Thoma enter through the gates and as soon as they enter the yard Manuchar asks:

Manuchar: Tell me what has happened, Uncle Batlome!

Batlome without stopping hewing the stick and without raising his head answers:

Batlome: Chekists took Theopile this morning; shortly after you went.

The boys stop abruptly and seem unable to utter a word through their faces show that they have to ask a lot of questions.

***

Aslan Oboladze's room design matches the style of the epoch. A big bulky table with appropriate objects on it from which we can single out a heavy grey paper-weight made of marble stone. One side of the table is laid for one person with some maize-bread, cheese, the salad made of tomatoes and cucumbers, Tkemali[34], pieces of boiled chicken and some other meat. Aslan Oboladze is sitting at the table; he is wearing a standard Chekist uniform, but he has his jacket unbuttoned, and the belt unfastened. He is eating greedily. He drinks some wine from a glass and calls in a loud voice:

Aslan Oboladze: Lazare!

Lazare immediately enters the room and stops by the door, waiting for a command.

Aslan Oboladze: What's he doing?

Lazare: Nothing. He is sitting quietly there. He's asked for neither food nor drink yet. He hasn't even asked why we hold him here. He is sitting and thinking.

---

[34] Georgian sour plum sauce made of such cherry plums

Aslan Oboladze: OK, OK! (He interrupts Lazare without stopping chewing food and after a short pause continues) In principle, his case is different - not our business. We have to send him to Tbilisi tomorrow morning. It seems that they are interested in him because of his German. They say he lived in Germany for 6 years. Clara told me, do you remember her? One who spied on that pseudo-archaeologist who disappeared so suddenly... So, we have nothing to do with him, but still bring him in; I might recall or find out why his face seems so familiar to me. And, at the same time, I'll have a little fun.

Lazare: Would you like me to bring him immediately or would you like me first to clear the table?

Aslan Oboladze: Clear the table? Are you kidding? I have just started. (He takes a handkerchief out of his pocket and wipes the sweat off from the back of his neck and says) the heat is unbearable, and it seems it will last forever… I wish it could suppress my appetite.

Lazare is walking out of the room when Aslan Oboladze says:

Aslan Oboladze: Don't enter there alone, Lazare, ask someone to follow you and don't forget to tie his hands.

Lazare: His hands are already tied. (His answer is heard from outside the room)

Aslan Oboladze (Says to himself): He might be sitting quietly there, but he doesn't seem to belong to the category who surrenders to fate… I should be watchful… (He says and continues eating with somehow renewed energy)

Some armed Chekists walk around the Chekists' yard, Lazare walks to the cattle-shed. On his way to the cattle-shed, a wolf-dog accosts him wagging its tail, but Lazare pays no attention to it. He comes to the cattle-shed, opens a padlock on the bar, looks back and calls one of the Chekists:

Lazare: Vano, come here! We have to take the prisoner to Oboladze.

Vano immediately comes to Lazare and asks:

Vano: Which prisoner?

Lazare: The one we have locked here. We have only one.

Lazare opens the door and cries in a semi-dark cattle-shed:

Lazare: Come out! Oboladze is waiting for you…

Theopile comes out of the darkness. His hands are tied. First, he looks at Lazare, then to Vano and walks towards the house. Lazare accelerates his steps and starts walking in front of him. Vano, holding his gun in his hand, walks behind Theopile. They walk up the stairs to the balcony and Lazare asks:

Lazare: Shall I bring him in?

Then he turns to Theopile, steps aside and says:

Lazare: Go in, Theopile!

Lazare walks in following Theopile and slams the door in Vano's face. Theopile stops as he enters the room. Lazare walks past him, stops and leans against the wall.

Aslan Oboladze looks at Theopile inquisitively: eating greedily and staring at him. Then he fills his glass with wine, sips it with his eyes screwed up until the glass is half-empty and says to Lazare:

Aslan Oboladze: Don't you have to offer a seat to our guests? Put a chair here, near the table; he must be hungry. It turns out that you brought him this morning, and I was informed about it only recently?! No matter how much I train you, you still can't tell a criminal from a suspect. You treat everyone the same way. People hate this place because of you.

Lazare moves a chair to the table, at the end of the table opposite to where Aslan Oboladze is sitting. Then he comes to Theopile and gently pushes him to the chair.

Lazare: Go and sit down!

Theopile looks at lazare up and down, then goes and takes the seat without uttering a word. He sits in an awkward pose, his back partly turned to the side of the table where Oboladze is sitting. He turns his head and looks at Oboladze unapologetically, in disgust! Aslan Oboladze is still eating and without stopping chewing he says:

Aslan Oboladze: Don't be ashamed, help yourself to something; you must be hungry.

Theopile doesn't reply or react. Lazare interrupts:

Lazare: How can he eat, Aslan, when he has his hands tied…

Aslan Oboladze is embarrassed because his subordinate has addressed him by his first name and replies with a irritated tone.

Aslan Oboladze: If you're clever enough to understand that then help him to have his hands untied.

Lazare comes to Theopile and unties his hands, but Theopile says nothing and touches no food.

Aslan Oboladze: Now when you have your hands untied what are you waiting for? Have something, I told you.

Theopile: I've always been wary of anything offered by an executioner and I wouldn't like to touch one.

On hearing this Oboladze startles and stops chewing food. He stays in this position for a while, with one of his cheeks full of food and his mouth open. Then he starts moving his jaws, looks at Lazare and asks him:

Aslan Oboladze: Lazare, tell me the truth, please! Do you see anybody in this room besides us?

Lazare: I can't see anybody, Dimitrich! (Lazare addresses Oboladze by his second name)

Aslan Oboladze: Then it appears that he meant me when calling someone an executioner, doesn't it? But Lazare, could you tell me how he might know whether I am an executioner or a lamb? (He laughs loudly and adds) How should he know I am not a victim?

Theopile: I know. I saw you shooting some innocent people locked in a carriage. Who else if not a genuine executioner could have committed the atrocity?

Aslan Oboladze: Wait a minute! What did you say? Did you saw me? Thank God! Nobody knows what I have been through! I was asking God to help me recall where I had seen his face and he has just reminded me! Thank God… (Then suddenly his tone becomes stricter and he continues) I do remember you… my dear! You were standing there on a platform and staring at me just like you are staring at me right now. And there was a child standing next to you. Is he the son of the woman whose grave in Germany you wanted to be decorated with flowers? Why? You are surprised I know about this, aren't you? So, we have come to the point… We are aware of everything… absolutely everything! Therefore, if you don't behave yourself and answer my questions appropriately, who knows, you may walk out of here alive or be returned to the cattle-shed… Everything is possible… Now, tell me what else you said to that foolish German! Why did he leave for Germany the very next day? Do you want me to believe that he rushed to take flowers to that whore's grave?

On hearing these words Theopile's facial expression changes; he grows pale and purses his lips, but he says nothing.

Aslan Oboladze: He said he had to see a Consul who was planning to go to Germany and he wanted him to take some preliminary results of his research to an archeological center. The bastard sounded so convincing that we even hired a coach for him to take him to Batumi[35]. He entered the consul's office, and that's it, no one has seen him walking out of the office. He might have got into his suitcase instead of his papers and escaped.

Aslan Oboladze stands up, goes to the window, looks out of it and then turns to Theopile again.

Aslan Oboladze: Now, let's say when all these happened. Shortly after you talked with him about God knows what; more precisely, the very next day... in the morning... This is a fact... the truth! And you can't run away from the truth just as you can't run away from Aslan Oboladze. Therefore, you have to tell me in detail what you told him that made him flee from here the very next day. Do you know that you've upset our biggest plan? Do you think you will be able to beat the rap?

Theopile: Yes, but didn't you say a minute ago, that you knew everything? Then why are you asking me if you already know the truth!

Aslan Oboladze: That might be true, but I am very much interested in your version of the story...

---

[35] A Black Sea resort and port city, in west Georgian region of Adjara.

Theopile: If you are well aware of everything, you should be aware of what one might discuss with a foreigner who he has met for the first time. We talked about who he was; where he from was; how long he was going to stay here; whether he liked Georgia or not and so on. That was it. As for the end of our meeting, you've just told us, haven't you? I really asked him to take flowers to the cemetery near Berlin ... but not to a whore's grave, as you said, but to the grave of the woman who is my son's mother. You shouldn't allow yourself to use words like this. But… (He throws up his hand and continues) By the way, do you know what interests me? If the German really disappeared the very next day and if you didn't talk to him, then how did you get to know what I asked him to do? The paper I wrote on and the pencil I wrote with was his. He gave them to me. So, it seems to me you are lying…

Aslan Oboladze first looks at Theopile persistently he seems to be trying to realize something. Then he turns back to Lazare and says:

Aslan Oboladze: Lazare, this man is either too naïve or a real knave[36]… What do you think of him?

Aslan: I don't know Dimitrich. If I were to guess this kind of thing so easily I wouldn't be leading a dog's life here standing by the door 24 hours a day. Anyway, they say Theopile Darchia is the most honest person in the whole region.

---

[36] A dishonest or unscrupulous man.

Aslan Oboladze: You mean him? OK! Then what can you say about yourself, Mr. Darchia? Are you an honest man or a sly old fox?

Theopile: Do you think it can change the situation anyhow?

Aslan Oboladze: No, of course, not! Not the situation but it can change my attitude.

Theopile: You probably mean your mood. You can't change your attitude. You can change anything in this world but for your attitude. That's why you should assume that you are already doomed.

Aslan Oboladze: Lazare, explain to me what rot this bastard is raving? Is it me who is doomed?! (Then he turns to Theopile and says) Have you got any idea of who I am and who you are talking with?!

Theopile: I do and I am not alone! Whole Guria knows who you are! That's why you are doomed. Would you like me to tell you what your biggest mistake is? You identify being doomed with death. I can somehow understand you, the mind of an executioner can't go beyond death; but that's OK, I'll try to explain it to you. You are not doomed to die; you are doomed to remain an executioner, Aslan Oboladze. Being an executioner is far worse than death. Sooner or later you'll realize that. And when you realize that you'll wish you were dead. It seems to me that troubled souls of the dead do not haunt you yet, do they? You don't have to wait long; they'll come and turn your life into hell. By the way, the people you are serving so devotedly will abandon you and leave you to your fate. Executioners are endured as long as they are needed; in general, what everyone feels when hearing their name is contempt and nothing else. So, I know well who you are; it's you who has yet to learn it.

Aslan Oboladze: Did you finish? Now you have to listen to me, be careful not to omit anything. From the times this world came into existence, this has always been true and will remain as such: people are divided into executioners and victims. But I am neither an executioner nor a victim; I am an extraordinary phenomenon for you and for everyone like you. Aslan Oboladze is only my name and nothing else; what matters is what is beyond this name - I am an extraordinary charge d'affaires in this region. Did you hear well? E-X-T-R-A-O-R-D-I-N-A-R-Y C-H-A-R-G-E D-A-F-F-A-I-R-E-S. Do you know what it means? Do you? That means that I have your life at my disposal. I may feel like giving it to you temporarily or not giving it to you.

Aslan Oboladze rushes to the table and starts looking for something in a rampageous manner.

Aslan Oboladze: I have here a directive for extraordinary Charge D'affairs like me. Ask me who the author is! Here it is! I have found it. (He turns and waves a sheet of paper) The author is Lenin[37]! Theopile! L-E-N-I-N! Lenin himself wrote to me, do you hear bastard?! I'll read it to you now, it's in Russian: С врагами будьте беспощадными! Подозреваемых расстреливать без суда![38] Do you now understand who gave me – Aslan Oboladze - your life? Lenin gave it to me! L-E-N-I-N! Because I am an extraordinary charge d'affairs; and as for you, you are a nonentity, not only your life, but your sons' lives also belong to me! And her… (He turns to Lazare) What's her name?

Lazare: Melita!

Aslan Oboladze: Yes, your Melita's life as well! But I won't directly kill her! First, I'll f…k her and only after I'll kill her… Call me executioner after that.

---

[37] A Russian revolutionary, politician, and political theorist. He served as head of government of Soviet Russia from 1917 to 1922 and of the Soviet Union from 1922 to 1924.

[38] Be ruthless with enemies! Shoot suspects without trial!

Theopile springs to his feet at incredible speed; rushes towards Aslan Oboladze like a strained spring and starts ruthlessly beating him up. Lazare is confused; first, he pulls his gun but then changes his mind and comes to Theopile, gets a hold on him from behind and tries to take him away from Aslan Oboladze, but in vain; Theopile kicks him in the chest and Lazare is thrown back against the door. Aslan Oboladze's face is shapeless and covered in blood. Lazare attacks Theopile again, but this time Theopile stops beating Aslan Oboladze, straightens up, turns to Lazare and strikes him hard across his face with his clenched fist and turns to Aslan Oboladze again, who loses consciousness. At this time, Lazare takes a marble ashtray from the table and hits Theophile on the head with it from behind. Theophile loses consciousness and falls right on Aslan Oboladze's body lying on the floor.

Lazare first moves Theophile to free Aslan Oboladze's body; then takes the bottle of wine from the table and pours wine on Aslan Oboladze's face. Oboladze starts snorting and tries to open his eyes but finds it difficult because of his eyelids glued together with his own blood. He looks terrible. Lazare is trying to help him get up and sit down on the chair but Oboladze resists.

Aslan Oboladze: leave me alone! (He stands up with difficulty and sits down in a wooden armchair, puffing and trying his face with his fingertips for a while. Then he says pausing and groaning after every single word) Tie his hands and throw him back into the cattle-shed. Leave him there until dawn. We have to set off early in the morning only you and me and we have to take him with us. He has to say good-bye to Tbilisi. Beware no one else should know about this besides you and me... And send people to bring his bulls here immediately... if anybody tries to stop them and resist, they may shoot them... They have to say that they are subject to... Wait! What's the word? EXPROPRIATION or something... They get confused and afraid when they hear this word. Say as if it is subject to confiscation for damage incurred by the state. First bring them here in the yard and afterward I will decide what to do with them. We have to set off very early to Rukhumela gorge; we have to go to the ravine. They won't even be able to find his dead body. I'll teach him the lesson! I'll show him how to demonstrate muscles. Go, call someone and lock him into the cattle-shed, now!

***

It's early morning. Theopile Darcha's yard... A dog is lying at the bottom of the stairs; it seems to be asleep. We hear the door being opened. The dog first raises its ears up then its head and then stands tall on its toes and stares at the balcony wagging its tail. Thoma is standing on the balcony; he seems to have just woken up. He comes down the stairs yawning; pets the dog and walks in the direction of the gate. He no longer pays attention to the dog, which runs joyfully around him and jumps up at him from time to time. Thoma walks through the gates and closes the gate just in the face of the dog that is eager to follow him. He walks to the road and towards the bond bridge. In his way he keeps on looking back as if he doesn't want anyone to notice him leaving house.

But he is noticed not by the people in the house but by Sisona who is coming to the house with a towel around his shoulders.

Thoma: Sisona, where have you been in these early morning hours?

Sisona: Are you asking me? As if you don't know that I go swimming in the river every morning.

Thoma: I do know, but I mean it is very early!

Sisona: Why? Rivers do not close at night, do they? And why did you get up so early? What's going on?

Thoma: Don't you remember what mom said last night? Today dried fish is being brought to the market from Batumi. Dad loves dried fish... I am going to the market to bring some.

Sisona: Now I understand. Dad loves dried fish, that's right, but can you tell me where he is? I'm asking about Dad. Maybe you know that as well? Is he already at home?

Thoma: No, he isn't but he'll come sooner or later. Dried fish don't go bad quickly…

Sisona: Ok, It seems to me that dried fish is only your alibi; you wouldn't have got up so early for dried fish. You might have some other reason, but that's Ok, you may go as long as you promise you won't be late. Manuchar and I have to go. We have to find out what's going on. The bulls didn't return home last night. We have to find them as well.

Sisona continues his way towards the house and Thoma goes running towards the bond bridge.

***

We see the Cheka yard from outside. Not far away there is the tree, which sheltered Thoma when he was watching his father arriving there in his cart to take arms to Ozurgeti. Thoma is now sitting high up in this very tree. He has perfectly disguised himself and is watching the yard. He carefully observes everything that is going on in the yard. But nothing interesting is going on there: only occasionally several armed men march up and down. Thoma tries to sit more comfortably, moves back, tries to put his arms around the tree trunk. He puts his cheek against the trunk of the tree; his eyes close by themselves and finally he falls asleep.

We do not know how long he has been asleep, but suddenly - still in his dream - he hears a desperate and loud bellowing of a bull; he's startled by the sound and opens his eyes. Thoma immediately looks through the branches to see the yard. His eyes widen as he sees Attila standing in the Cheka yard and bellowing nonstop. Then he hears Ocean bellowing and sees the bull standing nearby. The boy's eyes filled with sudden tears; then he starts hurriedly climbing down the tree; he clings to the lowest branch of the tree, jumps down on the ground and runs away.

***

A typical market place of a large village is overcrowded. The people there move around looking for different goods, bargaining, and haggling. In front of the farrier's shop a bull is lying on the ground and a farrier is trying to fit shoes to its hooves. A horse is standing nearby waiting for its turn. There is a barbershop next to the farrier's shop; a man is having his beard shaven and a dozen men are waiting outside talking, laughing and having fun. There are a lot of other things going on around. Thoma approaches the row of fish with wooden counters piled high with dried fish. Some of the products are hanging up at stalls and some are hanging from rope on hooks. Thoma moves down the rows looking at these things, then all of a sudden, he stops, inflates his nostrils and inhales air deeply and powerfully with his head slightly raised; he slowly turns his head to the side where he can smell the sweet odor. He heads in that direction and comes to the rows of tobacco with wooden counters piled high with finely-chopped tobacco leaves sold mainly by elderly men with white beards or mustaches and a kind look on their faces dressed in Chakuras[39] wearing Kabalakhis[40]. Some of them are chopping dried tobacco leaves with sharp knives in front of their customers. Thoma moves slowly down the row, stops at a counter with a pile of freshly chopped tobacco leaves, takes a pinch of it with his three fingers, brings it to his nose and inhales so he can smell the sweet smell of tobacco and a smile of pleasure appears on his face.

---

[39] a kind of Chokha – traditional Georgian male dress

[40] a hood, separate from the robe – a garment of the Chokha outfit

The man behind the counter: Do you smoke, boy? Isn't it too early for you?

Thoma: No, I don't smoke yet, but I love the smell of tobacco.

The man behind the counter: Well, it smells great, I do agree with you. But you shouldn't start smoking yet; I think it's too early for a boy of your age.

Thoma: I don't smoke, I'm not lying. If I smoked I would do that at home, I have plenty of tobacco at home...

The man behind the counter: OK, don't get angry with me. You may stand here and smell it as much as you want; when you get tired you can move down the row and start smelling tobacco there. Can't you see how much of it we have here?

Thoma understands the irony behind his words steps back and moves down the row. Suddenly he sees his father's friend - Batlome a knife-grinder in a stall; he is sitting, wearing his glasses on the tip of his nose; there is a foot pedal powered grinding machine in front of him and he is grinding something. Thoma watches glowing hot sparks flying off the grinding wheel as Batlome grinds. A man named Nikephore is sitting side by side with him and they are talking. Thoma did not want Batlome to notice him so he quickly hides behind the stall wall from outside.

Nikephore: This morning I witnessed such an infernal scene, Batlome, that I can hardly find words to narrate it.

Thoma standing behind the stall wall hears these words though they are said in a very low voice intended to be heard only by Batlome. Thoma looks interested and eager to hear well the rest of the conversation.

Nikephore: I fear it is even dangerous to tell anyone about it. It's dangerous for me. But my soul will find no rest unless I tell you what I've seen, and besides I can trust you and I'm sure you won't tell anyone. Let me tell you now and let's decide afterward what to do next. You know well, I'm fond of hunting. So, I went to the woods before dawn. I wanted to hunt woodcocks. They always fly over Rukhumela[41] gorge early in the morning. They can be clearly seen in the background of the sky illuminated by the light of the rising sun and it's easy to hunt them. I know there a more-or-less trodden path; I wanted to be there and to lie perdu before they flew over the gorge. I had walked quite a lot when roosters started crowing. I came to that place earlier than I intended, so I had nothing to do but to lie there and wait. You know, if you don't notice them from afar, they will flow over you so quickly that you won't even manage to raise your hand. And suddenly, wow! I see a dog starts fidgeting, but not the way it usually does. You know how? It runs towards me, then towards the ravine, stops there holding its breath and stares into the darkness. I followed it and it moved further ahead, looked at me and stopped again. I went after it further and so it led me to the brink of the ravine! Then it hid itself in the grass just at the end of the forest; it lay there still. I could see it had all of its muscles strained; it even stopped wagging its tail and remained in this position. I was about to shout at it "What's the matter with you?!" and to scold it when I had to pull up short as I heard someone talking. God saved me Batlome. If I had uttered a word I wouldn't have been sitting by your side now; beasts would have been gnawing my bones thrown into the ravine.

[41] A name of valley in western Georgia

Batlome: What are you talking about, Nikephore. Weren't they hunters like you? Who scared you to death, man?

Nikephore: No, they weren't hunters… they are a million times more dangerous than hunters. Hunters can kill a bird or two or a hog in winter. But they hunt humans, Batlome, and if they had noticed me there, they would have killed me, they would have taken care to leave behind no living witness. Do you understand now? And can you tell me why that dog didn't bark? Can dogs tell good from the bad? Maybe they can!

Batlome: Nikephore, I can't wait to learn what happened. Just tell me what you saw until someone walks into this stall, or you'll have to wait for them to go. Don't you say how many of those who have nothing to do, wander there, outside?

Nikephore: So, listen to what I saw there... It was quite light to see everything clearly. The sun hadn't yet risen, but its rays had already painted the sky pink. There were three of them. Two of them were carrying arms. The third one was not armed. From these two armed men one seemed to have been beaten hard. His face was swollen, but nevertheless I recognized him. The unarmed man's head was broken; I could see some dried blood in his hair and on his neck. They made him stop at the brink of the ravine. There is an old ash-tree standing there and they made him stand by that tree. Then they stepped back, stopped about five footsteps away from that man and got their firearms ready. One of them was carrying a rifle and the other – the one who was badly beaten – was carrying a Mauser, I saw that clearly enough. The one with a Mauser said: "Do you understand now which one of us is doomed? Now say... Is it me or you? We'll throw your dead body in this ravine with a bullet in the back of your head and no one will ever be able to find your corpse.

Batlome seems to be uptight. He stops rotating the grinding wheel and puts the knife down on the counter. Then he turns to Nikephore and says:

Batlome: Don't tell me they shoot him... Who was that unfortunate man? Did you recognize him?

Nikephore: I did, Batlome, I did recognize him and that's why I am here telling you all these...

A woman (Ninutsa) walks into the stall. She is smiling at Batlome.

Ninutsa: Good morning, Batlome. Have you ground the pair of scissors I gave you yesterday?

Batlome: Good morning! They are ready Ninutsa; wait a minute I'll find them.

Ninutsa: Shalva told me he had given you a knife as well…

Batlome: That's right; I have ground it as well. Here you are. I kept them together.

Ninutsa: Are they ground to the edge … I mean sharp enough?

Batlome: Ground to the edge? Tell your husband to take this knife and shave his fluffy beard. He will guess whether the knife is sharp enough. And tell him "Batlome says you don't need to apply any lather you can dry shave…

Ninutsa: (laughs and says) I'll tell him if I change my mind and don't cut his throat with this knife?

Batlome: why? Has he done anything wrong?

Ninutsa: Anything wrong? He drinks tea with a wine glass once a month and wine with a tea mug twice a day! That's why…

Batlome: Tell him to come and visit me. I'll give him a delicate hint and he will start drinking tea more often.

Ninutsa: What did you say? He will start drinking tea more often? My late mom was right when she used to tell me not to marry a Gurian. She said all Gurians were mad and even if one of them had serious mental disorders, they wouldn't worry because no one would ever notice it!

Batlome and Nikephore smile. Then Batlome gives her a knife and a pair of scissors.

Batlome: Take these! Shalva has already paid for them.

When Ninutsa leaves the stall, he says to himself:

Batlome: See! Gurians have just been roundly condemned for a cup of tea! What were you saying, Nikephore? You said you were here because you recognized him, didn't you?

Nikephore: That's right… I'll tell you in short. Theopile Darcha was that man, Batlome… your friend!

Batlome: Don't tell me! You must have mistaken someone else for Theopile… (Batlome's voice begins to tremble)

Nikephore: No, unfortunately, it was him. Do you want to know what he did? (Nikephore's voice begins to tremble too) He turned his back to them. Without saying anything, not a single word neither "Help" nor "Forgive me"… nothing of this kind. He turned calmly to the ravine as if he had come here for a walk. He threw his head back… looked at that pink sky and started to sing! Have you ever heard of anything like this?

Batlome: Don't tell me that, Nikephore, it made my blood run cold…

Nikephore: I felt the same. The scene made me hold my breath. I even pulled my gun, but felt there was nothing I could do. What could I have done with my duck-shot?! Theopile was standing there with his head raised and was singing... singing. I heard the other man telling the one with a rifle: "Shoot what are you waiting for, you bastard?"

Batlome: Then? I have my heart in my mouth...What happened then?

Nikephore: Then the one with a rifle raised his hand and aimed at him his rifle, but soon he pulled it down and said to the other man: "The man is singing I can't shoot him. Let him stop first and I'll shoot him then... The other replied: "You say to let him stop, don't you? Give this rifle to me" He got furious. He pretended to be angry with that man but I guessed what made him feel furious... Theopile's song made him furious. It meant that he failed to make Theopile surrender; it meant that he was defeated. Then he put his Mauser in his belt, snatched the rifle from the other man's hands, put it nearly against the back of Theopile's head and fired!

Batlome: My God! What do you say Nikephore ... (Batlome stands up)

Nikephore: (stands up instinctively and continues) I closed my eyes. No, I didn't close them; they closed themselves and when I opened them there was no one there; neither the men with arms nor the dead one. I think the bastard indeed threw him in the ravine.

Both men keep silence for a while. Then Batlome asks with his face and eyes lit with fury:

Batlome: Did you recognize those two men, Nikephore?... There is no need to ask… No one could have done it except Oboladze… Am I right?

Nikephore: Hush, Batlome! I haven't told you anything. It was you who mentioned his name… I came here to ask you what we shall do next. Shall we keep it as a secret or inform the family? Eh! Was Theopile Darchia the man to be thrown into the ravine and be left there to be torn by wild beasts?

Batlome: I don't know yet, Nikiphore… It's anything but easy to tell this to Melita. We may tell this only to the boys I mean elder boys, not Thoma.

Batlome is interrupted by the sound of somebody crying bitterly coming from outside. Batlome and Nikiphore rush out of the stall. Batlome stumbles on the grinding machine and turns it over. They find Thoma standing outside the stall, holding the toy his dad has given to him – a cardboard plate. He is crying and spinning the toy in his hand. We see the toy being spun and a bluebird in a cage. He doesn't stop sobbing and spinning the toy in his hand. He seems to be in a trance. Batlome comes close to him, hugs him tight and says:

Batlome: You've been standing here, Thoma, and heard everything, didn't you? I wish my hug were strong enough to take away your pain! (Batlome starts crying and tries to console him with all his heart) Come on; let's go inside the stall! Life is not fare at times and there is nothing we can do about it, my son…

Some people gather around them and keep on asking about the reason; they want to know why the boy is crying. Batlome tries to keep the curious people away from the boy and answers:

Batlome: Nothing serious! I overturned my grinding machine by accident and he cut his finger ... Come with me, Thoma, I'll wrap your finger and this will help you to calm down. Let's put some tobacco on your wound. It heals wounds, it stops bleeding and relieves pain; and it will help you to stop crying.

Thoma follows him, his crying gradually turns into a whimper and they enter the stall. The curious people leave the place. Batlome takes his seat and hugs Thoma again. Nikiphore heaves the machine up to its proper position and picks up several knives lying on the floor.

Batlome: Calm down, Thoma, calm down. You are a big boy and you have to withstand pain as men do.

Thoma: (sobbing) I know. Dad used to tell me that. (Then he turns to Nikiphore and asks him) I want to know which song Dad sang.

Nikephore: What can I do now, Batlome?! I don't have an answer to that question. Maybe you have heard about my gift of singing. Heavenly Father didn't give me the one, and what shall I do now?... The only thing I know is that he sang so magnificently; I heard him singing and that's why I say that. But I failed to realize which song he sang, I was so shocked watching all these. What can I do now, my son?

Batlome: Go home now, Thoma. God knows I didn't want you to learn about this misfortune like this, but there is nothing we can do about it now. Go home and be careful, Melita shouldn't know what happened, I feel so sorry for her! Tell Manuchar and Sisona only. I will come later... We have to find his body... And, when you get to the house, run down to the riverside and wash your face and wipe tears off your face. Your mother shouldn't notice that you've cried.

Thoma: And what about fish? I have to buy some fish. Mom said the father likes it and, she wants to prepare it for him.

Batlome and Nikephore look at each other for a while and at last Batlome says:

Batlome: You're right, Thoma, You have to prepare it for your dad. Waiting breeds hope, my son, and hope gives us the incentive to live. Sit down here, at my place and I'll be back in a minute I'll bring some fish. You can't go home empty-handed.

***

Aslan Oboladze is at home. He is looking at his face in a frameless simple mirror hanging on the wall. He looks awful. The scars on his face speak of him being beaten up. A view from the window shows that it is getting dark. He looks through the window as he can't see himself clearly in the mirror. He goes to a lamp standing on a low cupboard and lights it. He hears a knock on the door.

Aslan Oboladze: Who is it?

Lazare: It's me, Lazare!

Aslan Oboladze: Come in, what are you waiting for?

Lazare enters the room. He seems a bit nervous.

Lazare: Aslan, Theopile Darchia's youngest son is standing at the gates.

Aslan Oboladze: (turns abruptly) What did you say? Did he tell you what he wants? This cub might have suspected something!

Lazare: You might be surprised but… he wants to see you.

Aslan Oboladze: See me? Just look at him! You should have told him to get lost and that it's not so easy to see me.

Lazare: I tried everything but he wouldn't give a hoot. I can't beat him up he is a child…

Aslan Oboladze: Who told you that you can't beat him up... You might even be secretly going to church?! Listen, bring him here! I am really interested in what he wants.

Lazare is about to leave the room but Aslan Oboladze stops him.

Aslan Oboladze: Wait... Don't bring him here... I'll be waiting in my working room. First, light some lamps in the working room and place them so that their light doesn't fall on my face. Get it? I don't want him to see what his father did... to hell with his father and mother...

Lazare walks out of the room. Aslan Oboladze first looks at himself in the mirror; then he gets dressed in his full-dress-coat; puts on his headgear; puts his handgun into the handgun case and turns to the mirror again. He pulls down his headgear over his eyes and walks out of the room.

***

Manuchar and Sisona are having supper at home in silence. Manuchar pours wine into the glasses and says:

Manuchar: Let's drink some wine or food that gets stuck in my throat... At least we know that those bastards took Dad; but where is Thoma? Where's he gone? He left home early in the morning and hasn't returned yet... It's getting dark... Did mom say anything?

Sisona: Yes, she said Thoma had come home and had brought some dried fish and almost immediately rushed back. Mom said he had behaved weirdly… He had given inadequate answers to all her questions. He had sat at the stub in the yard and hadn't moved until he had gone. He had refused to have dinner. Mom said that's because they had taken the bulls…

Manuchar: Ok, but where is he now? It's dark outside.

Sisona: I think he's gone somewhere together with boys. When I was coming home I heard some boys having fun and making noise in the field just across the river. He might be with them. We have to help Dad somehow. As for Thoma, he will find his way home.

***

Aslan Oboladze is sitting at the desk in his working room. He takes his handgun out of the handgun case and puts it on the desk so that it can be noticed by everyone coming into the working room. He says through clenched teeth:

Aslan Oboladze: I wonder what that small scoundrel wants… Look! How he has put that lamp! I've told him to place it so that the light doesn't fall on my face! He's grown dull, that bastard!

He rises from the wooden armchair and moves the lamp away a little and takes his seat again. There is a knock on the door at this time.

Aslan Oboladze: Come in, come in!

Lazare comes in bringing Thoma.

Lazare: So, you were banging your head against the wall to see him, Here he is! Our boss! Go and report what you want.

Then Lazare closes the doors and stops leaned against the wall. Aslan Oboladze is sitting leaned against the back of the armchair, so that his face is hardly visible, but the observant eye will notice that he is severely beaten.

Aslan Oboladze: Did you hear what you've been told? Tell me quickly why you are here; quickly until I'm in the mood for you. See, I didn't refuse to let you in. By the way, you seem to be a tough guy! Only my name mentioned scares the hell out of all living beings on this side of the River Likh. They wish they didn't bump into me and you come here of your own free will?! You might either have very brave heart or still very weak mind...

Thoma is just looking at Aslan Oboladze and says nothing.

Aslan Oboladze: Are you really weak-minded, boy?! Or did fear made you dumb? Maybe your brothers sent you here to learn how your father is, in the hope that you are still very young and I can't do you any harm ... tell them they don't have to wait long, Aslan Oboladze will take care of them soon. Then, if you don't behave yourself, your turn will come. You're still very young; I'll give you some time… If the reason of your visit is to learn about your father, I will tell you frankly. We've sent your father to Tbilisi; they will find out some things about him and probably will release him. So, if there is nothing more you want to learn, you may go home now. Lazare will follow you to the gates. Remember what I told you and tell you, brothers, as well... what's the matter with you, boy? Why do you stare at me like this? Are you looking at my handgun? Don't tell me you know how to shoot a handgun...

Thoma: No! (At last, he manages to utter a single word. Then he tries to look directly into Aslan Oboladze's eyes and continues) I haven't come here to ask you where my dad is! I already know that… I came here… to… ask which song Dad sang before you shot him!

Aslan Oboladze's scarred face turns even uglier on hearing these words. His jaw drops open and he finds it impossible to utter a word. Then he looks askance at Lazare. Lazare puts his finger to his lips as if telling him that it's not him who has given off the secret. Then Aslan looks at Thoma again and says trying to hide the disappointment in his voice:

Aslan Oboladze: Why on earth, boy? (His voice sounds hoarse, he coughs and continues) What nonsense, how did you manage to come up with that one?! I've already told you, your father has been sent to Tbilisi. Shooting...song... there's been none of these. Your father is in Tbilisi. T-B-I-L-I-S-I. Got it?! Or do you want me to drive the point home?! (Aslan Oboladze gradually regains the self-confidence and impudence he's lost temporarily)

Thoma: Let it be as you say, but which song did he sing? (Tears well up in Thoma's eyes, but he tries to curb his emotions)

Aslan Oboladze: Lazare! Help me to get rid of that oddball right now! I am tired of his balderdash. Throw him out right now, or I'll do away with you instead of him. Throw him out and to hell with him.

Lazare goes close to Thoma, puts his arm around his shoulders loyally, even showing a kind of compassion and leads him to the door.

Lazare: Let's go, boy... do what he tells you. Your father is in Tbilisi. And I think he will be back soon. Come, let me follow you to the gates; it's already dark and the dog must be unchained.

As Thoma steps out the door, he can't help crying and bursts into tears.

Lazare: Calm down, boy. You're no longer a child and you have to gradually get used to things like this... Times got hard... Didn't you know it? Calm down, boy! Don't cry.

Thoma goes on sobbing until they come to the gates. Lazare opens the gates and lets the boy through them. Thoma walks away very slowly, sobbing, with his head cast down. When he starts walking along the road lit by the moonlight he hears a voice from behind him:

Lazare: Voisa[42]!

Thoma turns back abruptly to see Lazare standing at the gates. We see Thoma's big, sad and clever eyes full of tears shining in semidarkness. Lazare looks around, steps forward and says in a lower voice:

Lazare: Your dad sang Voisa before… The name of the song is Voisa, I mean. I didn't shoot, I couldn't. I was there, but I didn't shoot. Neither Oboladze planned that. He really planned to send him to Tbilisi, but your father beat him up in his working room, so severely… Didn't you see his face? Your dad might even have killed him if I hadn't been there. I saved his life. You didn't have to ask him which song your dad sang! Do you think he knows anything about music and songs? Nope! He couldn't answer anything even if he wanted to. Obolasze hears the song when he listens to bullets whizzing in the air! He knows nothing about a real song… Go now, go and remember your father sang Voisa before he died. Now go, get out of here quickly.

We see Thoma's eyes full of gratitude, but he does not say anything. He turns and disappears into the darkness.

Lazare watches him going away and then says to himself:

---

[42] A Georgian folk song (Guria)

Lazare: You should be proud of your father, boy…

With these words, Lazare closes the gates.

***

Manuchar and Sisona are sitting at the table. They have finished their supper and sit there talking with each other. They hear the noise of somebody running up the stairs. The door opens and Thoma, with a light blush dusting his cheeks, walks into the room lit with faint light thrown by a lamp. He casts a guilty glance at his brothers, stops by the wall and casts his head down.

Manuchar: What's the matter with you Thoma? What's that look on your face and where have you been so long? You know what Melita's going through and you are adding to her worries.

Sisona: Why do you stand there leaned against the wall as if you've done anything wrong? Come and sit down, have something to eat and then let's go to bed. We have a lot of work to do tomorrow morning: we should take tobacco to the retailer, and with this money, Manuchar and I will go to Tbilisi. I met the man Dad helped to carry arms to Ozurgeti and he told me that Dad had been taken to Tbilisi.

Thoma: That's not true! They didn't take Dad to Tbilisi.

Manuchar: How do you know that?

Thoma: I know!

Sisona: Where is he then? Do they keep him locked up at the Gugunava's cattle-shed?

Thoma: No, they killed him! They killed our dad!

Manuchar and Sisona look paralyzed. After a while, Sisona stands up, comes close to Thoma, puts his hands on Thoma's shoulders, looks into his eyes and asks in a very low voice:

Sisona: What are you saying, Thoma... Do you understand the meaning of the words you've just said?

Thoma: Oboladze shot him. Dad had beaten him first, severely... in his working room. I've been told that Dad nearly killed him. But there is a man called Lazare; he helped Oboladze and saved him from being killed.

Manuchar stands up and goes close to Thoma; first, he gives him an inquisitive look and then asks him:

Manuchar: Thoma look at me and answer; were you really told about it or did you make up this story?

Thoma: How can I make up a story like this? Did they kill our dad? Can one make up such a story? I saw Oboladze... I've just left his house.

Manuchar and Sisona look at each-other. Then Sisona says:

Sisona: You're driving me mad. How did you go there? How did you find the courage to go there? Did you want us to be condemned to even more torment?

Thoma: I found the courage! He told me I should have had a brave heart to come to him, but... I found the courage! I have nothing to hide, in fact, I was terrified, but I tried my best not to show my feelings to Oboladze...

Manuchar: Yes but, what did you want there. Did you expect him to admit to having killed our dad? You are not quite clear on this!

They hear somebody coming and Manuchar and Sisona rush to take their seats and try to pretend that nothing is going on. Melita walks into the room, sees Thoma and says to him in a voice and manner showing love and care for him.

Melita: Are you already here, my son? Manuchar and Sisona were asking about you and I couldn't answer. Where have you been so long? Come and have something to eat and wash your feet before you go to bed. I have already heated some water for you.

At the moment Sisona stands up, comes close to Thoma and says:

Sisona: Thoma and I are going to the kitchen garden. We have to pick some cucumbers. I saw they were ripe in the morning but then I forgot …

Melita: Why did you choose midnight to pick cucumbers, Sisona? How do you plan to distinguish cucumbers in the dark?! The cucumbers aren't going to run anywhere until morning, are they?!

Sisona: No they aren't but they may get overripe and inedible. Besides, it's not dark at all; can't you see that huge moon in the sky? It is hovering just over our kitchen garden looking at cucumbers. Come on Thoma, let's go… let's take the basket; it's outside on the balcony.

Sisona and Thoma walk out through the door. Melita turns to Manuchar and says:

Melita: He is so strange just like his father. In fact, you are all so similar. Why did he take Thoma in the kitchen garden, it's almost midnight? I'll go and prepare your bedrooms.

Melita walks out of the room. Manuchar is alone in the room. He seems thoughtful. After a while, he stands up and walks out of the room to the balcony. He looks up at the moon. Sisona and Thoma are coming back. Sisona stops under the balcony and asks Manuchar:

Sisona: Is Mom there?

Manuchar: No, she's gone to prepare our bedrooms... What did you learn?

Sisona: I learned that... Oboladze is responsible for our misfortune, Manuchar. Go, put on something, we have to go. I'll saddle the horses. I'll tell you all about it on our way. And fetch some rushlights, it's under the granary, we have to take it with us.

Manuchehr turns back without uttering a word, walks into the room and almost immediately comes out wearing his Kabalakhi round his neck. He runs down the stairs and towards the granary.

Sisona leads the horses to the gates. Manuchar appears out of darkness carrying a bunch of neatly cut pieces of rushlight, hangs the bunch on the saddle of one of the horses. Then Manuchar and Sisona climb on their horses and Manuchar say to Thoma:

Manuchar: Thoma open the gates...

Thoma rushes to the gates and opens them. As his brothers ride through the gates he asks:

Thoma: What should I say to Mom if she asks about you?

Sisona: I don't know. You have to think of something. You didn't find it difficult to think of visiting Oboladze, so you will find it easy to think of an alibi for us.

Manuchar and Sisona ride their horses away and they soon disappear in the darkness. Thoma is standing by the open gates and staring into the darkness. Soon the splashing noise made by horses' hooves can be heard which is followed by the clip-clop sound being gradually reduced to silence. Thoma closes the gates only after that.

***

It's night. Moonlight falls on the yards bordering one another and wooden houses in the middle of these yards. Two riders stop by the gates of one of these yards. We hear them calling:

Sisona: Uncle Batlome!

Manuchar: Uncle Batlome!

We hear a door being open with a squeak.

Batlome: Who is it?

Sisona: Manuchar and Sisona. We know it's late but we have to talk to you.

Batlome: I'm coming.... I've been waiting for you...

Batlome lights a kerosene lamp standing on a window-sill, takes the lamp and walks towards the gates.

Batlome: Come in, get off the horses and let's go into the house. I knew you would come and I asked the man you need to talk to come here. I wanted to come to your house but the man you're looking for told me he would rather wait for you here.

Sisona: No, Uncle Batlome, we want to set off right away. Tell him to follow us if there is a horse for him and show us the place. We'd better find Dad tonight, or beasts may smell his scent and tear the body…

Batlome: I'll tell him but, it's night, and can we find him in the darkness?

Manuchar: We've foreseen that, Uncle Batlome, and we fetched some rushlights. Here we have enough of them; that will suffice even if we have to search for him all through the night.

Batlome: OK, I'll go in and tell him…

Batlome turns but the man he is going to call is walking to the gates.

Nikiphore: It's them, I guess.

Batlome: Yes, they have come. They have just learned about that.

Nikiphore comes close to the gates and greets the young men with a slight nod of his head.

Nikophore: I would be happy to greet you differently but the misfortune has fallen upon us. I saw everything with my own eyes and I can show you the place. Batlome and I wanted to go there without you, but your youngest brother heard everything and… Batlome, can you bring the horse here? We will set off right away.

Batlome: Not a horse but horses. I'm coming with you. I'll fetch an ax and some rope; we may need them both. The boys have brought some rushlights.

Sisona: We don't want to bother you, Uncle Batlome. Three of us will manage to do the job. We wouldn't have bothered this person if we were able to find Dad without his help.

Batlome: You should mind what you're saying, Sisona. What do you mean when you say "bothering" me? You'll certainly manage to do the job by yourselves but there should be someone to console you when you find his body and I'm coming to do that. Actually it's not you who should be searching for his body, it's our duty, he was our friend, we had to find his body and bring him to your house, but we didn't want Melita to learn about this, that's why we waited for you.

Batlome goes and soon comes back bringing horses and we see the four figures disappearing into the darkness.

***

It is dawn. Thoma is lying asleep crouched from the cold on a bench standing on the balcony. Clopping sound made by horses' hooves striking the ground coming from a distance wakes him up; he immediately springs up from the bench, rubs his hands up and down his arms looking in the direction of the bond bridge. As soon as Sisona's and Manuchar's horses cross the river and, he catches the glimpse of his brothers, Thoma jumps over the guardrail into the yard, rushes to the gates, opens them, goes through them and waits for his brothers. Sisona and Manuchar soon come close to the gates and jump off their horses. Thoma says nothing, but his face shows that he is anxious to learn the news from his brothers; his eyes move from one of them to the other, but both of them seem to look away from him. In the end Sisona says:

Sisona: We have been looking for him the whole night, Thoma... The whole night, brother... but we couldn't find Dad.

Sisona hugs Thoma tight and starts crying. Thoma starts crying too.

Manuchar: Stop it right now... Stop crying like women. We'd better go in and decide what to do next. (He says that and we see his eyes filled with tears) But we can't talk about it at home. Melita shouldn't learn about it. We'd better have a nap for a couple of hours, and then Sisona and I will go to Kallisto's snack bar. Uncle Makharbel will come with us. Batlome will come and we will decide together what to do next.

Thoma: And what about me? May I go with you?

Manuchar: No Thoma, you can't. We can't leave home altogether. We can't leave Melita alone. Stay with Mom and be careful, don't let her suspect anything. OK! Let's go in until Melita wakes up and finds us here. Let's go in and pretend we are asleep.

The three of them walk towards the house. Until they enter the house they unbridle the horses but leave them saddled and let them go.

***

The market place… a small snack bar … no one is in the snack bar; the wooden tables are empty; only Kallisto can be seen at the lunch counter he seems busy placing cold breakfast foods neatly on a small wooden tray. Then he takes the tray and walks towards a back room; he opens the back-room door and walks inside, places the tray on a wooden table. Manuchar, Sisona, Makharbel, Batlome, and Nikiphore are sitting at the table. Kallisto puts the cold breakfast on the table and the table is laid. He puts the empty tray on the window-sill, pours wine in small glasses, takes his seat and asks:

Kallisto: Shall I close the bar? While we are here talking.

Manuchar: You don't have to, Uncle Kallisto. don't close your snack-bar. Besides, we aren't doing anything wrong. We want to find Dad, dead or alive, is it a crime?

Kallisto: How couldn't you find him I wonder?! It's incredible. Sometimes it dawns on me… what if… it was not the case… and Oboladze had changed his mind at the very last moment. But I can't question what Nikiphore says. He says he saw everything with his eyes…

Makharbel: I think the only person who can tell us everything is Oboladze himself. Only he knows where Thopile is; but how can we ask him? He is guarded by the Chekists all the time. I haven't counted them but there are roughly sixty of them in the yard of Cheka. They even have a machine-gun there on an open cart.

Sisona: Even if he were guarded by even twice as many of them, as long as he is the only person who can tell us the truth, we would call on him and make him give us the answer to our question. If Manuchar and I fail to find Dad's body, our own lives will be worth nothing to us.

***

Melita is sitting on a stump on the balcony of her house. She has some green beans on her lap; she is snapping the tops of the pods off and putting them into a saucepan. There is a wooden tray piled with some more green beans. Thoma walks through the door rubbing his eyes with his fists.

Thoma: Mom, have Manuchar and Sisona woken up?

Melita: Woken up? They said they had something to do and rushed out of the house like arrows from a bow. They nearly outran their horses. Go and wash your face. There is a glass of milk for you on the table.

Thoma: Yes, I saw it. I'll drink it later. (Thoma looks at the hens strolling around the yard and asks his mother) Mom, which of the hens did you mean when you said it was no longer laying eggs and would have to be boiled soon? Is it the black one over there?

Melita raises her head and says:

Melita: I can't see it from here. If it's black with a top knot, then it's the one.

Thoma: Yes, Mom. It's got a top knot.

Melita: So, it's the one. It hasn't laid an egg for two weeks now. It's only clucking and eating corn. Why are you interested in it? You didn't use to care about egg-laying hens...

Thoma: I'm not interested in it Mom, I've asked just for the sake of it. I have to talk to you about something. But if you ask me it's too beautiful to bother itself with laying eggs.

Melita: What would we have to do if the rest of them started thinking they are beautiful and stopped laying eggs? Now I guess ... you don't want to eat eggnog today, do you? If you don't, I'll tell your dad when he comes.

On hearing these words Thoma gets nervous, looks askance at Melita and says:

Thoma: I'll go and drink a glass of milk.

Thoma walks into the house.

***

The same snack bar... Manuchar, Sisona, Makharbel, Batlome, and Nikiphore are listening to Kallisto:

Kallisto: So, let's decide now what we're doing next. I'm sure Oboladze will rise to the bait. I'll arrange everything. I'll go there and tell whoever I meet there that two men their faces covered with Kabalakhis came to me this morning. I'll tell them that I couldn't see their faces and that they ordered three-day meals for six people. I'll tell them as if I have to deliver these meals to a hunters' hut until this evening; you know the hunter's hut that is uphill in the woods just along a ferry crossing on the Rioni River. I'll tell them that these two men paid a lot of money and that, on the one hand, I have to deliver the meals where they've told me and, on the other hand, I feel it is necessary to inform them about it. I think they'll ask me who these men might be to my mind and then I'll reply that although they had their faces covered with Kabalakhis, I could see their eyes and that one of them might have been Gogia Ghlonti. Oboladze is terrified whenever he hears the name of Gogia Ghlonti. I think he will rise to the bait. He will send all of his guards to the woods to lay siege to him around the hunters' hut. I bet he will. Manuchar either you or Sisona should be on the watch for them. If everything happens as I say, we'll have to decide what to do next. We'll have at least 24 hours for that.

Makharbel: Everything is clear, Kallisto, yours is a well-thought-out plan, but... what if Oboladze wants to go there with the squad? What shall we do then? We can't launch a war against them at the riverside...

Kallisto: It's quite likely, Makharbel...

Manuchar: No way… Uncle Kallisto. Oboladze won't follow them. He is so severely beaten he doesn't even enter his working room; he doesn't want anybody to look at his face. He appeared to have hidden his face from Thoma; he spoke to him in the darkness.

Batlome: God bless Theopile's soul for beating that son of a bitch and breaking his nose.

Kallisto: May God bless us all. Let's try our plan might work I think. I'll go now and prepare everything that I have to take with me and then I'll call on Oboladze.

Sisona: Uncle Kallisto, please calculate your costs we're going to pay for all these.

Kallisto: Why should I? Am I sending it to you? You shouldn't have said that, Sisona… Theophile Darchia was such a special man he was the best in the whole region. God bless his soul. I would do anything and sacrifice anything for his sake; I can even burn down this snack bar… (Tremor can be heard in his voice) You and Manuchar will have to take care of Oboladze if everything goes according to our plan. And I have to give you some bones for the dog they have in their yard. They unchain it at night and you'll need these bones to keep it quiet. The poor dog is half-starved. They don't feed it to make it aggressive and ready to attack people…

Kallisto walks out of the room.

***

Thoma is walking down the village road. He is carrying the very black hen, the one he talked about with Melita not long ago. The road leads to a small village church and Thoma goes in the direction of this church. He enters the yard surrounding a very old church and stops abruptly. He holds the clucking hen in his left hand and crosses himself with his right hand. Then he walks straight on, goes around the church and walks in the direction of one-storied cells. There he sees an old man. Thoma comes to the old man and asks:

Thoma: Excuse me; they say there is a person here who teaches chants. I would like to see him if it's possible.

The old man: Nobody seems to have time for chanting, my son; the country is falling apart. Communists haven't destroyed this church yet, but what's the use of it? No one is allowed to enter it any longer and who would care about chanting... anyway why did you ask about the teacher? Can you tell me?

Thoma: I want to study how to sing a song?

The old man: A single song? How's the song called, the song you've chosen?

Thoma: Voisa!

The old man: Voisa? That's a very good song, little gentleman. And if you tell me your name, I will try to help you somehow…

Thoma: Thoma, my name's Thoma.

The old man: Thoma? Nice to meet you, Thoma! Now listen to me little gentleman. Do you know that Voisa is not a chant to be sung in a church?

Thoma: I do. So what?

The old man: So, the person who teaches chanting won't teach you to sing this song. You need another teacher. I'll tell you where he lives but the place is a bit far away. Not very far but still; It's in a village next to ours. You have to go towards that mountain when you walk out of this churchyard. There is a road leading all through the woods and over that mountain. You have to take that road and when you reach the bottom of the mountain you will find a village there. Then you have to ask the way to Ivliane Vashalomidze's house. Anyone can tell you where it is and you'll easily find it. He is the one who can teach you the song you want to study, my son. He is the master. But first you have to do your best to win his favor. If you set off right now you'll be able to come back before it gets dark... By the way, the song you've chosen is a great song. You want to be able to sing Voisa of all other songs, don't you?

The old man giggles. Thoma doesn't say anything, nor thank the old man. He simply turns around and walks away. The old man watches him going away and says to himself:

The old man: Just look at him!

***

Oboladze's residence... It's late evening... The Sun is about to set... Lazare opens the big heavy gates and armed Chekists start riding their horses out of the yard; approximately fifty of them. They also lead a horse carrying an open cart with a machine-gun. The whole detachment heads towards the woods.

Manuchar and Sisona are lying on the ground among pomegranate shrubs at the riverside. They watch the scene with their eyes wide open. We see their faces light up with a smile of satisfaction. Sisona turns to his brother and whispers:

Sisona: Filthy snakes have crawled out from their hole. Uncle Kallisto's plan worked. We had to count them.

Manuchar: I have counted them. There were 46 or 48 men. A man or two more or less doesn't change anything. So they've left that damned Oboladze to the mercy of fate... Let's go Sisona; we have to get ready... We'll call on them at about 4 in the morning and catch them off guard while in the grips of deep sleep.

Manuchar and Sisona leave the place walking hunched over and heading in the direction of the riverside where their horses are waiting for them.

***

Thoma is standing at the gates. He is holding the hen with his both hands. He is looking in the yard and calling in not a very loud voice:

Thoma: Is anybody out there?

There is a small kitchen garden on the right side of the gates. An elderly woman called Domna is busy there planting some vegetable seedlings. On hearing someone calling she raises her head up, looks over the fence and says in an affectionate manner:

Domna: Do you want to see Ivliane, son? Come in and I'll call him now. He is in the backyard teaching some kids to sing a song; he might not hear you. Come in, don't be shy; I'll call him right now.

Domna hurries to the house, holding her dirty hands out to her sides. Thoma enters through the gates, closes the gates, moves a little forward and stops there, waiting for Ivliane. Ivliane appears soon from the side of the wooden house coming to the place where Thoma is standing; he stops halfway and says:

Ivliane: Come here, son!

Thoma comes close to Ivliane. Ivliane curiously looks at the boy and says reverently:

Ivliane: I am listening little gentleman, who are you and why did you trouble yourself to come here?

Thoma: I am Thoma Darchia. I want to study a song, Uncle Ivliane, only one song! That's why I am here. (Thoma's voice sounds sad) Please, don't refuse to help me. I've come here from afar; I've been told you might help me. And look… I've brought a hen, but it isn't an egg-laying hen; maybe you'll take it… I mean instead of money… I don't have any money and I thought this hen could cover the cost of just a single song… but it doesn't lay eggs.

Ivliane's facial expression changes a little. He looks carefully at the boy.

Ivliane: You said you'd come here from afar… but could you tell me where are you coming from?

Thoma: From Jumati[43].

Ivliane: I know a lot of people living there. Who's your father?

Thoma: Theopile Darchia is my father. Don't refuse to help me, please… I implore you…

Thoma's eyes filled with sudden tears.

Ivliane: You don't say! Are you really Theopile Darchia's son? And why have you come here to me to learn a song, aren't you on speaking terms with your father? Your father used to teach me how to sing! How's your dad doing?

Thoma: Dad is dead! They've killed him!

Ivliane is unable to utter a word. His facial expression changes once again. His wife Domna is coming from the side of the house saying:

Domna: Woe is me! Is what I've just heard true? Who did that? Who killed Theopile Darchia? I think there's no one here who could have killed such a man!

---

[43] The name of a Village

Thoma: Oboladze shot him. But Dad had beaten him before Oboladze shot him. They say he had beaten him to death.

Ivliane comes closer to Thoma, strokes his head and says:

Ivliane: How come I didn't hear about that? When did it happen, Thoma?

Thoma: Yesterday at dawn… at the Rukhumela ravine.

On hearing these words Ivliane looks abashed and confused and steps back.

Ivliane: Do you mean that your dad was killed yesterday and today you've come here to study a song? I don't quite understand what's going on! You can't be Theopile Darchia's son. He might be your father but you can't definitely be his son! Your dad was killed yesterday and today you are in the mood for singing?!

Thoma casts his eyes down and tries to say something… but his speech is not fluent; he speaks separate words and phrases.

Thoma: Dad had sung there ... before Oboladze shot him... he started singing... knowing that they were going to shoot him... but he sang ... the second man could not shoot, but, Oboladze did. That's why I came to you… I don't want any other song, only the one Dad sang before his death. I was told he'd sung Voisa. Lazare told me. He was also there, but he said he couldn't shoot him ... That's why I've come to you and I implore you, don't refuse to help me... Don't send me back like that… Here you are… Please take this hen... I implore you… If I don't study that song, I know I will die...

Ivliane seems moved. We can see tears rolling down Domna's cheeks. Ivliane goes close to Thoma, puts his hand around Thoma's shoulders and says:

Ivliane: I'll teach you, son. You don't have to beg me like that to teach you a song. And I'll teach you not only that song but all the songs I know. Theopile Darchia's son should know all the songs! I'll teach you how to sing bass, lead and higher. But we have to agree on one thing. First, tell me whether Melita knows that you've come here.

Thoma: No, Mom doesn't even know what happened to Dad!

Ivliane: Then let's do this way. You should go home now, take that hen with you and let it go where it should be, as if it has never left the place. I wouldn't take it; you said it doesn't lay eggs. Why should I take the hen which doesn't lay eggs? I'll write a letter to Melita now; you take that letter to her. She'll send you to me when she reads it. If you really want to learn singing, you'll have to stay here for at least three months. I'll go now and write a letter. You go with Domna, You must be hungry and you should have a snack.

Thoma: Thank you so much, Uncle Ivliane, but I don't want to eat anything... I'm afraid I need to find my way back before it gets dark. I'll wait for the letter and run away, but ... Do not mention what happened to my dad in the letter Uncle Ivliane, my mom doesn't know about it yet...

Ivliane: Don't worry, son. I know I don't have to. Domna, would you please bring a piece of Khachapuri to Thoma. If he can't wait, maybe he will have it on his way back?

Ivliane enters the house.

***

Manuchar and Sisona are sitting on the balcony of Theopile Darchia's house. It's already getting dark but the brothers can clearly see Thoma walking through the gates and holding something black in his hands. Manuchar and Sisona are watching carefully and only after Thoma puts that something on the ground and that "something" hurries to the hen-house clucking desperately they realize that Thoma was holding a black hen in his hands.

Thoma goes upstairs to the balcony and stops in front of his brothers.

Sisona: Where have you been Thoma? You have been wandering through the village just like a stray dog, for the last two days. Maybe you tell us where did you take that black hen?

Thoma: Mom said it no longer laid eggs and I took it for a walk, maybe it feels good after a walk and starts laying eggs.

Sisona: Just look at him, Manuchar! Who would believe he was born in Germany? He speaks like a genuine Gurian, doesn't he?

Manuchar: Come Thoma and take a seat next to me.

Thoma takes the seat next to Manuchar. Manuchar strokes his hair, then leans down and kisses him on the head and says:

Manuchar: Sisona and I are going hunting tonight. Let's go to the river, just the three of us, and go swimming there to relax a little. Run to the kitchen, Mom must be cooking something there and tell her you're coming with us.

Thoma: I have to give Mom something… a letter.

Sisona: A letter? Who is it from?

Thoma: Have you heard the name Ivliane Vashalomidze? I've just been to his house. He told me to give this letter to Mom.

Manuchar and Sisona look at each other with surprised faces. Then Sisona says:

Sisona: You're driving me crazy, Thoma. We've found out about Oboladze, but why did you go to Ivliane, so far away from home? What's going on? Did you get a message from him that he wanted to send Mom a letter?

Thoma: No, Sisona, he wrote this letter when I was leaving his house. I went there to ask him to teach me a song… the song Dad had sung before he was shot. I want to learn to sing that song.

Manuchar and Sisona (simultaneously): Voisa?

Then they look at each other again and Manuchar says:

Manuchar: That's a good idea, Thoma. But you must have told us first… Sisona and I would have taught it to you… though… (He stops and continues after a short pause) That's good that you went to him. I think he wants you to stay with him, doesn't he?

Thoma: I think so. I think the letter says so…

Manuchar: How long is he going to shelter you?

Thoma: He said I had to stay at his house for at least three months… He didn't take the hen I brought him. He was shocked when he learned about Dad.

Manuchar: Ok, Everything is clear… Go and give that letter to Mom… But wait, give it to me we'd better explain everything to her ourselves, Sisona and I. It'll be good for you if you go away from this place. You have to set off tomorrow morning. Don't wait for us. Don't wait till we return home from the 'hunt'. If we manage to kill something we'll call on you there at Ivliane's house.

Manuchar stands up and turns to Sisona:

Manuchar: Come on, Sisona, Let's explain everything to Melita.

Sisona stands up and they go downstairs.

Thoma is lying in his bed but he is not asleep. The moonlight coming through the window shines on his face and we see him lying with his eyes open. A very reserved and low-key conversation heard from the living room, adjacent to Thoma's bedroom, is sometimes accompanied by a noise made by somebody who is doing his best not to be heard but in vain. A stream of faint light is coming through the clearance between the closed-door bottom and the floor. Thoma gets up quietly, tiptoes to the door slightly open it and peep into the room through the small opening. Manuchar and Sisona are getting ready to go. Both of them are wearing Chakuras and Kabalakhis. They have ammunition pockets across their midriffs and chests filled with rifle bullets. They are both holding rifles in their hands. One of them has a Mauser in a loop of a piece of cloth tightly wrapped around his waist; the other has a Nagant revolver. Black sheaths can be clearly seen on the sides of the pieces of cloth around their waists with shining cross-shaped hafts. After a while Manuchar and Sisona look at each other, cross themselves; Sisona blows off the kerosene lamp and they leave the room.

Thoma is standing motionless for some time. His face can no longer be seen through the door clearance. Then he enters the living room; lights the lamp; takes it in his hand and tiptoes to the icon of Virgin Mary. He raises the lamp up and the icon will shine forth and he looks at the icon with beseeching eyes, for a long time, without uttering a single word.

***

It's night. In the faint moonlight, a Caucasian Shepherd can be seen growling and greedily gnawing on a large bone. Lazare is sitting on a wooden bench at the end of a long balcony of the house; he is sleeping. He is holding his rifle against his chest; his rhythmical snoring indicates that he is in a deep sleep. Only a faint light can be seen coming through one of the windows.

The silhouettes of two men move smoothly along the balcony as if gliding against the wall, without making any sound; the men stop at the door of the room, through the window of which the light is coming out. One of the men peeps in the room through the window. He sees Oboladze sleeping in a metal bed. His face, distorted by having been beaten, looks ugly in the faint light of a kerosene lamp. The man takes a quick glance around the room. He sees a belt hanging on the back of a chair; the gun holster on the belt is empty. Then he turns to the other man accompanying him; puts his finger to his lips and then points his finger at the man sleeping on a wooden sofa on the balcony, meaning that he should take care of that one. Then he puts his palms together rests his head on his hands and closes his eyes and simultaneously points his finger at the window, meaning that the man inside the room is asleep. The silhouettes start moving without making any noise. One of them goes close to the man sleeping on the balcony and stops by him leaned against the wall and nods to the other man. After a very short pause, the one standing at the door opens the door at an amazing speed, so that actually no squeak is heard and glides into the room. He is holding his gun in his hand. He approaches Oboladze's bed; points his gun muzzle at him in a way that it nearly touches Oboladze's forehead just above his black eye and says in a very calm voice:

Manuchar: Wake up Aslan! I have to talk to you.

Aslan Oboladze opens his eyes, looks at the unfamiliar face with a look of uncertainty on his face for a while. Then he turns his eyes up to see the gun muzzle, seems to have realized the situation and starts shouting:

Aslan Oboladze: Laza...

Manuchar doesn't let him finish the name. He puts his hand over his mouth silencing him and says:

Manuchar: Don't do it, Aslan, don't shout. Don't wake Lazare up. You don't want him to get into trouble, do you? He is being watched over and until he is sleeping and not moving, he won't be harmed. As for you, you have to listen to me very carefully. I will now slowly lift my hand, and you don't have to shout! Understood?! One sound out of you and I'll kill you right away!

Aslan Oboladze's eyes wide with fear indicate that he has understood what he has been told.

Manuchar: Well done!

Manuchar slowly removes his hand from Aslan Oboladze's mouth. Aslan Oboladze is not moving and is looking right into his eyes obediently.

Manuchar: That's much better now!

Manuchar smiles ironically. Then he moves a chair standing nearby close to the bed with his leg so that he has his gun pointed at Oboladze and doesn't take his eyes off him. Sits down on the chair and says:

Manuchar: Well ... now you have to sit up on the bed slowly. Go ahead! Well done! Now take the pillow with your one hand slowly, and put it on your knees...

Oboladze does everything the way he is being told. As he moves the pillow, a Mauser with a purple wooden-handle is exposed.

Manuchar: just as I expected. (Manuchar takes the Mauser, looks at it and continues) It's pretty nice! You might have killed somebody to take it from it, just like you killed my dad to take our bulls!

Oboladze startles looks at Manuchar, but says nothing.

Manuchar: Yes, it's really me! Theopile Darchia's son! You don't believe your eyes, do you?!

Aslan Oboladze: Lazare!

This time Oboladze manages to cry out the name in such a desperate voice that it must have woken up Lazare. Manuchar hits him in the face with a handle of his own Mauser, at the very moment, he cries. Aslan Oboladze's cheekbone is fractured and starts bleeding. His face is partially covered in blood.

Lazare who is sitting on a wooden bench on the balcony raises his head when he hears Oboladze calling his name. He listens for a brief moment, then quickly stands up and is about to rush towards the door leading to the room. When he takes the first step, Sisona, standing leaned against the wall nearby, grabs hold of his forehead with his left arm, jerks his head back a little and cuts his throat with his dagger holding in his right hand. Then he wraps his hands around Lazare's waist and helps his lifeless body to fall to the floor of the balcony without making any noise. Before he straightens himself, he cleans his dagger and his hands with Lazare's clothes; takes his rifle and enters the room.

The door is being opened and hope fills Oboladze's eyes momentarily, but it disappears as he sees Sisona coming through the door instead of Lazare. He feels overwhelmed with fear and his voice sounds hoarse as he speaks:

Aslan Oboladze: What do you want from me, whatever you might be planning will fail sixty men ... (all of a sudden he stops, the expression on his face changes the way as if it dawns on him what is actually going on and continues) So that rotten shopkeeper lied to me... my doubt was not without reason but ... you deserve it Aslan Oboladze, I shouldn't have believed him?! But I promise you, if you don't kill me, I will do everything you want me to… I wouldn't even touch that shopkeeper. Do you want money and gold? No problem, I'll give you as much as you desire... but please don't...

Manuchar doesn't even react to these words. He looks at Sisona for a brief moment. Sisona signals with his hand that he has killed Lazare and Manuchar turns back to Aslan Oboladze.

Manuchar: Listen to me you dirty rotten scoundrel! We did not come here to take your bloody loot. We are here to learn what you did with our dad's body. I wouldn't listen to you talking nonsense. We already know that you shot Dad at the old ash-tree on the verge of the ravine in the Rukhumela gorge. You shot him while he was singing, didn't you? But we couldn't find his body and we are here to ask you about this! We apologize disturbing you at such a late hour. But you have to forgive us. Where is his body?!… Answer you dirty bastard… Did you shoot him and throw him in the ravine?! Answer immediately or I'll show you what I am like when I really lose my temper!

Aslan Oboladze: Do you want me to believe that you won't kill me after I tell you that?

Manuchar looks at Sisona again. The later nods his head in agreement. Then Manuchar turns back to Aslan Oboladze.

Manuchar: What do you think about it, Aslan? Should anyone trust you? So, you have to get up and go with us to show us where Dad is... we can decide on what to do with your life only after we find him.

Aslan Oboladze: I can't... I can't find him. Lazare knows the place... Lazare buried him. He told me he couldn't leave a Christian man unburied for beasts to eat him there. He went back and must have buried him. He might be somewhere near in the yard. Bring him and he will tell you everything. He will go with you and show you the place to you.

Aslan Oboladze finds it extremely difficult to speak. His speech is not fluent and his voice sounds hoarse. He seems to be scared to death.

Manuchar looks at Sisona once again. Sisona spreads his hands in response, meaning: "I didn't know; it's too late".

Manuchar's face grows even gloomier. We see a few drops of sweat being formed on his forehead. He shoots a glance at Aslan Oboladze and says in a bloodcurdling voice:

Manuchar: Tell me, did you shoot Dad from this gun? (He shows Aslan Oboladze the Mauser) or... Sisona gives me that rifle, it's his, I guess (Now he shows him the rifle) from this? Tell me quickly, which weapon you used to shoot Dad? You bastard... Tell me quickly! (Manuchar looks furious; he springs up the chair and starts beating Aslan Oboladze first with the Mauser handle and then with the rifle butt, and goes on shouting to the rhythm of the beats) Tell me... Tell me... Tell me... The man was singing and you shot him, didn't you? You shot him, didn't you? You shot him!

Sisona tries to stop Manuchar by holding his arms. Oboladze is released from Manuchar's clutches but he no longer seems to be amongst the living. He falls to the bed all covered in blood. Manuchar calms down a little and says to Sisona:

Manuchar: OK, Sisona... Let me...

Manuchar frees himself from his brother's arms, gives him the Mauser and the rifle. He unsheathes his dagger, grabs hold of Oboladze's hair and cuts his throat.

Manuchar: Let's go, Sisona. We failed to find Dad. Let's take our bulls and get out of here. The dawn is near. We should cross the River Rioni until the sun rises.

***

A pretty wooden house is standing in the middle of a neat yard. Some voices singing can be heard from the house. According to the register of the voices, we can guess that young boys are singing. The boys stop singing and we hear a man (Ivliane Vashalomidze) speaking:

Ivliane Vashalomidze: OK, once again, from the beginning...

We see Thoma's face. He is smiling at someone and then starts singing in a very pleasant childish voice. He finishes singing his solo and the rest of the boys join him singing different voices. We see them sitting in a semicircle in an almost empty small room, singing and looking at Ivliane Vashalomidze standing in front of them. Chonguris of different size is hanging on the walls. Ivliane has his eyes semi-closed, his head cast back a little and is listening to the boys singing a song which finishes very soon. It seems that they haven't studied the song to the end yet.

Ivliane Vashalomidze: Very good, I have no comment. I can tell from the expression on your faces that you like it as well, don't you? Well, let's sing the same part once again before we start studying the remaining part of it...

***

A marketplace in a settlement... Different breeds of cattle have been brought here from many different places. They are kept separately in ad hoc open-air cages. Cows and bulls are kept together... sheep and goats together... pigs and piglets together, etc. people are busy buying and selling cattle. Theopile's bulls are there. They are standing separately. Kallistrate Kankava is selling them to three men who are standing in front of him. One of the men is busy counting money; the other two men are watching carefully. Kallistrate seems to be bored and is fidgeting. At last the man finishes counting money and says:

The buyer: Here you are, man, exactly the amount we agreed on. Now it's your turn to count it.

Kallistrate takes the money and seems a bit relieved. He folds a thick pack of money, takes a piece of cloth from his pocket; neatly wraps the money in that piece of cloth, puts it in his jacket pocket and says:

Kallistrate: There's no need to count it again. We've just counted it for the sixth time. Look at your lower lip; if you had counted it once more you would have dropped it. You'd better remember what I have to tell you now. The formal owner of these bulls used to take much care of them. They aren't used to inhuman treatment, I have to warn you. You have to treat them the same way, or one day they might gore you and you don't have to blame me. As for the money it is intended to be invested in the education of a very good boy. So you have to be proud that besides buying these bulls you're doing a good and kind job. Well, may God bless you and, as I've told you, don't show them a switch.

***

It is night. Thoma is asleep. He smiles in his sleep. He dreams and he dreams in black and white. Theopile is sitting under a lime-tree in the yard. There are some dry tobacco leaves on a low table in front of him. He has a thick plank on his lap and is cutting tobacco leaves on it with a sharp knife. He puts the cut tobacco leaves in a wooden box. Thoma is there with his dad greedily smelling tobacco odor. He hears somebody calling his name:

– Thoma!

Theopile startles at this sudden calling and cuts his finger. He puts some cut tobacco leaves on this cut presses them against the cut with his thumb, but bleeding doesn't stop; on the contrary, it bleeds more and more. Thoma takes some more tobacco leaves from the box and puts them on his dad's finger, but bleeding doesn't stop. Theopile's bulls are at the gates and are bellowing in turn.

- Thoma! We see Thoma again. He is still asleep. But this time he is not smiling; pain is depicted on his face. He looks relieved to be woken up. He sees Ivliane standing beside his bed holding a lit kerosene lamp and calling his name.

Ivliane: Thoma, don't be afraid, my boy. It's me, Ivliane. You have to get up; your brothers have come to see you. They are waiting in the living room.

Thoma immediately jumps out of bed.

Thoma: Manuchar and Sisona?

Ivliane: Yes, my boy, Manuchar and Sisona. Do you have any other brothers as well?

Thoma looks happy; he runs barefooted towards the living room.

Thoma: Manuchar! Sisona!

First, he runs towards Sisona and hugs him, then towards Manuchar and hugs him too. Manuchar and Sisona are wearing the same outfits they wore the night they went "hunting".

Manuchar: Thoma, you haven't quite learned yet to distinguish between your elder brother and the younger one! Did you have to hug him first and then me?

Manuchar says and smiles and hugs Thoma at the same time.

Sisona: You must be jealous Manuchar, that he loves me more...

Thoma: Says you! Just as before! Where have you been so long? You promised to see me after that "hunt", didn't you?

Manuchar: We had no choice, Thoma. We just couldn't come earlier and now we have to run away again. Can't you see, we've even woken up and disturbed Uncle Ivliane at midnight?

Ivliane: Don't worry about it! All the same, I can't fall asleep until morning. I'll go now and sit in the yard… you - brothers - might have something to talk about I guess. (Ivliane walks in the direction of the door, stops and says) If you're hungry, tell me. I won't even wake up Domna, I'll prepare everything on my own.

Manuchar: Thank you so much, Uncle Ivliane. We don't want to bother you anymore. We are neither hungry nor thirsty. We'll tell something to Thoma and go away.

Ivliane: OK!

Ivliane walks out of the room.

Manuchar stands up and starts walking in the room. He seems to be thinking hard about something and to find it difficult to start speaking. But he stops at last turns to Thoma and says:

Manuchar: Listen to me Thoma. You're already a big boy and a smart boy. You realize too many things. You've probably noticed that I find it hard to talk about what I have to tell you now, but I prefer to cut a long story short. We have to leave Thoma; Sisona and I have to leave Georgia... Forever, I'm afraid... You see, these bastard communists don't allow us to live together and enjoy our lives. We're going to Turkey, Thoma, my brother, and God know when we'll be able to see each other again. Or will we ever be able to?! If the Lord wills and everything change for the better we will be together again, but who knows when it will happen. Will we live to see it?! As for you, Thoma, you have to stay here with Uncle Ivliane till the end of August. We've already warned him. In no case should you go to our village. Our house is watched by Chekists 24 hours a day. We moved Mom to the house of her parents temporarily. She asked us to tell you that you don't have to go to her to say good-bye. She won't be upset, as you come to her dreams every night and she hugs you in her dreams. At the end of August, a friend of our dad, Kallistrate Kankava, will call on you and take you to Tbilisi. We'd given our bulls to Uncle Kallistrate and he already sold them and the money is yours. He'll give it to you when you're in Tbilisi. You'll live with Dad's friend in Tbilisi. He also knows about it and is waiting for you. He is Jewish, and he's going to take care of you. He'll decide which school you have to be enrolled and when you leave school, if you decide to continue your studies, he'll help you achieve your goals. You don't have to feel shy; you should think he's your father. If I were you, I would entrust him all the money I had. They are not like us; they never go on spending spree; they are well aware of the value of money and he'll help you spend it wisely. That's all I wanted to tell you.

Manuchar takes a deep breath as if he's been relieved of a heavy burden. Thoma stays silent for a while; then he raises his head and says in a very sad voice:

Thoma: I understand everything, Manuchar; but you haven't told me what I should do when I miss you very much!

Thoma comes close to Sisona, hugs him tightly and starts crying. We can also see tears running down Sisona's cheeks.

Manuchar: Oh no! ... Stop this collective mourning... (Manuchar tries to sound self-confident but his voice lets him down. In an attempt to hide his true feelings, he changes the topic and suddenly asks something completely different.

Manuchar: Thoma, did you learn how to sing Voisa?

Thoma wipes tears from his eyes and says sobbing after every single phrase.

Thoma: Not yet. Uncle Ivliane says we have to start learning it next week. We've started by learning simpler songs.

Sisona: Which song did you learn? It is night I understand, but you might sing one in a low voice. Who knows when we'll see each other again and Manuchar and I will keep the memory of it in a special place in our hearts.

Thoma doesn't say anything. He looks carefully at his brothers, one after the other and asks them:

Thoma: What did you do that night, when you went hunting? Did you kill the beast? Or did you fail to and that's why you are leaving for Turkey?

Manuchar and Sisona first look at each other with surprise, then both look at Thoma and Sisona says:

Sisona: No, Thoma. We did! We killed it and that's why we have to run away. Manuchar killed the dirty swine in his bed…

Thoma's facial expression changes on hearing these words. His face expresses the pleasure of accomplished revenge. He presses his lips together tight than his face beams with delight and suddenly he starts singing in a very sweet voice coming from the deepest depth of his heart. His brothers watch him and smile and then exactly when the song requires, both of them get down on their knees, with Thoma standing between them, put their arms around one another's shoulders and join him in singing and with this song they seem to be saying good-bye to one another.

We see the moonlight shining on Ivliane Vashalomidze's face. He is calmly smoking his pipe. He hears the boys singing and smiles. His smile gets gradually diluted in the smoke coming from his pipe.

End of part one

Part Two

***

June 1941. Tbilisi, Navtlughi Station… A train on the track is mainly composed of open carriages without roofs or seats; there is only one carriage with a roof but it is not a passenger carriage, it is for carrying cargo or maybe for some fragile cargo. Along the train there is a wide variety of people on the platform. Some vendors with baskets full of different types of savories walk around shouting. Locomotive breath can be heard. Among too many civilians some uniformed men can be seen, who is standing by the open carriages of the train; some of the carriages are full of manganese some - of yellow sand and the rest are packed with sacks; the uniformed men are guarding the cargo. Two of the open carriages are loaded by large wooden boxes carefully nailed and locked; nobody knows what they contain. Fragments of phrases mostly Georgian and a few Armenian and Azeri can be heard from all sides.

A young man dressed in lieutenant's uniform jumps onto the roofed carriage through its open door and turns around to face the platform brings the megaphone he is holding in his hand to his mouth and shouts for the whole station to hear in Russian:

Lieutenant: Construction crew members should gather in front of this carriage. I'll be calling their names in 10 minutes. I repeat all of the construction crew members…

A short and bald elderly man (called Moshe) with a pleasant face looks in the direction of the lieutenant and listens to him carefully. Some grey dots can be seen on his bald head. When the lieutenant finishes his announcement and stops, the bald man turns to a tall, well-built young man standing next to him and says:

Moshe: We've got 10 more minutes, Thoma.

We see Thoma, He is 18 or 19 years old. He is tall and well-built. He is handsome, with dark wavy hair and large black eyes. His appearance immediately attracts attention. Lying on the ground at his feet is a faded knapsack apparently with such a few belongings inside that it lays crumpled on the ground.

Thoma: We've actually got 10 more minutes, Uncle Moshe, but we'd better go close to the carriage and wait there.

Moshe: Ok, let's go. By the way, did they say you would have to wear a military uniform?

Thoma: I don't know, Uncle Moshe; they didn't say that, but they said it would be something like a paramilitary unit and I think we will have to wear uniforms.

Moshe and Thoma talk and walk slowly towards the carriage.

Moshe: What do you think Thoma, imagine a war started, would the wall built by you be strong enough to withstand attacks of German tanks?! Don't you feel it is a little funny, Thoma?!

Thoma smiles.

Thoma: I don't know what to answer, Uncle Moshe. I don't actually know what we are supposed to build there. I haven't even seen the project yet. I've told you before that as soon as I was given my diploma, this very lieutenant who shouted from the carriage came to me and told me they were looking for young specialists to help them build some fortifications along the borders of the Baltic States. They need some construction crews to build them. He told me he'd been to the Dean's office and they all recommended my candidature... did me a favor to say so... You already know all about this, Uncle Moshe, but you didn't have to say that "imagine a war started" I have learned through my experience that when someone says "imagine this or that happened"... it happens the way they say and now I have a premonition that something bad is going to happen...

Moshe: Don't worry, Thoma, if my words had the power of instigating a war, I would remain silent throughout my life. Now tell me where the crew is, are you going to meet the crew members after your arrival there?

Thoma: No, Uncle Moshe; haven't you heard what the man said? They'll call the names of the people on roll... the names of the crew members. I was told the crew members will be Georgians as well, but I don't know who they are, I haven't met them yet. We will get to know one another on the train. I hope they are all good guys and we'll make friends. You'll see them during the roll call. You know, there is something else I worry about. Well, I leave this place without saying good-bye to my mom. God knows when I will be able to come back. I asked the lieutenant to give me a couple of days to prepare but guess what he answered: I do understand you, but "Родина не может ждать"[44] - that's what he told me. He wanted to sound like a patriot.

Moshe: Don't worry about it, Thoma; you've already visited her twice this year, haven't you?

Thoma: I wouldn't call it a visit. I called on her at night and ran back the same night. I had a kind of a conspiratorial meeting with my mom. Uncle Moshe, would you do me a favor and send her a letter just to explain to her why I didn't see her to say good-bye? Would you promise me?

Moshe: Of course, I would. I don't have to promise as soon as I say good-bye and wave my hand at you, I'll run back home and write a letter to her. I was just thinking we've got some time before the train leaves and do you want me to go and buy something for you to take with you? A friend of mine works in a restaurant near here. He's Jewish. He always has some good sausages for his friends and relatives. Let me run and I will bring some.

---

[44] Motherland can't wait

Thoma: No need, Uncle Moshe, Aunt Helen has put so many things in my bag. She complains of pains in her legs, however, she spent the whole night cooking.

Moshe: Yes, and that's why she is not here to see you off… Listen to me Thoma, You have to write to me, write regularly; it's not me who has to make a promise, but you. I don't want you to forget your Uncle Moshe, my boy; you know well I love you like you were my own son… (Moshe's eyes fill with tears)

Thoma: Of course I will. Don't worry about it, Uncle Moshe?

The lieutenant's voice cuts him short.

The lieutenant: Please, listen, I'll call the names now!

Thoma: Let's listen to him. He's going to call the names on the roll.

Thoma looks at the lieutenant, who is holding his megaphone and shouting very loudly in Russian.

The lieutenant: Darchia! Thoma Theopilevich…

Thoma raises his hand to show his presence. The lieutenant looks at him, smiles at him and goes on reading the names.

The lieutenant: Ratiani! Odishar Maizerovich…

A tall good-looking young man standing on the right side of Thoma raises his hand and says: Here! The lieutenant looks at him, then back at the roll and goes on calling the following names:

The lieutenant: Jangirashvili! Kakhaber Giorgevich… Zeragia! Batsi Mironovich… Togonadze! Bessarion Euremovich… Dematrashvili! Gigi Zurabovich… Duduchava! Dachi Danielovich…

After each name being called we see the young men one by one standing on the platform with their family members seeing them off. The young men react differently, in their own manner, on their names being called; some of them even showing reluctance and simply letting the lieutenant know that they are here. The lieutenant calls only seven names, then removes the megaphone from his mouth and says to himself:

The lieutenant: All of them are here… Well done, Georgians... (Then again, he announces through his megaphone) You have… (He looks at his watch) three more minutes. You may kiss each-other good-bye and get on the train. That's all!

A hubbub on the platform near the carriage follows this announcement: kisses and embraces, occasional tears. The scene is emotionally loaded as characteristic of the Georgians.

Moshe looks at Thoma with sad eyes and says:

Moshe: Let me hug you once again…

Moshe and Thoma hug each other and Moshe start sobbing.

Thoma: That's Ok, Uncle Moshe… I'm not going to burn my bridges. I'll arrive there, build those fortifications or God knows what and come to you again. I think it will take us at most six months.

Moshe: I do know, Thoma, but... Lena and I will find it difficult without you. We'll be missing you...

Thoma: It's time to go, Uncle Moshe...

Thoma takes his knapsack with a swift move and throws it in the carriage through the open door; the lieutenant helps him to jump on board the train; Thoma is standing at the open door and helping others to get on, taking their language and giving his hand to help them jump on board. Almost all the young men are carrying only one bag, with the exception of Jangirashvili, Kakhaber. He stands on the platform and gives Thoma his bags of different sizes and colors one by one: one, two, three, four, five and a 10-liter wicker bottle. Thoma smiles and says:

Thoma: What's up man? Is a bride waiting for you anywhere? Are you planning to have a wedding party on our way?

Kakhaber Jangirashvili (Jango): That's a good question, sir, one never knows what the future holds, isn't it so? Give me your hand!

Thoma helps him to get on board and when Jango is in the carriage he turns to Thoma and says smiling:

Jango: If it happens as you say, you're going to be my best man!

The lieutenant is standing at the entrance putting ticks next to the names of those who get on the train on the roll. When the seven of them are on the train, he folds the piece of paper and puts it in his pocket; with the happy look on his face rubs his hands together and says in Russian:

The lieutenant: Oh! Georgians my brothers! You don't know how I love long journeys, especially when my companions are as nice people as you are.

The young men throw their belongings at random inside the carriage and rush back to the door with the exception of one of them - Bessarion Togonadze (Beso), who stays inside the carriage. Thoma notices this and says to him:

Thoma: Come on, there is a room for you as well. Don't you want to wave your hand at your kinsmen?

Beso: I would like to, but are you sure they'll see me waving my hand at them in Oni? I said good-bye to them a week ago and I am alone here.

The train starts slowly and leaves behind the platform and the people standing on it.

The lieutenant: Here we go! It's time to settle down... we've got plenty of hay here!

Thoma: How long will it take us to arrive there, lieutenant?

The lieutenant: I think at least 10 days. 10 days and we'll be there!

Thoma: 10 days?

The lieutenant: Exactly, and if we are not stopped on our way, as they sometimes do with trains like ours... There are plenty of crazy people out there! What you have to do is to look on the bright side and everything's going to be all right!

Thoma: I hope so! (Then he turns to the young men and says in Georgian) What shall we do guys? Don't you think it's time to get to know one another? As you might have heard I am Thoma Darchia. I'm from Guria; I was awarded my diploma the day before yesterday and today I am your team leader (Thoma smiles and continues) I have to know my team members, aren't I? (Then he turns to the lieutenant and says in Russian) I say it's high time to get to know one another.

The lieutenant: Of course, it is…

Jango: Wait a minute, lieutenant; we can't do it like this! First, we have to lay the table, sit down, drink a glass of wine, wish one another luck and that's it, we'll know one another.

The lieutenant: (Looks at Thoma and asks) What did he say?

Thoma: He says if we want to know one another better, we'll have to drink at least a glass of wine…

The lieutenant seems pleased with these words and promptly nods his head in agreement and says:

The lieutenant: The man is right, and we have to obey him.

Thoma: Ok, let's have a potluck party than. Let's see what we've got and let's cover this small heap of hay with a piece of cloth and lay a "table" here.

All of the young men hurry to reach to their bags to see what they can contribute but Jango stops them and says:

Jango: Wait a minute! We shouldn't devour everything at once. First, we have to partake of perishable food. Don't bring the food that won't be spoilt by tomorrow or the day after tomorrow. So let me… the chicken won't last long as it's too hot here.

Gigi Demetrashvili: And what about Khachapuri?

Jango: We can have it for breakfast and for supper as well.

The lieutenant looks at the wooden boxes piled at the corner of the carriage, goes and brings several of them and says:

The lieutenant: These will serve us as chairs. I'll bring some more.

He brings 8 boxes very quickly.

Jango takes a piece of cloth out of one of his bags and covers a small heap of hay with it. Then he starts taking out some food: pickled garlic, boiled chicken, bread loaves, some Guda[45], cucumbers, pink tomatoes, and tarragon. Jango puts all these on the piece of cloth one by one commenting on each of them.

---

[45] Cheese made from sheep milk

Jango: This is boiled chicken; this is another one; this is pickled garlic. Mmm, it's delicious; these are cucumbers; just look at the color of the cheese, it is amber, isn't it? (When he takes out salt and puts it on the piece of cloth he begins to hum a song) აღზევანს წავალ მარილზეეე... მარილს მოვიტან ბროლსაოოოო...[46] and glasses?! I have forgotten to take glasses; damn… if no one here has a glass it will prove to be a fly in the ointment; we can drink water from the bottles, but what shall we do with Chacha[47]?

Togonidze: I have a small horn for the wine… here you are… it's not for wine it's for vodka.

Jango: (heaves a sigh of relief, takes the horn and says) May God bless you... Come on! Let take our seats, eat something and bless God! Come here our team leader; take the head seat at the end of the "table". Let's reserve a seat for lieutenant in the center…

All of them take their seats. The lieutenant can't take his eyes off the wicker bottle; at last he asks:

The lieutenant: What's the wine called?

Jango: (starts in Georgian) What do you say, man, if it were wine, we would be doomed. 10 liters of wine won't suffice so many of us?! (Then he adds in Russian) Чача это, товарищ лейтенант, Чача![48]

---

[46] Aghzevans Tsaval marilzeee ... marils movitan brolsaoooo – I'll go to Aghzevani to bring some crystal salt

[47] grape vodka

[48] This is Chacha Comrade Lieutenant, Chacha!

The lieutenant: Самогон?[49]

Jango: Не самогон! огонь![50] (Then he says in Georgian again) It has 80^0, it is real fire!

The lieutenant seems very pleased he smiles and says:

The lieutenant: Да, это надо попробовать...[51]

The train wheels roll along the track. We hear it making a monotonous sound. Jango pours Chacha in the horn and passes it to Thoma.

Jango: Help yourself, chief…

Thoma takes the horn, seems to be thinking about something for a brief moment and then says:

Thoma: Let's do it this way, guys! We have to pass this horn around, anyway; so each of us will have to say something about himself when it's his turn… something like who we are and where we come from… and offer a toast! Deal? (The young men all agree with Thoma) Ok, then I'll interpret this to the lieutenant and then I'll introduce myself to you. (Thoma turns to the lieutenant) Lieutenant, we agreed to say a couple of words about ourselves when it's our turn to drink from this horn…

---

[49] Alkie? (Vodka)

[50] Not Alkie, but fire!

[51] Well, then we must taste it…

The lieutenant: (literally fidgeting with impatience) Да, ладно вам! Я на все согласен, лишь бы поскорее…[52]

Jango: Ok, start, chief, the man is dying of thirst, can't you see? We are all ears!

Thoma: In fact, I've already told you who I am and where I come from. My name is Thoma and my father was called Theophile. Theo... He is no longer alive. I have my mother, who lives in a village in Guria. I also have older brothers, two brothers, but I have not seen them for a long time. What else can I say? In short, that's all about me.... Yeah, I'm not married yet.

Batsi Zeragia: So, you say your dad is no longer alive; then who was that man who accompanied you to the station?

Thoma: You're asking about Uncle Moshe? He is an old friend of my dad. He is Jewish and he lives in Tbilisi. I have been living with him for the past decade… He's a very nice man. I dare say he is like a father to me… Well, so let's drink to the people who came to see us off today, as Uncle Moshe did... those who could not come here but found it hard to let us go and cried when saying good-bye. May God bless all our kinsmen and let's pray to our Father in Heaven for our peaceful existence in this world, for helping us in treading our path in peace and for the joy of reunion to surpass the pain of our separation soon... Amen!

---

[52] Come on! I agree to anything, as far as we get everything done quickly…

The young men altogether: Amen! Amen! May God hear you! Thoma drinks the Chacha, stands still for a brief moment, then takes a deep breath and says:

Thoma: It's like fire indeed but it tastes good!

Thoma passes the empty horn to Jango, who fills it with Chacha then looks at the young men as if scanning them with his eyes, fixes his gaze on the lieutenant and says:

Jango: (first in Georgian) According to the way he looks at me, he'll definitely throw me off the train if I don't pass this horn to him immediately. (Then He smiles at the lieutenant, passes the horn to him and says) It's your turn, lieutenant!

The lieutenant: (grabs hold of the horn and starts almost immediately) I have nothing special to say. I don't remember my parents. I grew up in an orphanage. There was a small hill behind our orphanage and in winter we used to ride a toboggan there. So, that's how I got my nickname – Podgorni[53]. Then as it always happens, I served in the army followed by continuous service and now I am here with you. So to us all... (He takes a deep breath and empties the horn in a single shot) That's really something like fire... and how much of it do we have?

Jango: Just enough to have a little every day till we arrive in the Baltic states, Comrade Lieutenant, don't worry; and we'll manage to get some there as well.

Rapidly changing scenes follow a person, his toast.

---

[53] Foothill

Beso: Your slave Bessarion Togonadze! Beso... I'm from Oni! I have parents and twelve siblings. They all live in Oni. So, from now on, you are my brothers and friends and I want to drink to our friendship and brotherhood. (Beso empties the horn)

Gigi: I'm Gigi Demetrashvili from Zemo Imereti. My dad accompanied me to Tbilisi and went to the station with me to see me off. When the lieutenant was calling your names, he was carefully studying each of you and it seems to me he liked all of you very much as he told me to invite you to my village when we come back. So, you have to start preparing now... (The young men laugh... Thoma interprets Gigi's speech to the lieutenant. Gigi Demetrashvili continues) Like all the Imeretians my dad is silver-tongued. When he sees someone walking pass his gates he can cajole them into his yard and they eventually find themselves sitting at the table having forgotten where they wanted to go... So let us drink a toast to sweet words – words that serve as a remedy when we worry, words that add to our joy when we are happy. May we always say and hear sweet words and never feel the slightest sting of envy of each other. May God bless you! (Gigi empties the horn)

Dachi: I'm Dachi Daduchava from Tbilisi. You'll learn about me later. I want to drink a toast to the wheels of this train. I want them to take us safe and sound to the place we are heading and bring us back to our motherland safe and sound as well. (Dachi empties the horn)

Ushba: Have you ever heard of Ushguli in Svanetia? I am from there. I've been nicknamed Ushba, just because I'm tall. You may call me Ushba as well. I might not react to my real name. Trust me, I'll always be there for you and May the prayers and blessings of Saint George abide with you all… (Ushba empties the horn)

Batsi: I'm from Tbilisi as well. My name is Batsi Zeragia. My dad is a military doctor. He is a well-known surgeon, maybe you have even heard of him. He used to tell me my brain needed to be operated on as it hanged upside down and needed to be inverted... So, I took it and ran away. Now I'm here with you, together with my brain hanging upside down. So, that's exactly what I want to say, long live the people, who have their brains hanging upside down but still do nothing wrong... the people who are ready to sacrifice their lives for the wellbeing of their friends and never surrender to the enemy… (Batsi empties the horn, turns it over and saying the traditional words) So many drops in the glass, so many enemies!

Thoma: At last it's your turn, brother; fill the horn and start.

Jango: (fills the horn with Chacha and says) I will, certainly. You already know that I am from Kakheti. So, to be more precise I live in Telavi. My grandfather Berdo moved from Mtiuleti to Telavi. His family name was Jangirashvili and I am Jangirashvili too. My name is Kakhaber, but just like Ushba, nobody calls me my real name. They call me Jango. You can call me Jango as well. I like it, not that it's better than Kakhaber; but I still like it. As for my toast, I want to drink it to our Motherland, brothers. Our Motherland that tastes sweet like mom's breast milk. And you don't quite understand why it is so sweet and still, you're happy that it is. Whenever you try to go deeper and study its essence, tears come to your eyes. I am ready to cry now; we haven't yet gone beyond its borders and I miss it badly. Let me drink to our Motherland, guys; to those invisible strings that tie us to it and pull us back home no matter how much better the place you are is. That's it. (Jango empties the horn)

The train wheels roll along, the track and through the opening of the carriage we can see the Earth running somewhere with the tail between the legs.

***

It's dark inside the carriage. Only shadows darting can be seen through the opening of the carriage. The moon in the sky looks lonely and sad. Its pale light shines on a part of the carriage, and we see the young men sleeping there. We see the faces of all of them and finally that of Thoma's, who has his eyes wide open and seems to be thinking about something. The remains of food can't be seen anywhere. The squelch of the liquid in the wicker bottle not completely full can be heard against the background of monotonous noise made by train.

***

The young men are again in the carriage. It's daytime. Everything in the carriage is the same as it was before but the landscapes along the train tracks have changed dramatically. Space stretches into the dull yellow steppe as far as the eye can see. The monotony is a bit scary. We look at his huge expanse from above and see the train like a piece of thread moving in some vague direction.

Jango is sitting on a wooden box. The box doesn't stand firm on the floor of the compartment and it jerks in rhythm with the train. That's why Jango finds it difficult to pour Chacha from the well-known bottle. He has put it on his lap and is doing his best to accurately pour the liquid in the horn. The lieutenant is standing in front of him, impatiently waiting for the horn to be filled.

Jango: Comrade Lieutenant, is the seven of us supposed to build that fortification alone?

The lieutenant: Of course, not. There will be 15 more teams besides yours… Pour it quickly… You're not going to wait till the train stops, are you? It can go non-stop for three days and nights… A team per fraternal republic… They know well there (He points upward with his finger and says) ...about the national principles and such things... competition! What can I say; smart people are sitting in the Kremlin. They understand the psychology of ordinary people. Wait, I'll drink and tell you a secret…

Jango fills the horn at last and passes it to the lieutenant. The lieutenant takes a deep breath and empties the horn in a single shot.

The lieutenant: уф! красота![54] Ok, what will be, will be! When you arrive there, you'll see yourselves and let me tell you now. Guess what they have planned there (He points upward with his finger again). You see well that there are only seven of you in your team. All the other teams – the fifteen in all – consist of ten people each. Can you guess why? Because… as I've told you they are good psychologists… they know Georgians love when they take priority or a kind of show-off. They say you'll work hard to prevail upon ten-member teams. In turn, the 10-member teams will be ashamed of lagging behind a 7-member team and start working harder. That's the whole logic! Eventually the job will be done well. Besides, the fewer the Georgians, the less is the likelihood of fights! Why don't we have another drink?!

Jango fills the horn. Thoma turns to the lieutenant.

Thoma: What do you think, Comrade Lieutenant, are we Georgians fight mongers?!

The lieutenant: I don't know! I know that I enjoy your company… (He empties the horn in a single shot).

Thoma: I think that it isn't true. We are not fight mongers. We have a bit more heightened sense of dignity than others. You say that Georgians are hot-tempered, don't you? Actually, what matters to us is dignity. We care much for it and can't tolerate when we are disrespected or treated unworthily. That's why we were labeled fight mongers. What do you think, Lieutenant, don't you have to react when someone insults your family?!

---

[54] Delicious!

The lieutenant: I don't know, I don't know. I don't have a wife yet… Jango, man, is there anything left in the bottle?

Thoma: Let me tell you a real story, Lieutenant. It happened in the 19th century, in Kutaisi. Have you heard of Kutaisi, a town in Georgia? A Russian governor had his residence there ruling over the whole region. A Georgian noble, they say, visited him to ask for something. Dadeshkeliani was his surname. He was from the region in Georgia where Ushba comes from, and he was very tall and well-built just like Ushba. All of a sudden, the governor got a screw loose; no one knows why, perhaps the noble's outstanding appearance made him have an idea of humiliating him. Anyway, when the noble was about to leave his room the governor put his leg on a table or chair and ordered him to creep under it. Quite an odd whim, isn't it?!

The lieutenant: And, what happened then? Don't tell me that he refused? He couldn't have refused to obey the governor's order!

Thoma: See, Comrade Lieutenant! That is exactly what matters! You, like thousands of others, would have crept under it… They would have thought it was Ok, if they'd crept under his legs and then continued their life as usual. Is that what you meant?

The lieutenant: Exactly…

Thoma: But Dadeshkeliani didn't think that way. He was the man of merit and he couldn't simply have thought that way. To tell you the truth he didn't even try to think of anything at all. He unsheathed his sword and cut the governor into pieces in his own place of residence in front of everyone. Then he calmly walked out of the room and went to Svanetia.

We hear the young men's reactions: Good job!... He did what he had to ... I would have done the same...

The lieutenant: (seems surprised unlike all of them) Do you mean he killed him... the governor? You might be kidding! And what happened then? Didn't they punish him? He might have been put to death for that.

Thoma: That's the most uninteresting part of the story, but I'll tell you, if you wish. Of course, he was executed, but that was exactly what he wished for... to die with dignity... but it's probably going to be even more difficult for you to understand.

The lieutenant: You're right. I don't understand what you are talking about. Therefore, Jango, let me have one more ... it's so much simpler... pour and drink... just one more and that's all till evening. Jango pours Chacha into the horn singing a Kakhetian tune:

Jango: This man's going to die of drinking so much... Arlaloo!

***

It's night. This time Thoma is sleeping. He sees the same dream he once saw when he was staying at Ivliane Varshalonidze's house; that night his brothers came to say good-bye to him. Thoma wakes up. He looks at the ceiling for a while. Then he puts his hand into the pocket and pulls out a cardboard toy well-known to us. He unties the strings of the toy and looks at it in a thoughtful way – at the bluebird and the cage, in turn - for a long time as the moonlight is shining on it.

The train goes on spinning rails around its wheels.

***

It is daytime. The train is standing at an empty platform. Everything around seems to have died. Some of the young men are wandering around the train; some are sitting at the open door of the carriage their legs hanging out. Two of them are gone to fetch some drinking water. A Gypsy woman appears as if from nowhere, holding a baby pressed against her and a dirty child following her and holding to the end of her long multi-colored skirt. She walks up to the young men and offers them to read their palms for money:

The Gypsy woman: Give me a ruble, only one ruble and I'll tell all of you your fortune.

The young men laugh and try to get rid of her. But the woman stands there and keeps repeating one and the same phrases. The lieutenant comes through the carriage door and as the Gypsy woman sees that he is the only person wearing uniform, she asks:

The Gypsy woman: Are you prisoners?

Young men start laughing.

Batsi: She's a great fortuneteller, isn't she? She promises to tell us our fortune for a ruble and she can't even guess who we are...

Thoma jumps off the carriage, walks to the woman and says:

Thoma: Here you are, take these three rubles and here's my palm... tell me what awaits me...

The Gypsy woman hides the 3-ruble note with one swift lightning-fast move; then she looks at Thoma's palm and stares at it for a while; she looks into his eyes a couple of times and we see her facial expression changing; then she makes him close his hand into a fist and says with a sad expression on her face:

The Gypsy woman: I've changed my mind, young man. You're so handsome and brave.

She turns and walks away. The child follows her. Thoma looks surprised; he opens his fist and finds the 3-ruble note he has given to the woman.

The train starts moving slowly along the track. The young men start jumping on the carriage one by one. We see Dachi and Beso, who has been sent to bring some water, running towards the carriage. Thoma is the last to jump on the board of train and standing there he shouts at Dachi and Beso:

Thoma: Hurry up, guys, or you'll have to stay here in this desert...

Dachi and Beso come up to the carriage running; first, they give some bottles full of water to Thoma and then jump on board of the carriage.

Dachi: Why on earth did you make me go with that deadbeat... That was because of him that we nearly missed the train...

Beso: It wasn't my fault... The well was too deep, and it was difficult to get water out of it...

Batsi: What did that woman tell you Thoma? Why didn't she tell you about your fortune?

Thoma: I don't know, Batsi... She said the lines on my palm are so entangled she'd better walk her way.

Jango: We have one there in Telavi, I mean Gypsy, but not a woman but a man, a one-eyed man, and he isn't a fortuneteller... He used to hang out with us. Do you want me to tell you how he lost his eye? In summer I used to go to the river bank with boys and he would follow us everywhere we go. We would sit there by the river and sunbathe. He used to try to do the same; though he didn't have to, as he was black as pitch. We used to throw small stones across the River Alazani. And once he threw a stone but not across the river but up in the sky, then he knelt down, and looked up at the falling stone his one eye closed and started shouting: Look, it's falling so straight down! He didn't manage to express himself properly, as the stone fell straight on his open eye.

The young men start laughing. Jango looks at them and adds:

Jango: The same thing happened there... The poor boy was grunting and squirming with pain, and we were laughing. Don't think that we didn't feel pity for him we just couldn't help laughing. You laugh at hearing his story and imagine what we might have felt. We did our best but failed to save his eye. So, he is one-eyed now.

Batsi: Is that guitar lying flat there yours, Dachi?

Dachi: Yes, it's mine; you may take it if you wish and play.

Batsi: Why me? The guitar is yours so take it and play something. If you don't want to play it, use it as a pillow when you sleep. You've both been lying there for four days now.

Dachi: No problem; as you wish. Gigi, can you pass me the guitar?

Gigi passes the guitar. Dachi plays several chords and feels it needs to be tuned. He tunes it quickly and starts playing a popular Georgian song: საქათმეში შეპარულა მელა.[55] Several of the young men join him in singing the simple melody of the song. Then Dachi starts playing a Russian song:

"Полюбить ты меня не сумела
оцениць ты меня не смогла!"

And the young men join him again and they start singing louder:

"так смотри чтоб потом не жалела
ухожу от тебя навсегда..."

The lieutenant's face shines in delight and he says: – правильно![56]

---

[55] Title of a Georgian song

[56] That's right!

Dachi (to Thoma): Why don't you join us, chief, is it because you don't like singing or you do but you can't?

Thoma: Well, your guess is wrong! I love songs and I can sing a little, but I sing different and a bit more difficult songs - Georgian folk songs.

Dachi: Which songs? Start one and we'll try to join you… maybe we can sing those songs as well

Thoma: I don't think so. It took me three months to learn one. Maybe later, when you are willing to learn it, I'll teach you. We're going to have plenty of time for that… It's called Voisa!

Dachi: Voisa? It must be a Gurian song. My forefathers came from Guria, but I have been there only once. I'll be glad to learn about it. Besides I've just listened to the boys and I think there's no one who can't sing well. (Then he turns to the lieutenant and asks in Russian) And what about you, Comrade Lieutenant, do you like singing?

The lieutenant: Of course, I do. But you sing so well that one might want to drink something. They say one out of two in Georgia can sing well… It seems to be true.

Batsi: Dachi, can I borrow your guitar for a while? I'll try to play it if I remember how to.

Dachi passes the guitar to Batsi. Batsi plays some chords and then starts playing the guitar and singing a Russian romance, but he stops abruptly and says:

Batsi: I want to dedicate the song to that fortuneteller and sing a Gypsy song. Though, I don't quite know whether it is a Gypsy song or a Russian one. But anyway, I love this song.

Then he starts playing the guitar again and singing in a very pleasant voice. The sound of the train wheels gets stronger and stronger and eventually the sound made by a train passing by overlaps with the sound of his voice.

***

The train is moving onward. It's the break of dawn. The lieutenant is standing at the opening of the carriage and is looking outside. The train moves past a building. The lieutenant tries to read the inscription on the building in the dark, he sticks his head out and follows the building with his eyes but in vain. We see his blonde hair blowing in the wind. Then he looks around studying the surroundings and shortly after he turns to the sleeping young men.

The lieutenant: That's it, my Georgian brothers. We've come. Our journey will end in half an hour.

We see the young men stretching themselves; some of them look reluctant to open their eyes. Thoma sits up and leaned against the back of the carriage looks at the lieutenant. He has a stalk of hay clung to his hair; it's hanging just in front of his right eye. He looks at it and peaks it out of his hair by his hand.

A noise comes from outside; that noise adds up to the noise made by the train wheels. The lieutenant sticks his head out of the carriage and looks at the sky to see two German planes with one of them floating down in the direction of the train. The lieutenant's eyes are wide open with astonishment.

The lieutenant: It's unbelievable! Did we cross the border?

He's hardly finished his words that the first explosion is heard. The train rocks vigorously making some of the young men spring to their feet, others just sit up. For some reason, everyone is looking at Thoma.

One of the young men: What's going on? Was it the noise of explosion I've heard or did I just had a dream?

Thoma and the lieutenant are about to answer but they are interrupted by the noise of the second explosion. The second bomb hits the carriage preceding theirs and a real nightmare starts. We see the carriage being turned over, but before that the lieutenant standing at the opening of the carriage literary flies out of the carriage. The wooden boxes on the open carriage preceding their carriage start exploding one after another, they appear to have been loaded with cannon shells. A deafening noise is heard around. The lieutenant's body flies in the air just above the exploding shells, the explosion tearing his body apart and sending his limbs flying through the air. The train derails and the carriages start to overturn falling on both sides of the track. The carriage falls upside down and the young men inside are thrown to one end of the carriage; shell debris keeps falling on the carriage wall, making terrible noise.

The wreckage stops as unexpectedly as it has started and all of a sudden eerie silence reigns over the surrounding. Only the sound of planes can be heard from a distance that gradually subsides; they are leaving the blown-up train as they might have considered they've done their part. We see the young men moving and trying to get to their feet. We see that all are alive and safe and sound. Only Thoma has a minor bleeding cut on his forehead. Thoma feels the cut with his hand; looks at the blood on his palm and then asks:

Thoma: Are you all alive?

Jango: I think so, but I don't know where to put my feet. We have to manage to get out of here… What's the matter with you? What's there on your forehead?

Thoma: Nothing a minor cut… But I wonder what's going on, what has happened to us. The single person who could answer our questions and make decisions flew out of the carriage. Unfortunate guy! I don't think he could have survived the train wreck… But, you're right, Jango, let's first get out of here and then we'll see, he might be alive… miracles happen once in a blue moon.

Batsi: Yes, we have to get out of here if we manage to… (He tries to climb the carriage wall up to the opening)

Dachi: We no longer have the guitar… just look at it…

Jango: And the bottle is also broken… to hell with it… it was already empty. The lieutenant couldn't take his eyes of it until the last drop. If only it had done him something good. Poor man…

The young men climb out of the opening of the carriage carefully one by one, carrying their belongings: their knapsacks and some food. When all of them are out they get a bit away from the train wreck site and look around. Literary nothing can be seen around, but for a typical gloom of north showing no trace of life. The young men are silent all of a sudden, a crash is heard from the side of the train. All of them startle and look in that direction.

Ushba: My heart skipped a beat… Can anyone tell me what's going on here? Who's bombed us?

Thoma: Didn't you hear the lieutenant's words when he looked up in the sky? He said it was unbelievable… Who else if not Germans could have bombed the train? I think it's started…

Beso: What do you mean, man? What might have started so unexpectedly?

Thoma: War, Beso, a war has started!

Gigi: So, what shall we do now?

Thoma: We should think of a plan... this track couldn't have been laid only for us… seven Georgians coming to work on the border... other trains must be running on the track. So, sooner or later, someone will appear… at least to see what has happened here if not for repairing the track. So, in my opinion, it makes no sense to leave this place. We have to wait here. Even if we decide to leave this place do we have any idea where we should go? In short, we have to stay here and wait. Until then, I'll go and try to find the lieutenant dead or alive.

Jango: I'm coming with you, Thoma…

Ushba: I'll go with you guys!

Beso: It seems to me I have nothing to do here, so I'll join you!

Batsi: (to Thoma) Wait a minute, chief, can you see a construction site near here?

Thoma: I don't understand why you're asking Batsi...

Batsi: I'll tell you now. You were supposed to be our team leader in case we had to work as a construction team. Look around and tell me, can you see anything here besides that damn wrecked train? Why on earth then do you decide for us... what we have to do? Has anyone asked you to do so? You say we have to stay here... what if I don't want to stay here? We all want to survive and I'm not an exception, but I have to decide how to save my own life. So, I'll choose whether to stay here or go. Got it? I'll go back to where we've come from. Maybe you've never seen that there are roads running along railways. I'll go along this track and find that road. I'll take that road and as our lieutenant used to say all the roads lead to some settlements. So, I am leaving this place. As for you, you have to decide what to do. If you want to go with me, you're welcome, if you don't, you may stay here and look for the lieutenant. I'm not quite sure but, say, the war has really started, do you think Germans would manage to occupy Moscow? So, we'll walk and come across our men in a couple of hours, I assure you.

Thoma: Who do you mean when you say, "our men"?... And besides, if you want to go, nobody is going to make you stay; you didn't have to deliver such a long speech to let me know you want to go. I'm not going to tell anyone what they should do. For God's sake; I was asked my opinion and I just said what I thought. Go, brother, and have a safe journey! And all of you who decide to go, you too have a safe journey!

Batsi: So, I'm off, does anyone want to join me?

Dachi: I think I'll go with you… Not because I don't trust Thoma, simply, it's because of my character. I'd rather act and fail than sit and wait, that's it.

Gigi: Thoma don't be angry with me, I think I'd better go. I am a little impatient just like Dachi. I can't stand waiting for anything. (He addresses the rest of the young men) What are you going to do, guys?

Jango: I think I'd rather stay!

Ushba: Me too!

Beso: And I am staying here!

Batsi: That's it! Everything is clear. So, let's go. We won't walk fast, so if you change your mind you can catch us up.

Thoma: Good-bye, Batsi, Good-bye, guys… Wish you luck.

Batsi: Farewell, Thoma.

Batsi, Dachi and Gigi start walking. Thoma, Jango, Ushba and Beso watch them walking away for a while.

Ushba: Batsi said "farewell", but my heart is telling me, we'll meet them soon.

Jango: What is your heart telling you about our lieutenant, Ushba?

Ushba: My heart is telling me, we are looking for him in vain. If he were alive, we would hear him calling us for help or at least groaning.

Thoma: He might be lying somewhere unconscious…

Ushba: I wish it were true and we found him alive.

Beso: You said, Thoma, that you had seen him flying out of the carriage, didn't you? So, did you notice which direction he flew? We have to look for him there.

Thoma: Which direction might he have flown, Beso? Forward! It's the law of inertia! Jango and I will start searching this territory and you and Ushba can start searching the territory beyond these ruins. I think he can't have flown there but still…

The young men start searching the territory: Thoma and Jango are searching the piles of iron and wood mixed together. Thoma says to himself:

Thoma: Oh, Uncle Moshe, didn't I tell you? ... Why did you say that "imagine a war started" … I had a misgiving that something wrong was going to happen. And here it is… Every time it comes true…

***

Two men dressed in uniform are walking down the path. One of them is an aizsargs[57]. The second man is his subordinate. Therefore, he walks slightly behind at a distance required by the difference between their ranks. A derailed train with its carriages forming a mass of distorted and wrecked stock can be seen from where they walk. The policemen speak to each-other in Lithuanian.

Police officer: Look at that mass. The Germans blew it up early in the morning, an hour after the war began. It's a baggage train ... let's go and have a look at it. Maybe we can find something interesting...

The police officer turns from the path and walks across the field towards the train wreck site. The other policeman follows him.

Thoma and Jango see the policemen walking towards them and look askance at them.

Jango: (whispering)You were right… some men in uniforms are coming. What shall we do?

---

[57] A member of the Lithuanian Paramilitary formation; a police officer

Thoma: As they are coming, there's nothing else left for us to do but to meet them. I see they are wearing uniforms, but they don't look like Germans… and as I can see from here they aren't carrying guns. Well, just in case, let's do it this way. First, I'll walk up to them alone. You don't show up. Ushba and Beso aren't here anyway. I'll talk to them and find out what's going on and if I see that everything is all right, I'll call you. Maybe there is no war at all and the train was bombed by accident. Everything is possible...

Jango: But what if it's not all right?

Thoma: I can't say beforehand… I'll act according to the situation… Ok, I'll go now.

Thoma emerges out of the remnants of the wreck and stops on an open area for the men in uniforms to see him. They immediately notice Thoma, stop and the aizsargs produces his firearm from the gun holster on his belt, which Thoma couldn't notice because he's carried it on the back of his belt. He points the firearm at Thoma and simultaneously looks around examining the surroundings. He approaches Thoma step by step in tall grass with his gun pointed at him. Thoma raises his hands to show that they don't have to be afraid of him as he is unarmed. The aizsargs stops 7 steps away from Thoma and says something in Lithuanian. Thoma, naturally, can't understand anything and responds in German.

Thoma: Sorry, I don't understand what you're saying; I don't speak your language. Do you speak German or Russian?

The policemen look at each-other on hearing Thoma speaking German and then the aizsargs asks him in German:

The aizsargs: Who are you? Where have you come from?

Thoma: I'm an engineer from Tbilisi. I traveled on this train and now I don't even know where I am. We were sent here to build some fortifications along the borders, but you see we've been bombed. What's going on? Has the war started?

The aizsargs: Do you really mean that you've heard nothing?! The Baltics are already in the hands of the German forces. Goddamned Russian Communists ran away with their tails between their legs... As for you, if you are saying the truth, then where are the others? You didn't intend to build fortifications alone, did you?!

Thoma: No, of course not. Some have gone… in that direction, some are nearby. I'm sure they are watching us right now.

On hearing these words, the policemen get agitated. They take their eye off Thoma and start looking in the direction of the remains of the train.

Thoma: you've misunderstood me. They are watching, I mean… We don't have any guns. We're not soldiers. Cannot you see what I am wearing?! They are watching and hope that you'll be able to help us. We have to do something to get out of this stalemate somehow.

The aizsargs: Ok, so let's say I believed you, say things really were, as you say, and you really were builders and not soldiers disguised as civilians, then I wonder, how you would explain that... (He stoops to the ground and takes a piece of the lieutenant's hand from the grass, with a fragment of a military uniform cuff round the wrist) Judging from this shirt cuff, the owner must have been a lieutenant.

Thoma: (His eyes widen at the sight of the lieutenant's hand and he says in Georgian) Oh my God! (Then he regains his composure and says in German) He was our guide – lieutenant; he was the only person who knew where to lead us. Yeah, and he's been killed.

The aizsargs: (all of a sudden says in Russian with a specific accent) You just don't look like somebody from Russia…

Thoma: Why should I? I'm not Russian.

The aizsargs: Are you Jewish?

Thoma: No, I am neither Russian nor Jewish. Haven't I told you that I am from Tbilisi? I'm Georgian. And they are Georgian too. (Thoma points back with his hand)

The aizsargs: Aha! I see now! You're Stalin's fellow men. (He says contemptuously and then continues) Ok, ok. Tell them to come out. We'll take you to the police station and if you can prove that you are really builders, i.e. civilians, we'll let you go, and you'll have to take care of yourselves. What are you waiting for? Call the others and behave yourselves!

***

The yard of a military garrison abandoned by the Soviet army is full of prisoners of war. Soviet propaganda posters can be seen here and there. A billboard for top performers in garrison is in place with Lenin's image at the top. A German soldier is standing in front of it and shooting from a belt fed machine gun at the photographs posted on the board, shouting something in German. A crowd of buzzing and bustling solders is gathered behind his back. A long line of gloomy looking single-storied barracks surround the yard on three sides. The fourth side serves as a place for a checkpoint with a boom barrier. A truck loaded with another bunch of prisoners drives to the boom barrier and into the yard. German gunmen are standing in all four corners of the truck body. They jump off the truck open the tailgate and order the prisoners to get off.

We see Thoma, Jango, Ushba and Beso among other prisoners sitting leaned against the barrack wall and watching the truck being driven into the yard.

Beso: It's already the fourth truck today. They're bringing prisoners in non-stop.

Jango: Yeah, but all of them are wearing military uniforms and it's understandable why they are brought here, but I don't quite understand why on earth they brought us here; we aren't soldiers, we haven't even shot a bullet…

Thoma: That aizsargs was so kind to us. Lithuanians hate Russians like sin, and, apparently, neither Georgians appeal to them, because of Stalin. Did you notice that grimace on his face when I told him we were from Georgia? "Aha!" - he said, "You're Stalin's fellow men?!" – and he brought us here.

Ushba: You shouldn't have said that then…

Thoma: Then tell me what I should have said, Ushba?!

Ushba: You should have said we were Svanetians… providing him with a conundrum to solve… Just look there… Here they are… Didn't I say my heart was telling me, we'd meet them soon?

We see Dachi, Gigi and Batsi jumping off the truck.

Jango: What luck! Now we are going to have more fun. Let's go and meet them, they'll be happy to see us. At least that will give them a grain of hope.

Thoma: If we believe scientists, what's just happened to us is so to say achieving the same results by different means. We're all together again. Maybe that's because of that war that our Heavenly Father can't find time for improvisation.

Dachi, Gigi and Batsi also see Thoma, Jango, Ushba and Beso among prisoners, they start walking towards them smiling at having snatched a piece of joy from the hands of misfortune.

Two German soldiers standing nearby pay attention to their joy of coming together and one of them asks the other:

First German soldier: Hans! Look at these fools! What do you think the reason for their joy is? (The second soldier says nothing, and the first soldier answers his own question) Maybe that they are still alive?! (He spits out)

Batsi: We had hardly covered three kilometers when they caught us. We weren't wearing military uniforms, but we might be looking so different from the locals that we attracted their attention and besides we failed to make them understand what we were doing there... Thoma your mission is to save us... you are the only one who speaks their language and you have to explain to them...

Thoma: What do I have to explain to them, Batsi. Speak with them in German or Svanetian language; it's all the same. They wouldn't listen. War has its logic. They have waged war against Russians; and they identify us with Russians. That's it!

Jango: Do you mean that we're doomed?

Thoma: Can you see that German over there… the one who isn't wearing a cap? Do you know what he said when he saw us happy and excited about meeting each other? He said: "Look at these fools! What do you think the reason for their joy is?" and then he answered his own question: "that they are still alive?! So, we are still alive, guys, and for the moment this is what matters.

***

Prisoners of war are busy cleaning ruins of a destroyed factory. They are collecting bricks and carrying the garbage put in carts towards the end of the yard and throwing it there. Some soldiers can be seen here and there sheltered under the shadow. They are smoking cigarettes, talking with each other and shooting side-glance at the prisoners from time to time.

The Georgians are among the prisoners. They have already cleaned half of the concrete floor of a big plant with high ceilings and are now cleaning the second part; but a huge log of wood fallen from the ceiling and lying in the mass of construction and demolition debris hinders them to get their work done. Thoma tries to move the log but in vain as it is trapped under the debris of concrete structures.

Thoma shouts to a soldier standing nearby.

Thoma: Sir, if we don't pull this huge log out of here, we won't be able to continue cleaning the place. It is pulling us back!

The soldier: So, what do you want from me? Do you expect me to issue you a license?! Pull it out and (He looks around) drop it there. We'll sit on it while we are here.

Thoma: We've already tried but it's too heavy.

The German soldier gets interested and starts walking in the direction where Thoma is standing, walks up to the log, slings the rifle over his shoulder and in a business-like manner taps in the old tree trunk grown black.

The soldier: It's really huge. When the truck comes to take us, we'll have to attach a chain to it and pull it out of there …

Batsi: What does he say Thoma?

Thoma: He says we have to pull it out with a truck chain…

Batsi: No need, man, let's ask Ushba to do this… I bet Ushba can pull it out.

Jango: You're right; where is he?

The young men find Ushba and bring him to the place where the log is trapped.

Jango: Batsi says Ushba won't manage to pull out that log (He turns to Batsi, gives him a wink and continues) I say you can, in short, I bet him that you would move that log… Now it's your turn to say, will you pull it out or not?

Ushba: (looks at the log and says) This one? (Then he goes close to it, watches it for a while as if measuring it visually and asks) And what does the one who wins the bet get?

Jango: Well the one who loses the bet is to fulfill three wishes of the winner. If you manage to pull this log out, I'll let you have one of these wishes, what else do you want?

Ushba: And what if I fail to? How many of the three wishes are you ready to let me have, Batsi? (Ushba keeps on examining the log with his hands)

Batsi: Pull that log out and let us boast about you, and I'll let you have all the three of them, brother…

Ushba: Ok, I don't want anything from you. I'll pull it out for free…

Jango: Wait a minute, Ushba. It won't work this way. We have to benefit from this somehow. Three out of seven of us are smokers, aren't we? Thoma, ask the German, standing there all day and getting on our nerves... if this man pulls this log out of here and… (He turns to Ushba and asks him) Ushba, can you bring it to that place?

Ushba: I can!

Jango: May God help you… if he pulls this log out and brings it there, without anyone's help, will he give us three cigarettes?

Thoma smiles and interprets Jango's suggestion to the German soldier.

The soldier: That log? Without anyone's help? It's just impossible... (He looks him up and down sizing him up and asks) Are you Hercules?

Ushba looks at Thoma.

Thoma: He wants to know whether you are Hercules.

Ushba: Who is Hercules? I'm not Hercules, I'm Ushba.

Thoma: (Smiles and interprets Ushba's words to the soldier) He's not Hercules, he's Ushba...

The German soldier doesn't understand why Thoma smiles but neglects it and calls other soldiers to explains to them what's going to happen. All the prisoners and soldiers gather around to watch Ushba performing the feat. All of them learn what Ushba is going to do and watch him with great interest. Ushba takes of his shirt, stands there naked waist up, then walks close to the log, bends down trying putting his shoulder under the log, but then, all of a sudden, he changes his mind, takes his shirt lying on the floor, folds it a few times, puts it on his bare shoulder and gets down to the log again; he puts his shoulder under it and straightens himself up slowly using all the strength and energy he has and letting out an enormous roar. We see the debris of concrete structures falling from the top of the log to the ground and the log being moved with horrible squeaking sound. The prisoners and the soldiers cry out in surprise and cheer watching the scene with their eyes wide open. The Georgians are encouraging him with their frequent exclamations. Ushba now straightened up puts his arms around the trunk of the log slightly forward, holds his arms around it like leverages and pulls it forward with a loud roar. The log moves along with him a little. Then he pulls it again and again and so gradually moves it forward enough to free it from the debris and lets it down to the ground. Then he walks to the middle length of the log, raises it up slightly, puts his arms round it, takes it into his arms, raises it up to his knees with another roar and goes running to the place where he has to put it. All the people, standing around, step backwards making way for him to pass. Ushba reaches his destination safely. Throws down the log and turns around with an amazingly kind smile on his face.

The people shout loudly. The German soldier holds out a pack of cigarettes for Thoma. Thoma starts taking three cigarettes out of the pack but the soldier gives him the whole pack and says:

The soldier: Take the whole pack, you deserved it.

Jango comes running to Thoma.

Jango: Give it to me quickly, Thoma, until Dachi and Gigi see it.

Thoma: Why, Jango, do you really plan to give only a cigarette to each of them?

Jango: No, I'll give two cigarettes to each of them, but only because you want me to. They were drinking my Chacha on our way here, don't you remember?

***

Convoys of prisoners are led by soldiers into the garrison yard. There are a lot of them, all wearing dirty and torn military uniforms devoid of shoulder straps; the only ones not wearing uniforms are the seven Georgians. They all first gather in the yard and then hurry towards their barracks after they are ordered to do so; and in a few seconds we see them running back with bowls and spoons in their hands and arranging themselves in a queue in front of a small opening in the wall of a building. A Russian cook, a prisoner himself, is standing there and is pouring something resembling swill with a ladle from a huge pot into the bowls stretched out by the prisoners. The queue is enormous, forming several zigzags throughout the yard. The Georgian prisoners are the last ones who come to join the queue at the very end of it. The German soldier who gave them a pack of cigarettes comes to them and addresses Thoma:

The soldier: Tell your Hercules that the commandant wants to see him, immediately. You have to go with us to be our interpreter. You'll have your dinner later.

Thoma interprets the message to Ushba and both of them leave the queue holding their bowls in their hands.

The soldier: You can't take your bowls with you. Leave them to your friends. Don't worry; you're not going to be left without dinner. I'll personally tell the cook to put aside two portions of it.

Thoma and Ushba give their bowls to their friends standing in the queue and follow the soldier. A German officer with an intelligent face is sitting at a small table in front of the Headquarters. The soldier walks up to this officer, straightens up and is about to report to him but the officer stops him with a hand gesture and looks at the prisoners.

The commandant: They look rather cheerful, more cheerful then the rest of them here, but why aren't they wearing military uniforms? Did anyone interrogate them? They might as well be disguised commissars.

The soldier: No, Commandant, they were brought here by local policemen. They are builders. They were sent here to build fortifications, but they failed to; they were late.

The commandant: But if they are civilians why they were brought here. This camp is for prisoners of war and not for builders.

The soldier: The aizsargs said they were to join a paramilitary construction unit and were intended to take a military oath...

The commandant: So, you say the aizsargs has brought them... the aizsargs says... He seems to be a great swindler your aizsargs. According to his logics he should be here, alongside the prisoners, sooner or later, Communists would have urged him as well to take a military oath. Or maybe he has already done so...

The soldier: I don't know, Commandant!

The commandant: Ok, I'll find out myself. (Then he turns to the prisoners) So, here's our Hercules! He's built like Hercules!

Ushba: Why on earth they keep repeating that Hercules! Hercules! I'm Ushba!

The commandant looks at Thoma and the latter quickly interprets Ushba's words.

Thoma: He says that he's not Hercules but an ordinary man, Commandant.

The commandant: Certainly, he's an ordinary man, but as I've been told the one with extraordinary strength. I wanted to have a look at him. The man who possesses such tremendous strength should be treated with respect (He turns to the soldiers again) Go to the cook and tell him to send us a loaf of bread and a whole sausage. Let's award our Hercules.

The soldier immediately runs away. Thoma is looking at the open chessboard on the table with interest; he seems to be studying the position on the chessboard and trying to analyze it. The commandant notices this and asks:

The commandant: Do you play chess?

Thoma: Yes, I do. I love playing chess…

The commandant seems a bit surprised. Then he looks down at the chessboard, takes a knight in his hand, holds it for Thoma to see and says:

The commandant: This piece is made of wood; it weighs almost nothing, but taking it in your hand and placing it on an appropriate square, needs much more strength than pulling the log your friend has moved today, because it requires absolutely different strength… (He taps his forehead with his finger and continues) the strength of your grey matter.

Thoma: I do agree with you. Can we play a game? If you don't mind of course…

The commandant seems even more surprised. He gives him a long, inquisitive look and, all of a sudden, answers:

The commandant: Why not! But to make the game more interesting let's make a bet. (He pauses for a while and seems to be thinking, and then he continues) If you win, I'll tell them to bring a loaf of bread and a whole sausage for you as well. But what if I win… What do you have to offer?

Thoma: (bitter smile crosses his face) Unfortunately, I have nothing to offer you. My present possessions are limited to these clothes and… my life. And both are in your hands anyway. You can take them away from me any time. Though, there is one thing that I definitely can't be deprived of by you or anyone else on this earth, but unfortunately it neither can be subject to win-lose even if I wished it were.

The commandant: Your judgment has intrigued me, would you tell me, what exactly you mean?!

Thoma: I mean my will, Commandant, my goodwill, or a lack of it. Today the only thing I have control over is my will. It's mine and nobody can take it away from me by force. One's will can only be subject to relations.

The commandant: An interesting theory… but have you ever thought who needs your will or set of your mind?

Thoma: That's up to the person, Commandant. There are people who rejoice in others' goodwill.

The commandant: How old are you, young man? Your judgment makes me think that you reason as if you were older than you actually are.

Thoma: I am 21, Commandant.

The commandant: And where are you from? The language you and your friend speak is definitely not Russian.

Thoma: We are from Georgia.

The commandant: I see, the country of the Golden Fleece. And you seem to be very well educated.

Thoma: I'm an engineer. I graduated from the Tbilisi Technical Institute… 12 days ago.

The commandant: You say 12 days ago? And you are here now? Those Communists surprise me a lot. What did they want from you? Where did you learn German?

Thoma: My dad taught me. To be more precise I was born here... not here, I meant I was born in Germany. My mother was German, but she died in childbirth, after giving birth to me. When I was two years old, my dad went back to his homeland and brought me with him. I've lived in Georgia since then. I was told I had a house somewhere in Germany, but I don't know where.

The commandant: Can you show me a kind of document that will prove what you've just told me? If you can, I'll take care and help you to leave this place, and if you manage to find your house, you can claim and gain ownership of your property. What would you say; can you provide the documents confirming all that?

Thoma: I'm afraid I can't, Commandant. Though even if I could, it wouldn't make any sense. If I were allowed to leave this place, it would mean that my only crime was my origin and nothing else. If it's so, I can tell you without delay that in spite of the fact that I was born in Germany, I am and always will be Georgian.

The commandant says nothing, he just looks at Thoma. Then he turns to the soldier who has long been standing there and tells him.

The commandant: Put what you've brought on the table and go and tell the cook to send the same meal. Hurry up. (Then he turns to Thoma again) And how many of you are here, I mean builders?

Thoma: There are seven of us, Commandant.

The commandant: Well, ok, I'll send you back to your barracks as soon as the soldier returns. As for the game of chess, I promise, we'll play it sometime later. I don't want to quit this etude…

It's getting dark. Thoma and Ushba are returning to their barracks. Not a single person can be seen in the yard. Exhausted prisoners are lying in their beds in the barracks. Thoma and Ushba enter their barracks. Beso meets them at the entrance.

Beso: Where have you been so long? I thought I was the only person from Racha here. Your meals are on your beds waiting for you, but it's already got cold.

Thoma: Beso, we hate eating it when it's hot and how can we eat it now?

Beso: Don't be so sure! Russian looked at it like at prey. Guys have been guarding it.

Thoma: Tell those guys to come here and join us. We're going to have a party; and be so kind as to give that swill to someone…

***

It is evening. The prisoners are in the yard. They are arranged in such a way, as if they are getting ready for a parade. Though, their appearance is not suitable for a parade, dressed in dirty rags, they look pitifully. The seven Georgians are among them standing in a group together. German military men and Lithuanian policemen stride up and down the lines in which prisoners are arranged. Lithuanians are particularly active shouting at the prisoners in strongly accented Russian. The same aizsargs, the young men ran into near the exploded train, is in charge of leading Lithuanian policemen and he is the most aggressive one. He strides in front of the young men and looks at them with his eyes filled with hostility.

The commandant walks out of the headquarters building accompanying a young charming lady dressed in black clothes. They are walking towards the prisoners standing in lines and talking calmly.

The woman: Let me guess which one of them he is. Please don't prompt... Actually, you've described him to me in such details that I shouldn't find it difficult to recognize him... A tall man with an intelligent face, I don't see many of them here who match this description. Oh, they look awful.

The commandant: I'm absolutely sure you'll know him when you see him. In case you choose someone else, he'll be one of them. There are seven of them as I've told you.

They approach the prisoners. The woman walks a bit ahead of the commandant and looks at the prisoners' faces. They walk for a while and finally the woman stops in front of Ushba. She looks at him for a longer time than she looked at others; then she turns her glance to the prisoner standing next to Ushba. The man standing next to Ushba is Thoma. She stares at him for a while, then turns to the commandant and says firmly almost categorically:

The woman: It's him.

The commandant smiles claps his hand lightly a few times and says:

The commandant: Bravo, Maria! Bravo! (Then he turns to Thoma) Tell your friends that I have carefully considered your case and decided to let you leave the camp. All of you have to go with this lady, immediately. You'll work for her and you'll live in her house. You're given 5 minutes. You should be standing in front of the headquarters building in 5 minutes, all of you. (Then he finds the aizsargs and says) Order others to fall out! (Then he takes Maria by the arm, leads her to the building and says) Let's walk in Maria; I would like to offer you a cup of coffee. In five minutes, you can take your Caucasians with you.

***

A small tractor, with a platform body with low sides for carrying goods, is standing at the boom barrier. A black BMW is standing in front of the tractor. The young men are getting on the platform body. Maria is standing nearby watching them. When all the seven young men get on the platform, she walks towards the BMW and takes the seat behind the wheel. She drives slowly away of the POW camp and the tractor follows her car.

After a while they can be seen on a gravel road between trees. First, we see the car and not very far away the tractor following it. The car turns into the road running between broad-leaved trees. The road is as straight as an arrow and leads to huge gates. The gates are open. The car drives in the yard and stops at the entrance of a two-storied house. An elderly man (called Alex) walks out of a shed, approaches the woman and addresses her with respect:

Alex: So, you're back, Madam. Where is the tractor?

Maria: It'll be here in a minute and will bring the prisoners. Did you prepare everything in the shed?

Alex: Yes Madam. As you've told me, everything is ready in the shed and upstairs.

The tractor drives into the yard, stops and the young men jump off the platform. They are standing awkwardly there and looking at Maria. Maria addresses them in Russian with Lithuanian accent.

Maria: This is Alex, my right-hand man. You have to follow him and he's going to show you around and tell you where you have to sleep, have your dinner, supper and so on. He'll answer all your questions. You'll rest today and get to work from tomorrow morning.

Maria looks at Thoma, gives him her charming smile and asks him in German:

Maria: Do you understand everything?

Thoma: Yes, we do, Madam.

He nods his head, turns around and follows Alex together with the rest of the young men. He says in Georgian:

Thoma: Let's see what they have to offer us; but anything will do… Nothing will be worse than those putrid barracks. Now, that we have escaped that place, we can even spend the night outside, in the fresh air. The commandant was so nice to us!

Jango: You bet! Had Ushba not pulled out that log…

Jango is interrupted by Alex, who says in Russian.

Alex: Guys, try to speak your language less, especially when Madam is around, she is so incredulous…

Jango: Don't worry, we'll teach her Georgian soon.

Everybody laughs on hearing these words. Alex laughs too and says:

Alex: You seem to be so funny, guys. I think we'll get on…

Alex walks down the yard and the young men go after him. Besides a rather large long house with an attached shed there are some accessory buildings in the yard. It looks like a traditional German farm, more or less clean and well-ordered.

Alex leads the young men into the shed and we see a large, bright and long room. There is a long wooden table with two wooden benches of the same length in the room. There are six beds made of iron and a solid wooden chair stands by each bed. There are some necessary pieces of furniture as well: a closet, a stove, etc. the tap water is in the yard. All six beds have been prepared and look inviting.

Alex: This is your residence. You're going to have your breakfast and dinner here and… you can see beds over there. We provide self-catering service. I'll supply you with food products and the rest is up to you, you may want to have a rotation shift, or you may choose a cook. In short, as you decide. You may choose the beds as well some of you may like sleeping by the window and some by the wall…

Thoma: But there are only six beds and seven of us here…

Alex: That's true, but Madam says you're going to be the team leader and the team leader should live in a separate room.

The young men start laughing.

Batsi: This man is born to be a leader…

Alex gives them an incredulous look and Thoma is obliged to explain to him the boy's reaction in Russian.

Thoma: I used to be their leader until they took us in that camp; that's why they're laughing.

Alex: really? Than it seems that Madam was right when she ordered to give you a separate room…

Thoma: But, what if I want to be together with my friends?

Alex: You should discuss thief with Madam tomorrow. Now follow me, I'll show you your room. Hurry up; I have a lot to do. I have to find uniforms for you. (He looks at Ushba) This man is too tall I don't think I'll find anything of his size…

Thoma turns to the young men and says in Russian:

Thoma: I'll go with him and I hope to be joining you soon. What on earth I'm supposed to be doing there alone!

Jango: (in Georgian) Don't worry a lot, Thoma, it seems to me you're not going to be all alone there. You'll be offered something else besides the rank of a leader and don't dare to bring shame on us Georgians!

The young men laugh again.

Thoma: I think we have to stop now; we don't have to embarrass them… the camp is not very far away.

Thoma turns and follows Alex. They enter the house, go upstairs and Alex opens the door of one of the rooms. He enters the room and Thoma follows him. It is a cozy room; there's a wooden bed with canopy, a very thick mattress and some embroidered pillows on it. Some towels are on the chair standing near the bed. A bathrobe is hanging behind the door.

Alex: The bathroom is at the end of the hall. Madam said you should have a bath and go downstairs to have supper. There are some clothes in this wardrobe, choose any and get dressed.

Thoma: And what about my friends?

Alex: Your friends won't be left without supper, don't worry. I have to go now. I'll be back tomorrow morning.

Alex walks out of the room. Thoma looks around the room, goes close to the bed, takes a pillow, brings it to his face and inhales deeply with his eyes closed and with a look of pleasure on his face.

***

It's late in the evening. Maria is in the dining room sitting in an armchair and looking through some papers; she is wearing a black luxurious evening dress. The table in the middle of the room is laid for two persons. There are candles burning in the lampstands.

Thoma is walking downstairs. On hearing the footsteps Maria looks in the direction of the door and smiles as she sees Thoma looking like a real gentleman: he looks neat and tidy, wearing the outfit that he has chosen from the clothes in the wardrobe and that suits him very much. Maria stands up, goes close to the table and says:

Maria: Come to the table, please, don't be so shy. It's high time we knew each-other closer. Rainer - your commandant has told me much about you, but he didn't tell me your name.

Thoma: Thoma is my name.

Maria: Thoma? It sounds like our name Thomas! Shall we take our seats, Thoma?

Thoma waits until Maria takes her seat and only after he takes his.

Maria: Rainer visited me yesterday evening. My late husband and he studied together in Germany, in Halle… So he came to me yesterday evening and told me about you. You must have charmed him. It was he who recommended moving you here. I hope it's better for you as well.

Thoma: You said better, Madam? How can one compare? It feels like heavens here.

Maria: I wonder if they drink wine in the heavens. As for me, I'll have some pleasure if you pour some in my glass.

Thoma stands up goes to the place where Maria is sitting and pours some wine into her glass. He pours some wine in his glass as well, puts the bottle on the table, takes his seat and smells the wine in his glass. We can see by the expression on his face that he is pleased.

Maria: Help yourself, please, and don't be shy. You must be hungry and very tired. Your single goal right now might be to reach your bed. I'll let you go as soon as you finish your supper. All of you have to get a good rest today… and tomorrow morning… (She smiles) you'll have to start working.

Thoma only listens and doesn't say anything. He empties his glass of wine and starts eating. Maria stops talking not to interrupt him, looks at him and smiles.

***

It's morning. Thoma is lying asleep in his new bed. There is a knock on the door. Thoma wakes up, gets up and opens the door. Alex is standing there with a neatly folded blue uniform.

Alex: Take this and get dressed. Your friends are already ready waiting for you in the yard. They've had their breakfast. You were so deeply asleep that we didn't want to wake you up earlier. I'll be waiting for you downstairs.

Thoma closes the door, goes to the window and looks through it. The young men are standing there wearing the uniforms of the same color. Ushba's trousers are too short and he looks funny in them. Thoma smiles. There is a little boy standing there with the young men. Thoma stops looking through the window; he turns around, swiftly makes the bed and goes running to the bathroom, washed his face, runs back to his room and we see him running out of it in the blink of an eye wearing the uniform. He runs downstairs and sees Maria in the dining room. He runs into the dining room and says:

Thoma: I apologize, Madam, I promise I won't behave this way again.

Maria: Not a big problem. We have enough time to manage everything. Please, sit down and have your breakfast.

Thoma: No I'm afraid I don't have time for this, Boys are waiting for me.

Thoma goes to the table, takes two slices of bread and some sausage slices and walks out of the house chewing his breakfast. The young men are all looking at him and Thoma looks at them. They look a little funny in their uniforms. One of them chuckles and all of a sudden all of them burst out laughing. Thoma laughs too. They look at each-other roaring with laughter. Alex can't help laughing and the little boy is very amused. Maria walks out of the house, looks at the boys having fun and laughs.

After a while Thoma regains some composure and asks in Georgian:

Thoma: Tell me, please, what you're laughing at?

Beso: First you tell us what you are laughing at, as you're asking us…

Thoma: I don't know. Everyone was laughing, and laughter is contagious. Who is this little gentleman?

Jango: He's Maria's son. He's five. Look, isn't he a great boy? He's been with us since morning. He speaks to us non-stop, but we don't understand a word of what he says.

Thoma: (in Georgian) Hello, young man!

The little boy shakes his hand with Thoma in a manly manner and says something in Lithuanian. Thoma asks him in, German:

Thoma: Are you coming with us?

Matthias: Mom won't let me go with you…

Thoma: Then tell me what your name is.

Matthias: Matthias!

Thoma: Matthias! Matthias! It's a good name, sounds manly…

Maria comes close to them and says to Matthias:

Maria: Matthias, I see you've already got acquainted with our guests. (Then she turns to the young men) Good morning, everybody! How did you sleep? I think it's better here than in that camp.

The young men answer together: "Of course, it is." "We can't even compare." "It's like heavens here!"

Beso: We, Georgians, are hardworking people and we know how to express our gratitude. You have to wait a bit and I promise you, this place will soon look like the Garden of Eden. (Beso looks at his friends and says in Georgian) You have to wait to see what Beso is able to do!

The young men smile.

Maria: (in Russian) Спасибо ребята! Поживем, увидим![58]

The young men get on the platform body attached to the tractor. Alex is coming to the platform body, currying some scythes. He gives the scythes to the young men who are already on the platform body. Thoma is about to get on it, but Alex stops him.

---

[58] Thanks, guys! We have to wait to see!

Alex: The team leader should sit beside me in the cab… I'll explain to you what our plans are for today.

Thoma follows him and soon we see the tractor driving out of the yard.

***

A gravel road runs on one side of a vast field of tall, yellow grass. A black car appears on the road from a distance. When it drives closer, we can see that it is Maria's BMW. The car stops, and Maria gets out of it together with her son. Alex dives out of the tall grass and walks in Maria's direction to meet her.

Maria: How's the work going? What are our Georgians doing?

Alex: Everything's fine, Madam, we're lucky! You have to watch them working. They are so diligent. Only one of them didn't know how to mow but he was pretty quick to pick it up and is mowing grass now like he's been doing it for the year. I just can't take my eyes off them. You should come and see them; your presence can give them an additional incentive…

Maria: Do you mean that they haven't stopped since morning?

Alex: Exactly! They occasionally stop to sharpen a scythe blade. And they sang once or twice. They sing so beautifully.

Maria: Really? Now I regret not coming earlier. I should have come with you and taken Matthias with me. And what about the team leader, was it the right decision to choose him as a leader?

Alex: It was, Madam, it was the right choice. It seems that the young man is born to be a leader. Everyone treats him with respect.

Maria: Well, ok, tell them they may take a break and go to the river to wash themelves and you take this basket. There is some food there and find a place to have lunch. (Then she turns to her son) Matthias, do you want to go with Alex? You can join the young men there.

Matthias starts jumping for joy and asks.

Matthias: Does that mean that you let me swim in the river, Mom?

Maria: Well, you can swim in the river, but be careful. Alex, tell the boys to look after him.

Alex: I will, Madam.

Alex and Matthias go away. Maria gets in her car, opens the opposite door as well and seats herself gracefully on the car seat, enjoying the cool breeze blowing past her face. Soon she hears the young men making noise on the river bank; she smiles and closes her eyes.

***

It's late in the evening. Maria and Thoma are alone in the dining room. They have just finished their supper and are now talking.

Maria: Alex told me you had been singing while mowing the field. He said you had sung beautifully. I wish I had been there.

Thoma: Really? But you can't call it singing! The boys shouted some extracts from different songs. By the way, we're going to learn a real song. Our songs are polyphonic. It's not very easy to sing them. When we traveled here by train I promised the boys to teach them a song. We had a kind of plan that we would rehearse a song every evening when we settled in. But the war started and who would care about the song. Today they reminded me of my promise when we were by the river. A promise is a promise. So, we are going to have the first rehearsal tomorrow evening, unless you have something against this, of course. We plan to practice singing in the shed.

Maria: My God! What might I have against this? Shall I attend your rehearsals? I mean Matthias and me. We'll be quiet there; I promise we won't interrupt you.

Thoma: You are welcome, and besides, we don't have the right to refuse you, but the first two rehearsals won't be very interesting for you. First, we have to learn the song.

Maria: I don't agree with you; I will gladly attend all your rehearsals: from the beginning to the end. I used to sing when I studied at the University of Tartu I was a member of a students' chorus there. They said I had a good ear for music. So, I may even learn something. What would you say about it?

Thoma smiles.

Thoma: Ok, Madam. It is your choice. You're welcome… tomorrow, after supper. However, if you do not get angry with me, I'd rather have supper together with my friends. I don't think it's fair that I'm not with them…

Maria: I have nothing against it, but only if you stop addressing me like that, don't call me Madam. I'm Maria. So, you refuse to have supper with me, don't you?

Thoma: At other times and in other situations, I would have been honored to... but now ... you know Madam... sorry, it just slipped my tongue, I wanted to say, Maria. You know, Maria, I have been brought up in a country with absolutely different traditions. Any man must be longing for the relationship with you, but what sets limits for me is that initiative does not belong to me and that I am completely dependent on you. I can't enjoy the freedom to choose. I don't want to be misunderstood; I am not levying reproach against you, God forbid. On the contrary, you helped us and practically saved us from dying of starvation. That's why I am so shy. I don't even dare to compliment you. I'm afraid this might sound ridiculous to you.

Maria: I guess what you mean, Thoma, but neither me nor you possess any power to do anything about this. War destroys everything in its path and doesn't spare harmony and beauty of relations either. The only weapon against war is perhaps love. As when you love someone and is loved you forget a lot, the war and that you might sound ridiculous to someone... What do you think about this?

Thoma: I do agree with you. Love makes us forget a lot of things... but the inconvenience that tortures me can be relieved in a simpler way. Let's have a meal together, I mean all of us, you and me and my friends... if you don't mind, of course. I'm sure you'll like them a lot. You'll like it when we are all together; the area of happiness that builds is thus expanded...

Maria: How? What do you mean when you say that the area of happiness is expanded? I've never heard of anything like this.

Thoma: Maybe, but that's true. It can be expanded.

Maria: And what about love? What happens to the love area in this case? Does it shrink or what?

Thoma gives Maria an inquisitive look, and after a short pause says:

Thoma: Love requires only two people… But who do you think are the two people here?...

Thoma blushes.

Lola: Who are the two people here? Tell me honestly... do you like me?

Thoma: But I've just told you that there are several factors that set limits to my relations with you and particularly me feelings towards you, Madam.

Thoma blushes again, casts down his eyes, takes his glass and sips some wine. Maria stands up all of a sudden and says somehow bluntly:

Maria: It's too late. We have to get up early in the morning.

Thoma stands up immediately and looks at her.

Maria: Goodnight, Thoma.

Thoma: Goodnight, Maria.

Maria leaves the room and shortly after we see Thoma going upstairs slowly. He seems to be thinking about something.

***

It's night. Moonlight shines through the window of Thoma's room; the faint light falls on Thoma's face and we can see him lying with hands under his head and thinking about something. There is a knock on the door. Thoma bends over the bed, switches on the light and says in a calm voice.

Thoma: Alex, is that you? come in…

There is no answer from behind the door. Thoma gets up goes to the door and opens it. Maria is standing there her hair down, wearing a silk nightdress; she looks amazingly passionate. Thoma looks startled for a moment and then whispers:

Thoma: Maria, is that you?

Maria smiles.

Maria: Yes, it's me. You're going to be my first man since my husband died… Would you let me in?

Thoma draws her closer, holds her pressed against his chest and closes the door with his left hand. They switch off the light and we hear them breathing heavily and passionately in the darkness.

***

It's late in the evening. All the windows of the shed are open, and light is coming out of the windows and some voices singing fragments of songs can be heard from inside. Thoma is teaching a song to the young men inside the shed. The young men are listening to him attentively. Maria is sitting on the chair in the corner and Matthias is standing by his mother. Thoma asks the boys to sing some parts of the song and says:

Thoma: I think that's enough for today. We are all tired. Tomorrow after supper we have to rehearse what we studied today and then we'll try to sing it from the beginning to the end. Do you think we can manage?

Batsi: We can sing it now, but let it be tomorrow as you say, but without any rehearsal.

Maria looks Thoma.

Thoma: Ok, we'll sing it from the beginning to the end tomorrow.

Maria: Then I'll have a surprise for you tomorrow. So, you mean that's all for today?

Thoma: That's it. We're so tired we can't even think... Did Matthias learn anything? Matthias, would you like to sing together with us?

Matthias doesn't understand a word but he smiles. Maria says something to him in Lithuanian and the boy looks happy and nods his head.

***

A tractor with a platform body drives in the yard. The young men are jumping off the platform. One of them standing on the platform is handing scythes to the men who have already got off. Alex and Thoma get out of the cab.

Jango: (signs out) Supper, supper… რივორერა ვორერაა[59]. They made me – a man from Telavi – sing Gurian songs.

Gigi: (signs out) First we have to wash our hands, wash our hands რივო-რივორერა ვორერა…[60]

Thoma: What's going on? Have you already started rehearsing?

Jango: It's simply warming up, chief.

Maria walks out of the house and says in a loud voice for everyone to hear:

Maria: Today we are having supper together in the dining room. The table is already laid and waiting for you. Then we'll move to the shed and you'll sing there.

The young men are delighted, and we hear them expressing their joy by shouts. Maria smiles and continues.

---

[59] /Riworera Woreraa/ - a song refrain

[60] /Riwo-Roworera Worera…/- a song refrain

Maria: Nobody is allowed to enter the shed. Alex and I have something to do there. Please, come this way. You'll wash your hands here and go straight to the table. I'll join you soon. Thoma, show your friends where to go.

Thoma goes into the house and the young men follow him. Maria and Alex walk towards the shed. There is a rather big box on the table in the shed.

Alex: Shall I open it, Madam?

Maria: Of course, we have to assemble it until the boys come, and we have to check whether it records a voice.

Alex starts opening the box; and when the box is open he takes a tape-recorder out of it, puts it on the table and takes the box and the paper, in which the tape-recorder was wrapped, out of the shed. He returns soon and asks:

Alex: Would you like me to leave it here or shall I place it on the window-sill and leave only the microphone on the table? Where are they going to sing?

Maria: We'll see and put the microphone near the place they will be singing; it's not a problem. We'd better turn on this tape-recorder and see how it works.

Maria and Alex turn on the tape-recorder and check the microphone as well, prepare everything and Maria leaves the shed. Alex picks up some pieces of paper left there and takes them out.

The young men are having supper.

Beso: Can we have another glass of wine?

Dachi: Help yourself, Beso, but don't blame wine if you strike a false note while singing...

Beso: Don't worry about it, Dachi, Besarion Togonadze has never stricken a false note... See, Madam has come.

Beso stands up and the rest of the boys stand up along him. Beso continues:

Beso: This time you can't refuse to drink one more glass as I want to offer to drink it to Maria, our queen...

The young men drink a toast to Maria, they praise her, and Maria is standing there a bit confused. She likes the situation but doesn't know what to do.

Maria: Don't stand there, please, sit down and have your supper. Don't pay attention to me... Thank you, thank you so much. I love you all too.

After all the young men have drunk the toast, Thoma asks:

Thoma: As we're already standing here, shall we go now? Maria, are we allowed to enter the shed now?

Maria: Yes, you may go. Everything is ready there. Alex and I have a small surprise there for you.

Thoma: let's go then and see... if we like the surprise we'll drink another toast to you.

The young men walk out of the dining room and head towards the shed noisily, led by Maria. Maria enters the shed and the young men follow her. When all the young men are inside Maria turns to Thoma and says:

Maria: I've been to the town today and I bought this. This is a tape-recorder. I decided to record your first performance, the historic moment of you singing together for the first time. They told me the microphone is very sensitive. Let's first examine it and then... can you stand by the table in a semi-circle?

Thoma: we must stand in semi-circle anyway.

Maria presses some buttons; the bobbins start rotating and Maria says:

Maria: Would someone speak... or better sing something? Let's see how it records voices.

Thoma: Ushba can start; he has a very strong voice.

Jango: For God's sake, no. If he sings at the top of his lungs, the explosion of the tape-recorder will be inevitable.

Maria turns off the tape-recorder and rewinds the tape. Then she turns it on in the play mode and the young men hear the whole dialogue they've just had. They listen to it with interest and after Jango's words they express their excitement.

Maria: I think that's good; shall we try now, Thoma?

Thoma: Why not, come on guys, let's stand here around the microphone. (The young men take their places and Thoma adds) We're ready, Maria, turn it on and we'll start.

Maria turns on the tape-recorder in a record mode and gives them the signal to begin.

Thoma's face becomes serious; he seems to be thinking about something for a brief moment, then he coughs and starts singing his dad's song in a beautiful and warm voice. Gigi immediately joins him; he sings higher, and Ushba joins them with his bass, but Gigi's voice cracks as he tries to sing higher and his voice sounds something like "cock-a-doodle-doo". The young men start laughing. Thoma and Gigi stop singing and they start laughing too. Only Ushba goes on singing bass alone. Finally, he stops and asks:

Ushba: What are you laughing at?

Thoma turns to Maria.

Thoma: Maria, don't stop recording. We'll start from the beginning.

The young men stop laughing and Thoma starts the song from the beginning with even more enthusiasm. Gigi joins him, and his voice sounds perfect this time. Ushba joins them with his bass and they sing one verse of the song to the end and move to the other. We go out of the shed and see the beautiful landscape. A flock of some blackbirds flying towards the west high up in the sky can be seen against the background of a beautiful sunset over the horizon. The calls they make join the voices heard from the shed and eventually prevail.

***

It is snowing. Snowflakes are falling from the sky. A caption appears on the screen: "Six months later"

Suddenly a chestnut-colored horse's head gnawing a bridle appears in the white snow and its heavy breathing breaks the silence reigning around. We hear someone speaking Lithuanian language and then we see Alex talking to a Lithuanian police officer called Rokas, the one who sent Thoma and his friends to the POW camp after he found them at the place of train wreck. There is a sheepskin rug on the sledge and there is Rokas half lying down on it and listening to Alex.

Alex: In the beginning everything was perfect, Rocas. They behaved just as the people in their situation should behave. I kept them busy from early morning till late evening, but then Maria let them slide. Now they behave as if they were owners of the place. I feel totally left out. I cannot say that they do not work. They work hard but they nearly always find something to amuse themselves and they drew Maria into their vortex. They are together day and night… something should be done about it; you are the police chief and that's your business… we should stop these Georgians somehow... otherwise, they will probably expel me out of here soon.

Rocas: And what about Maria? Have you noticed that whore meeting with any of them in secret?

Alex: I don't know. I'm not allowed to enter the house after she goes to bed. Though I do suspect something is going on there. Maria ordered to accommodate six of them in the shed, and the one she's chosen as a team leader has a separate room upstairs, next to Maria's room. Who knows what's going on there at night.

Rocas: What? Why didn't you tell me about it earlier? It's bad news. And she's promised to marry me…

Alex: I haven't paid much attention to it until recently, as she gave him a separate room when they were brought from the camp. I thought it was normal. If she had accommodated him in the shed first and then had moved him to the house, I would have suspected something. I would have asked myself: "what's going on here, Alex? Is Madam pulling pranks?" But, as I've told you, he's been there since the day they came to the house. That's what confused me.

Rocas: I don't approve of that, either. You know well I plan to marry Maria and I'm not going to change my plans because of a Georgian prisoner. And where… in my own country?! I'll blow his balls off. Where are they now?

Alex: Where should they be? As a rule, they are all in the shed singing silly songs. Maria is there with her son. Can you imagine? They even have supper together. Then she goes to her house together with her chosen one and God knows what they do there till morning… No, no, Rocas, we have to put an end to all these somehow.

Rocas: That's good!

Alex: what's good? Do you mean that it's good that Maria has supper together with them?

Rocas: Have you gone nuts, Alex? I don't give a damn whether they have supper together or not! I mean that's good that they are together in the shed. I'll go now and will be back in half an hour... I'll bring some guys and bring some firearms as well; I'll make them pee in their pants. I'm not going to take any cartridges. We won't shoot. We must provoke them somehow. Georgians, in general, become reckless when it comes to their silly ambitions. We won't find it difficult to provoke them; your task is to phone in commandant's office in about ten minutes after our arrival and tell them that the Lithuanian national police forces are being attacked by Georgian prisoners. When they come, we will say that we could have killed them as they deserved it, but we didn't do it without their permission. We can kill two birds with one stone, and not only two, but I think tree at a time: we'll flatter Germans, batter the Georgians and get rid of them.

Alex: You are very smart Rocas. Well you said in half an hour, didn't you? I'll open the gates right now and you can drive directly into the yard.

The aizsargs pulls the reins and makes the horse turn and rides it forward breaking virgin snow. We see the horse and the sledge diluting in the whiteness. Alex opens the gates. It is still snowing heavily.

Blue Smoke coming from the roof of the shed goes drifting by into the sky. Inside the shed Maria, Matthias and all of the young men are gathered around the tape-recorder. The last chords of a song are heard, and the song ends in unison. The young men straighten themselves, with their faces showing satisfaction. All of them are trying to say something at once, and so we hear them exclaiming:

- It is a very good record, isn't it?
- To tell you the truth, I didn't expect it to be so good!
- What about Ushba? Did you hear his voice, wasn't it a bit loud?
- It was not because of the tape-recorder; it was because of Ushba.
- He should have stood a bit further… It would have been better…
- Further? What do you mean should he have sung bass from the yard? There was no room to move further.

Maria joins in.

Maria: I have to go now guys; it's time Matthias was in bed. I'll put him to bed and I'll join you again. (She looks at Thoma)

Thoma: Ok, Maria; I'll stay here and will be waiting for you. Then we shall go together.

Maria walks to the door together with Matthias; she plucks a hat off the peg, puts it on Matthias' head; she puts on a headscarf and they walk out of the room into the snow.

Ushba first looks through the open door, then through the window and says gloomily:

Ushba: Nobody can deny that singing is pleasure, but I wonder what's happening in Ushguli now. If only I took a glance at the view from the Ratiani tower-house...

Jango: What would you do then?

Ushba: I wouldn't mention Ushguli for the next six months.

Beso: My kinsmen must be boiling ham... or beans together with ham. They must be gathered by the fireplace and outside must be snowing just like here. When neighbors visit us, we can hear their footsteps in crunchy snow. They love being together when it's snowing; you should listen to them singing there... Khvanchkara[61] makes you sing.

Batsi: Tower-houses, Khvanchkara... sounds good, but I wish anyone could tell us what the situation on the front is.

Thoma: I've asked Maria about it as if randomly not long ago...

Batsi: And what did she say?

Thoma: She said she had no good news ... That's all she said. One has to guess what she meant... no good news for her or for us...

Jango: Meanwhile, the fire is dying out... If we don't go to the "front" to bring some firewood, we'll be freezing soon.

Dachi: I'll go out, Jango, or it will be better if Gigi and I go out and bring some more firewood.

---

[61] semi-sweet red wine

Dachi and Gigi go out of the shed. They collect firewood and are about to curry armfuls of firewood to the shed when they hear a truck driving into the yard. The truck stops and armed policemen wearing black uniforms jump off the platform. The aizsargs gets out of the cab. The platform is covered with canvas and Dachi and Gigi are not able to see from outside how many policemen are there, but they watch them jumping off the platform thick and fast, they jump and jump… one by one, in pairs… the yard soon gets crowded. Dachi and Gigi drop firewood on the ground and run towards the shed. They rush into the room and Gigi says:

Gigi: Some unbidden guests have come to visit us, guys; the yard is full of policemen.

Jango: How do you know that they've come to visit us? Maybe they want to see Maria…

Dachi: The whole police detachment wouldn't have come to Maria, Jango. They must have something else in mind. I recognized one of them, the man who brought the boys to the camp.

Thoma: We'll see.

Gigi: Here they are…

The door of the shed opens and the aizsargs with a mischievous smile on his face enters the room accompanied by several policemen. The rest of the policemen are standing outside the shed. Beso quietly looks through the break in the curtains trying to remain unnoticed; then he casts his eyes down and says in Georgian:

Beso: There are a lot of them; they are standing at the door…

The aizsargs move a chair takes a seat and starts talking with an insolent expression and his mouth curved into an ironic smile. He starts speaking in a strongly accented Russian.

Rokas: Good evening! Do you remember me, or do I have to introduce myself to you again?

Thoma: I think you're the one we asked for help when our train had been bombed.

Rokas: So you remember me! That's good! And I helped you, didn't I? If you hadn't encountered me there, you wouldn't be here living like lords. Others like you die of cold in the camp in large numbers and you sleep here by a warm fireplace. Though, I see only six beds in this room… the seventh? Where is the seventh? Well don't tell me anything. I'll try to guess… Do you sleep in turns? No! No! Not in turns. One of you must be a pederast moving from bed to bed at night. I think I guessed, didn't I? As you say nothing, then it must be true. Silence gives consent. You know, if you are fed up of him, tell me which of you is the one and I'll take him with me in the barracks and serve him better. Just look at my guys, don't you like them?

Thoma: You'd better tell us what the real reason for your coming here is… if you've been told anything bad about us you may go and ask our landlady.

Rokas: Calm down and stop talking so much. I've already seen your landlady and she told me that you are very funny people and sing well. We've come here to listen to you singing. That's the real reason for our visit. We need to be entertained from time to time, don't we? I'll ask my men standing outside to come in now. You go and stand against the wall there at the end of the room, between the beds and wait till I give you the signal to start singing; I'll be your conductor today. So, we will see … we might even clap our hands. Nothing is impossible. What would you say, guys, shall we clap our hands?

One of the policemen: First they should sing and then we'll see… if they deserve it, we can clap our hands.

Rokas: Maybe you're right. Well, what are you waiting for? Go… quickly…

The young men stand and don't move. They stand still like the Sphinx. Some of them have their eyes cast down. Some stare into the aizsargs' eyes. Thoma breaks the silence and says calmly:

Thoma: No way, sir!

Rokas: No way, you say? Does that mean that you can't sing or that you can't stand against the wall?!

Thoma: That means that we can't sing. And does it make sense to stand against the wall if we can't sing? I'll try to speak on behalf of all of us and explain to you what I mean. Singing is a means of expressing our spiritual condition. It comes with the mood. Life is not a stage; you can't simply stand there and sing. Life makes you sing either when you are very happy or when you are miserable. I apologize, but our state of mind is far from either of these conditions, not to mention the third reason…

Rokas: Wait a minute. What's that third reason that you've just mentioned? So, it goes that you've got some other claims besides that silly philosophy? Please, until I make a decision, would you inform us about your third reason? I see my guys are extremely interested in it…

Thoma: No problem, I'll tell you, sir, since you are so interested… When you come so unexpectedly, point your guns and demand from us to stand against the wall and sing… suppose we sang, would you expect us to sing properly? Would our song sound like a real song?

Rokas: I see! Everything is clear now! From the beginning to the end! See guys? They think they are real musicians. They have a kind of creative approach to the issue and that is why they trade with us. But they appear to have forgotten one thing, one negligible detail. They've forgotten that they are prisoners. And on top of that my prisoners as I have imprisoned them. And the prisoners are not allowed to make decisions. What they are supposed and required to do is to comply with commands. If I tell you: sing, you should sing! If I tell you: dance, you should dance! If I tell you: take off your pants, you should take them off! If I tell you: die, you should die! But, as you can see, they've forgotten all these. Such forgetfulness is often characteristic to a six-month trip from hell to heaven. But, no problem! They'll soon be returned to hell to improve their memory. Until then ... Until then just do as I tell you: stand against the wall and start singing… or else…

Thoma: Or else what, sir? Tell us what you intend to do with us…

Rokas: Or else I'll do away with all seven of you!

Thoma gives him an inquisitive look. He starts breathing heavily but he says trying hard to suppress his anger:

Thoma: We understand everything, sir, absolutely everything but allow me to add something… People don't always make decisions by considering the situation; their decisions are quite frequently determined by their character… And I have to admit, not without a certain degree of chagrin, that we… (He looks at his friends) can't boast of having good characters…

Rokas: To whose chagrin?

Thoma: Much to our chagrin, of course, but to your chagrin as well.

Thoma's face becomes even gloomier and he even flushes. The aizsargs call out a very short phrase in Lithuanian and immediately the door is smashed in and the room gets overcrowded with policemen on a spur of a moment. They enter the room one by one in an endless line. Some of them stand behind the young men with their guns pointing on them. Thoma takes his last chance and says:

Thoma: Everything is clear, we see there are a lot of you, all armed, but what then? Do you plan to launch a war against the seven of us? And you want me to believe you that you're doing it just because of a song? If it's the case, you may come tomorrow; we can have supper together and sing together as well. Can't you see the situation is evolving into a stalemate? We should leave a loophole to find a way out of it.

The aizsargs: (to himself in Lithuanian) My God! They keep on bargaining with me. These Georgians are the strangest people of all! (Then he leaps out of his chair and shouts in Russian) I say that's enough! I don't want to hear any more excuses! You have to sing immediately, or I'll order to beat you to death.

Ushba, who's been only listening to their dialogue, turns to Thoma and asks him in Georgian:

Ushba: May I say a word or two to them, Thoma?

Thoma: As you like Ushba, they don't understand a word of what I'm saying.

Ushba stands up, looks down at everyone there, turns to the aizsargs and says in Russian with a very funny Georgian-Svanetian accent:

Ushba: Да идите вы все в жопу![62]

These words were so momentous and so unexpected that they cause a kind of double reaction among those in the room. The policemen don't quite understand what they have been told and it takes them a while to realize them and get angry. The Georgians are amused not so much at what Ushba has said but at his accent and all of them, except Ushba, start laughing leaving the policemen even more shocked.

---

[62] / Go where the sun don't shine!/

Meanwhile, one of the policemen comes up behind Ushba and is about to hit him in the back of his head with the butt of his gun when Thoma jumps out of his seat in the blink of an eye and hits the policeman right in the solar plexus with his elbow even before straightening himself up. All of a sudden it becomes a free-for-all and the policemen and the Georgians attack each-other and a brutal fight starts. They are beating each other violently, but the Georgians are obviously in a fit of rage, fighting vigorously, having lost control over their behavior, ready to fight to the death. Some of them seize guns from the hands of the policemen and hit the policemen on the head with them. Several policemen escape the battlefield by running out of the shed into the yard. The Georgians gradually seem to be gaining the advantage over their enemies in this fierce fight, despite the fact that there are three or four times more Lithuanians. The Georgians are beating the aizsargs – the major player - severely and mercilessly.

We see Maria rushing out of the house and running towards the shed. She rushes into the room, pushes her way through the crowd of the policemen, tries to approach Thoma and shouts:

Maria: Oh, my God… What's going on here, Thoma?!

Thoma catches the glimpse of her and shouts at her without stopping fighting:

Thoma: Maria, go out of the shed!

Maria obeys him, goes out of the shed and sees a truck driving into the yard followed by a car. The yard is lightened up by the car and truck lights. A German officer comes out of the car and gunmen jump off the truck platform. The officer walks towards the shed and produces a parabellum from the gun holster on his belt; then he raises his hand holding the parabellum to shoot up into the air, but then he changes his mind and calls out:

The German officer: Gunther!

One of the gunners comes running to the officer. The officer puts the parabellum back into its holster with a swift movement of his hand, snatches the automatic rifle out of the gunner's hands, reloads it and shoots it up into the air several times.

We see the fighters stop fighting on hearing a shot. The aizsargs, his face covered in blood, rushes out of the shed, runs into the officer standing behind the door and tries to explain something to him panting for breath. He starts:

Rokas: Officer, I'll explain everything to you…

The officer interrupts him with a move of his hand, returns the automatic rifle to Gunther and says:

The officer: I'll find out myself.

The officer enters the shed accompanied by several of the gunners including Gunther. Other gunners take their positions by the door and the windows. Maria enters the shed, pushes her way through the crowd of German gunmen and beaten policemen and hugs Thoma. She is crying and telling Thoma:

Maria: Don't try to explain to me what has happened, I understand what's going on and why. What matters is that you're alive… and the guys as well. I had a kind of premonition but not of this scale! He's been asking me to marry him since my husband died. I mean Rokas… I'd rather be with you in the camp for prisoners than marry him.

Thoma doesn't say a word for a while, at last he says:

Thoma: Calm down!

Thoma gently strokes her hair. The officer walks around the room stops by each of the Georgian men and studies their faces. All of the young men are flushed and panting for breath. Maria turns to the officer:

Maria: Officer, I am Maria Kushner, the owner of this farm… I'll try to explain everything to you…

The officer: I know, Madam ... I think your presence here is not necessary. Calm down, we'll investigate everything. Gunther walk her to the house.

Maria: Officer, the camp commandant is my…

The officer: I've already told you that I know everything. I know that Rainer is a close friend of your late husband. By the way, he was transferred to another region a couple of days ago. As I've been informed he returned to Germany… Madam, you must leave this room now… Gunther will walk you to the house. I don't quite understand why you are so nervous; I hope that's not because of these prisoners. Moreover, nothing bad is going to happen to them; they will just be brought back to the camp from where we sent them to you. As for the spring works, we'll send you new ones; we have so many of them there in the camp that we don't even know what to do with them. If you wish, you may say good-bye to them and leave us.

Maria goes to each of the young men one by one and kisses them good-bye. At last, she goes to Thoma and says in a quiet gentle voice:

Maria: Don't worry. You'll see everything will be cleared up soon and everything will be fine again.

Thoma smiles bitterly and says:

Thoma: Everything was too good to be true and that's why all these happened, Maria. Go, leave us here; don't embarrass them.

Maria is about to walk away, but Thoma stops her with his hand, turns to the officer and says in German:

Thoma: Officer, in the front pocket of my jacket I have a toy that belongs to Madam's son. I took it in the morning and forgot to give it back to him. As you intend to take us from here, let me take the toy out of my pocket and give it to Madam.

The officer listens to Thoma attentively. He is a little surprised at his German. Then he takes the parabellum out of the gun holster, goes close to Thoma, shoves the barrel of the parabellum against Thoma's chest near his heart and asks him:

The officer: Do you have that toy here?

Thoma shakes his head in negation. The officer moves the barrel of the parabellum along his chest and shoves it against the right side of his chest and asks him:

The officer: Here?

Thoma nods his head this time. The officer stays in this position for a while staring into Thoma's eyes. Then he lets his right hand down, in which he is holding his parabellum. With a smile on his face, he takes the parabellum in his left hand, puts his right hand into Thoma's pocket and pulls the familiar cardboard toy with a bluebird and a cage out of it. He looks at it on both sides shrugs his shoulders and gives it to Maria with a cold and indifferent look on his face; then he turns to Gunther:

The officer: Gunther, walk Madam to her house and come straight to the car.

The officer turns around and walks towards the door and before walking out of the shed he turns and says:

The Officer: Throw all of them into the car.

The German gunners start moving immediately with their guns pointed at the prisoners, pushing them towards the door and out in the yard. The young men manage to take their coats off the pegs at the door while walking through it.

Batsi: I think we should have sung a song! It was not going to be the end of the world!

Thoma: Then they would have blamed us in something else. They've come here to do exactly that.

***

A train is meandering through a valley covered with snow like a black snake. Here and there the heads of cattle can be seen through the openings of the carriages made of rough wood boards, steam coming out of their nostrils. Only the last carriage looks relatively normal, but it is for carrying cargo and the door is locked from outside. The seven young men are inside the carriage; six of them are sitting right on the floor shivering from the cold. Only Jango is standing with his back pressed against the carriage wall.

Dachi: The bastards might have told us where they are taking us... Jango, get your back off the wall and look through that hole, maybe this time you can see something different...

Jango: I looked through it a couple of minutes ago, Dachi! We might be riding through the woods again... Besides, as soon as I take my back off this hole, the carriage freezes... cold air starts coming whistling through it. I think I have a hole in my back... As for you, you can't sit there half-lying down; you'd better stand up and play something; your blood will start flowing through your bodies and you won't feel so cold.

Gigi: Jango is right. We just must do something about it or we'll be frozen to death... Let's wrestle with Ushba. How many of us would you like to wrestle with altogether, Ushba?

Ushba: All of you.

The young men laugh when they hear Ushba's response.

Beso: He is like a lion; he can do this!

Dachi: Not all of us; Jango will stay where he is covering the hole, you have to wrestle with the rest of us... can you resist the five of us?

Ushba: I've told you, I am ready to wrestle with all of you together... Jango can join you as well...

Jango: Wrestle with them, Ushba, if they fail to defeat you, then we can wrestle, only you and me... It seems to me that you think you can rely on your muscles alone to win... But this is where you make a big mistake... wrestling is not a battle of strength, Ushba, it's a battle of brains and skills! You have probably heard the expression "work smarter, not harder"; or maybe you don't have such expressions and proverbs in Svanetia...

Ushba: we'll see. First, I'll beat them up and then I'll take care of you. When I tuck you in that hole, you may tell me other proverbs from the outside.

Ushba stands up. The rest of the young men except Batsi stand up. Thoma asks Batsi:

Thoma: Batsi, don't you want to wrestle?

Batsi: I've had enough of wrestling with those Lithuanians. You go and wrestle with him first. There are already four of you. If you couldn't defeat one man, then we should think that those Lithuanians were all beaten by Ushba and the rest of us were put here for having done nothing wrong. Do it, I'll join you later; I'll try to help Jango when he wrestles with Ushba.

The young men start wrestling, but they can't stand firm as the carriage is jolting and they are thrown from side to side, fall and beat against the carriage walls. However, they are exhilarated. They are no longer the same guys that were shivering from the cold and looking sad; their mood has changed in the spar of a moment, as is characteristic to Georgians. Eventually, the four men manage to defeat Ushba, and he doesn't show resistance, sprawls face up all over the floor and shouts:

Ushba: You the men! Leave me alone!

Jango: Is that all you can? We heard you boasting you would beat us up, inviting all of us together to wrestle with you and so on... So, you've got no choice but to surrender.

Ushba: Well I admit they've won but I'll defeat you I swear!

The train stops unexpectedly with a great noise and those who are standing in the carriage are thrown forward by inertia. Jango is also thrown off the wall and a cold wind blows in through the large hole he's been covering with his back.

Jango: The damn train wrestles with us instead of Ushba. It laid us all low. I wonder what's going on.

He goes closer to the hole and looks through it with one of his eyes. The train is still running but slower and the view is seen through the opening changes at a slow pace.

Jango: We've come somewhere. There are some gloomy buildings with narrow windows covered with metal grilles.

Dachi: If only we were to leave this train, I don't mind grilles.

Jango takes his face off the opening.

Jango: I have my eye frozen. What winter! Alex said there hadn't been such a cold winter for 60 years. It seems nature is against us as well. Alas, I'm missing Maria's shed...

Batsi: You're missing Maria's shed but can you imagine what Thoma might be feeling? He's lost Maria with her shed. I wonder whether he is in the mood to teach us singing now.

Thoma: Batsi! I've already told you to stop joking about this. We can't quarrel with each other. (He frowns, and his face becomes gloomy, he continues) If you mean we should have sung there, I've already explained to you, there was nobody who could have prevented you from singing your solo there.

Batsi: Ok, ok. I apologize. It just slipped off of my tongue. I promise I won't speak of her like that and I won't mention that song either. That's it.

The train enters the territory of a huge camp, slows down and eventually stops. The German military-run to the train and immediately start opening the primitive locks with short metal clubs, along the whole length of the train, and then they place some wooden planks in an inclined position at the openings of the carriages, lead the cattle of the carriages and towards the middle of the yard. When they have emptied all the carriages they gather around the last carriage of a train, in which the young men standstill. The young men hear them trying to open the door and when the door is open we see the scene from above: there are some German gunners; one of them goes to the open door and shouts in German:

The gunner: Get off the train, immediately! Quickly! Quickly!

Thoma: Let's get off, guys. May God have mercy on us!

The young men jump off the train one by one. They realize immediately that they are in the territory of a concentration camp. Prisoners, who seem to be so weak that they could hardly stand on their feet, wander around; some of them are standing and looking at the newcomers with empty eyes. The Georgians are led to a long gloomy one-storied building by gunners. They are pushed inside this building and the door closes behind them. Inside the semi-dark barracks, the young men can barely discern two-tier scaffolds made of wood with rough wooden boards placed on both levels; the place is overcrowded with prisoners. The young men are standing confused. A prisoner from the second tier watches them and after a while says:

The prisoner: Do you speak Russian?

The young men nod their heads and Jango says:

Jango: Of course, we do; we are from Georgia.

The prisoner: I guess, you are newcomers… there are all sorts of people there, you can't trust anyone. Walk to the end there might be some free beds for you. You'll manage to settle there.

Thoma: Thank you for your piece of advice. Would you tell us where we are now?

The prisoner: So, you don't even know where you have been brought?

Thoma: How could we learn? They pushed us in a carriage without telling us anything.

The prisoner: Congratulations, men… (He says in a low voice with a teasing tone and continues) Welcome to a slow death factory…

He starts giggling but suddenly his giggle turns into a coughing fit and he's about to suffocate. His face becomes red and he's unable to utter a sound, but he makes some gestures with his hand telling the young men to go to the end of the building.

The boys walk and they hear the prisoner saying:

The prisoner: Again… it's started again…

***

A vast plain land... A feeble bonfire is burning at the edge of a sparse young forest; the bonfire is surrounded by some German gunners warming their hands by it. Other gunners are standing along a long trench watching prisoners working there. It seems that the prisoners have just started digging the trench because they are still digging the surface of the ground. The prisoners seem to be freezing; they look weak and miserable; they seem to find it difficult to work on frozen ground but they're doing their best and are hovering along with the trench-like ghosts from the other world. The man who talked to the young men in the barracks is working near the gunners by the bonfire. He goes into another coughing fit. One of the German gunners seems to be fed up of his endless coughing, he gives the prisoner a hostile look a couple of times, then he gets up and points his gun at him, but fortunately the Russian prisoner stops coughing at that moment and the German gunner returns to his place by the fire.

The Georgian prisoners are working on a stretch at the end of the trench. They look healthier and less exhausted than the rest of the prisoners and, naturally, they work better and harder.

Thoma is trying to break up a clod of frozen earth with an iron bar and says:

Thoma: Ushba, and all of you, guys, we should perform our work perfunctorily: pretend to be working hard and simultaneously spare our energy. Have you heard what that man had said to us? The one who nearly died of coughing? He said we were in a slow death factory… We have to survive till spring; to live with the hope that one day we'll be able to follow the single way we've got…

Beso: Which way are you speaking about, Thoma?

Thoma: Which way you ask? We must run out of here… to escape our death. Can't you see? They make us dig our own graves.

***

A caption appears on the screen: "Six months later"

The winter is over. It's June. It is warm, and nature rejoices in the beauties. The prisoners, who survived the winter, look even more miserable; they are returning from field works to the camp, they can hardly walk, and the muddy road makes it for them even more difficult to walk. They all walk with their faces downcast looking exhausted and indifferent. The Georgian prisoners are among them; they seem to hold traces of winter; they are almost skinny; they can be distinguished from others only by their eyes; the light in their eyes has not extinguished yet. Several German gunners with German Shepherds are standing at the gates of the camp. The convoys of prisoners pass by them and walk through the yard of the concentration camp and towards their barracks. Two soldiers push the gates with full force and securely lock them.

A low-ranking young officer is standing by the barracks where the young men are accommodated. He is holding a rod in his right hand and is beating with it on the palm of his left hand monotonously. He is watching the prisoners entering the barracks and is looking at their faces. When Thoma passes by, the officer stops him with the rod and says:

The officer: Walk with me!

Thoma stops and the young men stop along the door and look at the officer with concern on their faces. Thoma asks in German:

Thoma: Only me?

The officer: Why? Do you need an escort?! I've told you clearly, you must walk with me.

Thoma: As you wish.

The officer: This way, to the headquarters, forward, march!

Thoma walks in the direction of the headquarters and the officer walks behind him, beating his rod against his boot this time.

When they walk up to the building door, the officer stops Thoma and looks him up and down. He stops his look at Thoma's boots and says:

The officer: Can you see a water-cask over there? Go and wash the mud off your boots! Quickly! I can't let you in like this.

Thoma obeys him without uttering any word and walks to the water-cask. He first cleans his boots with a chip of wood he finds there; then he washes his hands and splashes some water on his face as well, runs his hands through his hair brushing it back with his wet hands and goes back to the officer.

The officer looks up and down him once more and spells in Russian:

The officer: Хо-ро-шо![63]

They enter the building, walk along a clean corridor and stop at one of the doors.

The officer: Wait here!

The officer enters the room. Thoma is standing by the door and looking at another officer who is sitting at the table near the door. There are some telephones on the table. The officer who accompanied him walks out of the room and says to Thoma:

The officer: Go in!

Thoma opens the door gently and enters the room. The room is large with two wide windows. A high-ranking German officer is standing by one of the windows; Thoma can see only his back as he is looking through the window. Thoma is standing there and waiting for the officer to turn around. The officer turns around at last and Thoma recognizes him at once. The officer is Rainer - a friend of Maria's husband. Thoma feels relieved. Rainer looks up and down Thoma and says:

Rainer: You look awful. A common diagnosis – starvation and forced labor– the result is obvious... Sit down. I wouldn't have recognized you if I had seen you somewhere else. As for me, I haven't changed, have I?

Thoma: No, sir, you haven't.

---

[63] Not bad!

Rainer: Do you remember I promised to play chess with you someday? I would like to fulfill my promise today and play a game with you.

Thoma looks around and notices a chessboard laid out on a small table.

Rainer: I was moved here a few days ago. I'm in charge of this camp – a chief or a commandant. You may call me whichever you want. It's been only two days since I was moved here. I caught a glimpse of you this morning when you were taken to work. You are all alive, that's good! By the way Maria has asked me several times to find you and help you. No, she didn't ASK me she implored with tears in her eyes... She loves you so much... Thomas! As I remember your name is Thomas, isn't it?

Thoma: In German, it sounds like this I think, Thomas. Actually, my name's Thoma in Georgian, without [es]...

Rainer: Thoma and Thomas! Have you heard Thoma that your name is no longer popular in Germany? No one will dare to call their babies Thomas in Germany until the Third Reich exists, because of Thomas Mann. He is a German writer; He criticized Hitler and was forced to move to America. Führer gets furious on hearing that name so beware of running into him somewhere.

Reiner smiles, then suddenly his face becomes serious and he says:

Reiner: You must be hungry. You can't play chess if you're hungry. You might think about bread instead of moves.

Reiner walks to the old-fashioned cupboard, takes a bottle of cognac, a glass and an opened box of chocolates. He puts everything on the table next to the chessboard, pours some cognac in the glass and calls Thoma:

Reiner: Come here, have a glass of cognac. It's French. And here is some chocolate. But don't eat too much of it, or you'll risk getting sick. A glass of cognac will help refresh your mind and you might even win the game.

Thoma takes the glass. His hand is shaking slightly but he manages to take the glass to his lips and drinks cognac slowly tasting each mouthful of it. Reiner offers him the chocolate, Thoma takes a bit and his face expresses pleasure as he tastes it. The officer is looking at the young man with a kind smile on his face and then says:

Reiner: I'll pour you some more…

Thoma: No sir, thank you. We can start the game if you wish.

Reiner: Let's start!

Reiner and Thoma take their seats at the table where the chessboard is laid. They choose the color of chess pieces using traditional method. Thoma has to play with the white pieces. The officer turns the chessboard on the table and says:

Reiner: The conditions remain the same… I'll have to give you some food and you'll have to give me your goodwill. Wasn't it so? (He laughs loudly and adds) The first move is yours; you may start…

***

The young men are gathered at the far end of a semi-dark and smelly barrack. Two of them are sitting up facing each other in a wooden plank serving as a bed. The rest are sitting around. The young men look worried because Thoma hasn't appeared.

Beso: Where might he have gone so long? I don't quite like all these. I wonder why they might have taken him at these late hours.

Gigi: He might be made to translate something for them-as an interpreter – I mean. I just can't think of anything else.

Jango: Let's assume that it's the case, what might be they translating there so long. Is anyone delivering a lecture there?

Ushba: Calm down! My heart is telling me that he'll be back soon. We've done nothing wrong. If they had taken Thoma to accuse him of beating those policemen, then they would have taken us as well.

Batsi: What if Maria had found him and visited him?

Jango: Come on! What nonsense…

Batsi: Why do you exclude this possibility? She might have found him and called on him here.

Jango: Yeah, she's been traveling from camp to camp throughout the whole of Europe and tonight she found us and now they've been given a room with a warm bed… It sounds just too good to be true. Maybe Gigi's right and they've taken him because they needed an interpreter?

***

Thoma and Reiner are still playing chess in Reiner's room. The officer seems to be pondering over the situation on the chessboard. He raises his head, smiles at Thoma broadly and says:

Reiner: Nothing is going to save my king… he's doomed… Congratulations!

Reiner extends his hand for him to shake it. Thoma stands up and shakes his hand with him. The officer stands up and walks to the cupboard; He takes a whole wheat bread loaf from the cupboard.

Reiner: You see, how prudent I am... Take it; I'll call you soon to play revenge. You may go now.

Thoma takes the loaf and thanks to the officer; he is about to walk to the door but stops and turns to Reiner.

Thoma: Sir, would you lend me a knife?

Reiner: A knife? (Reiner seems to be surprised)

Thoma: Yes, knife… Otherwise, I can't divide this loaf into seven parts.

Thoma extends his hand in which he holds the loaf. The officer says nothing for a while; he only looks at Thoma. Then his facial expression changes, he goes to his desk and calls for a duty officer. The officer, who Thoma saw sitting by the desk full of phones comes in the room immediately. The commandant orders him to come closer and whispers something in his ear. The duty officer nods his head and leaves the room.

Reiner: He'll come back soon and bring a knife.

The duty officer comes back soon but he brings six more loaves of bread of the same size instead of a knife. He gives the loaves to Thoma. Thoma looks surprised and moved. He looks at the commandant and says in a brittle voice:

Thoma: Sir, it was you who won today's game.

We see Thoma going out of the building and heading to the barracks, holding the seven loaves of bread against his chest. When he comes up to the door, he stops, manages to take off his shirt, covers the loaves with it and enters through the door.

***

It's evening. The prisoners are wandering around the concentration camp yard. Water is dripping from the roof of a one-storied building of a barrack. After watching some drops of water falling from the roof we follow them and see Thoma standing there with his eyes closed and his forehead exposed to the drops. The drops fall right in the center of his forehead and run down between the eyebrows and down to his cheeks. He is smiling. Nearby Jango and Beso are sitting on the ground with their backs leaned against the wall.

Jango: What's up Thoma, you seem to be overwhelmed by playing chess.

Thoma: Worse than that, Jango! The commandant told me something last night that has been haunting and torturing me the whole day. I can't decide whether to tell you that or not. Right now, I am keeping my wits cool to make the right decision.

Jango: Oh, come on, man! I can guess from the expression on your face that you've got some good news... Tell us and if it proves to be good I promise you won't have to stand there waiting for that drops to keep your wits cool ... I'll pour a bucket of water on your head...

Thoma: I would if I could, Jango, but I am afraid of something, I don't want you to feel disappointed if it doesn't come true. That's why I don't want to tell you that. Let me be the only one with a broken heart among you.

Beso: Why do you want to be the only one? We are together, so if it comes to disappointment, let's share it as well. Go, man, tell us...

Thoma: Ok, I'll tell you, but... tell the guys to come. I'm not going to tell it to each of you separately.

Beso: They are inside, I'll bring them right now. (Beso stands up and goes)

Jango: Thoma, tell me in a few words what's going on until they come; don't you see I can't wait... Just give me a hint.

Thoma: Nothing special, Jango, nothing of the kind to be on cloud nine, but if we manage to change a little that damned situation we'll have the reason to rejoice, won't we?

Jango: You're right.

We see sparks in Jango's eyes fading away. We hear Beso calling from afar and see him coming.

Beso: They're coming.

Ushba, Batsi, Gigi, and Dachi appear soon. When the young men are all together, Batsi says:

Batsi: Beso told us you had some good news... what's it, do they plan to release us?

Thoma: Yeah, as you say... and they're organizing a farewell party for us and asked us to choose the kind of wine we would like to be served there. That's why I've asked you to come.

A bitter smile covers their faces.

Jango: If only I might live to see the day when it comes true and I'll bring so much wine from Telavi that the whole camp will be swept away.

Thoma: Well, it seems that we've somehow earned the commandant's good-will. If I manage to return to my homeland, I'll erect a statue in his honor in my own yard. He plans to send all seven of us to the Alps tomorrow morning. Well, at least he said so. I did not want to tell you until tomorrow morning. I thought, if they called on us and take us there in the morning, you'd learn about this yourself, but Jango convinced me otherwise. We'll be doing absolutely nothing there for a week; it's so to say, for our rehabilitation. We'll have to regain our strength and then start mowing, in the mountains. They say the grass there is very rich and a German official feeds his cattle on that grass only. The commandant says when they milk those cows they get not milk but pure chocolate. Of course, we are going to be watched by guards there and will be confined at night but, we'll be eating as normal men do and breathe fresh air.

Gigi: What are you saying, Thoma, I don't mind being confined in case we leave this damn place.

Thoma: Yes, the commandant says we'll regain our health. We'll have to stay there till the fall and then he'll decide what to do with us. But, I think, if what we have agreed on is still valid, we'll run away from that place till fall comes. Do you remember what we have agreed on? We agreed on to survive till spring... and that's it, we've done it. Summer is near, and the situation has turned the tide in our favor. The Alps runs through Switzerland. We must head to Switzerland. If we manage to cross the border, we'll find a haven for us there. I already have some plans for my mind, but it is too early. If we indeed find ourselves in the Alps, I will tell you about them there.

Ushba: You don't say so! As Gigi says, I wish we were in the mountains, there I won't find it difficult to decide what to do. I'll pull all of you over my shoulder and carry you all the way through the Alps to Switzerland. It's much easier to make your escape in the mountains. No chaser can find you within the perimeter of ten meters. I've trekked such dangerous paths in the Caucasus that you'll never find in the Alps.

Thoma: So, we must wait till tomorrow morning and we'll see what we'll have to do next.

Beso: What did he say, what time they plan to call on us?

Thoma: He didn't say. They would not scruple to come and wake us up at any time.

Ushba: My heart is telling me that everything...

Batsi: Leave your heart alone, Ushba. Whenever you say the phrase something disastrous happens to us.

Ushba: On the contrary! Don't you remember the other day when Thoma was late? I said then that my heart was telling me that he would come soon, and he did! And now my heart is telling me that...

Jango: Blessed be your heart! You've got not a heart but an oracle in your massive chest.

The young men laugh. Ushba smiles and says:

Ushba: You've got no understanding of me. There are so many things my heart is telling me, but I'd rather don't disclose them to you. You start laughing when I do.

The words make the young men laugh even harder.

***

A spellbinding Alpine panorama... Divine music is heard. The peace and quiet there give the impression of universal idyll reigning the whole wide world. No traits of more than half of the world are engaged in a bloody war can be found there. We see a vast plateau. We see high grass waving on the wind. There is a steep and bare slope on the edge of the plateau; far away down a coniferous forest starts at the bottom of the slope. A high-pitched loud call accompanied by echoes coming from the mountains is heard against the background of the music.

"Hey! Hey! Hey!" - The echoes can be heard from the mountains. We are led to the source of this loud calling and see Ushba – a highlander standing on the edge of the plateau and calling in the wilderness. Then we see the rest of the young men holding scythes and Germans carrying their guns. The Germans smile at hearing Ushba's calling.

Jango: Hey, Ushba, stop yelling, take your scythe and let's start.

We get a closer look at the young men and see that they look better; all of them are naked waist up and even though they are rather thin their bodies are still wiry radiating youth and vigor. They stand in a row holding scythes; they look at one another and as if having received an invisible order, start mowing down grass together. They proceed at an equal pace; only Ushba takes a lead after a while, because of his long and strong arms, but Dachi says to him:

Dachi: Don't do it Ushba; spare your energy; don't go ahead of us!

Ushba follows his advice. We hear the same divine music and look at this picturesque scene for a while.

Dachi: Thoma, what were these bastards trying to tell us before we started mowing?

Thoma: Nothing special… A traditional threat that they would shoot us without warning if they saw us doing what we aren't supposed to be doing. So, we must be careful… the bastards might smell a rat. We must win their trust gradually and methodically.

Beso: We can check right now how close we are watched over…

Thoma: How do you plan to check it?

Beso: I'll hide in the grass. Let's see how quickly they'll be to discover that there are six of us instead of seven.

Jango: A good idea… But what if they start shooting?... bullet is blind, have you heard about this?

Beso: Who will they shoot, Jango? They'll see you working and as logic says they must shoot the one who tries to escape; but to shoot they have first to see and identify their target. But I'll be lying in the grass and they can't see me… If they start shouting, I'll stand up immediately; I feel that my own life is still of some value…

Dachi: A good judgment, Beso. Look I'm going to count to three and you hide in the grass when you hear "three" … Let's see how they'll react.

Batsi: Wait a minute; we'd better first ask Ushba what his heart is telling him…

The young men laugh.

Ushba: Leave me alone… Mind your own hearts… Besides, why is he so obsessed with the idea of hiding himself? He can hardly be seen in this high grass, anyway. So, it doesn't make a difference whether he is standing or lying there. If you want them to see the difference you should ask me to hide.

Jango: That's absolutely excluded, Ushba. You serve as their landmark beacon. If you hide, they'll immediately notice that the horizon has become too bleak and they'll start shooting; that's for sure.

Ushba: Then, what is he waiting for? One doesn't need to count to three to lie down in the grass. Go, Beso, hide.

Beso: You're right, Ushba! Please be careful not to mow me with your scythes.

Beso disappears in the grass. One of the Germans starts shouting virtually at the same time.

The German guard: Stay where you are… all of you, or I'll shoot you. Put down your scythes and raise your hands up.

All the German guards immediately start shouting and running towards boys. Beso stands up, but the German guards surround the young men and one of them asks Thoma with a strict voice:

The German guard: Was it an attempt to escape? We've already warned you…

Thoma: No, sir! Where should he have escaped? Can't you see the open space around? He slipped on the wet grass. It's early morning and the grass is all clothed with dew.

The German guard slips flat his boot sole against the ground a couple of times and says:

The German guard: Ok, Go on! (He looks at his watch and adds) In an hour and a half, you may have a half-an-hour break and you'll be given something to eat.

Thoma: That's good, sir! But shall we have some water before that? It's getting hot!

The German guard: Water is over there; can you see it? Those who are thirsty may go and drink some. But you have to warn us beforehand that you're going to drink some water… or…

The German guard walks away leaving the young men there, who immediately start mowing the grass.

Beso: Well, it seems that we are being closely watched over by these dirty rotten guards. But believe me, they'll soon be tired of it. (He starts humming a song and adjusting it to the rhythm of mowing) "ჰერი ბიჭოო, ჰერიოო, იმითვინა ვმღერიოო"[64]

Jango: (In the same rhythm) უშბას გული ეუბნება, რას დაგვაკლებს მტერიო[65]

The young men start laughing. Ushba smiles and says in his typical friendly tone:

Ushba: Go to hell…

---

[64] /Hey, guys, hey… that's why I'm singing as I have sung/

[65] /Ushba's heart is saying, the enemy can do us no harm/

***

It's evening. The last rays of the setting sun glow and light up the mountain ridge. We see a small group of people walking along the path overlooking a ravine. The young men with their guards are heading to their dwelling place. Soon they appear on a small meadow. There are two almost identical ugly buildings resembling luggage vans in the center of the meadow. One of them is a dwelling place for the guards and the other for the prisoners. A field kitchen can be seen nearby. The building where the prisoners live is locked from outside and guarded by two German soldiers; one of them patrolling the door and the other back side of the building where there is a single-window covered by an iron grate.

The young men are inside the building getting ready to go to bed.

Batsi: Thoma, do you remember telling us that you had been considering a plan. As for me, I haven't stopped thinking about our escape, but these mountains and bare rocks discourage me a lot. Well, say, we managed to escape, what are we supposed to do next? How can we find our way through these mountains? We neither have a map nor know the route.

Gigi: Batsi is right. We don't even know which direction we should go in. We just can't rely on fortune alone…

Jango: Neither can we rely on what Ushba's heart is telling him.

Ushba: You're driving me mad. I've already told you to mind your own hearts, or…

The boys laugh. Thoma turns to Gigi.

Thoma: Your misgivings are justified in case we don't know where to go. But if we do, it won't be a problem; isn't it so?

Beso: Maybe, but how do you plan to learn which direction we have to go. Shall we come to the Germans and tell them: We are going to flee from here and be so kind as to tell us which direction we should take?!

Thoma: Not as directly as you say, though we must learn the route from them. Maybe we'll have to organize a small performance... but not yet, maybe a little later when we get to know them better. What would you say about performance with Jango and Ushba as main characters?

Ushba: Are you a bit insane? I'm not an actor...

Thoma: But you don't have to be one to do what I'm going to tell you now. For example, Jango will point to a direction saying that there is Italy there. You must reply that he's a bit stupid and that there is Austria there and not Italy. That's what you'll have to perform. Is it very difficult?

Jango: No, it's not, Thoma, but if Ushba says I'm stupid, will I have to put up with it? If so, won't it be a little artificial?

Thoma: But you won't have to put up with it. That's what I want you to do. You'll have to fight but not using your fists but have a kind of a verbal fight over it. You must perform this after dinner and so that the Germans see you. So, while you are having a discussion, they'll ask me what is going on. So, the rest is up to me; I know what to do next.

Batsi: Maybe you do, but wouldn't you share it with us?

Thoma: I'll make them tell us where we should run, which is which route leads to Switzerland.

Ushba: That's a well-thought-out plan, Thoma. Everything's going to be fine. My heart is telling me...

Hearing the word "heart", the young men can't help laughing.

Thoma: There is one more thing we should remember: we don't have to mention Switzerland. We must pretend that we know nothing about that country. We must show them that we've heard only about Italy, Austria and we can add to this list only France. We must pretend that we have no knowledge of Geography.

A guard standing at the door of the building where the prisoners are locked takes a pack of cigarettes out of his pocket, takes a cigarette out of, puts it in his mouth and starts searching his pockets but in vain, he can't find anything to light up the cigarette. He calls the other guard patrolling the backside of the building:

The first guard: Ian, have you got a match?

Nobody answers, but we see Ian walking towards him and handing him a match. The first guard takes the match and lights the cigarette, pulls on it and says:

The first guard: These Georgians are very funny people. They laugh all the time.

He's hardly finished these words that a loud and hearty laugh is heard from inside the building.

The first guard: Do you hear them? I wish I understood what they are talking about.

We hear Batsi speaking:

Batsi: Let's assume we succeed in wheedling the information out of them, what we are supposed to do next? We can't kiss them good-buy and walk away. (We hear half of Batsi's words from outside then we enter the building and see the young men talking)

Ushba: If we consider everything and plan well, it won't be a problem to disarm them. After all, there are only seven of them. I know, I know that you are going to tell me that there are not seven but three times seven of them, but I mean that we are watched over by seven of them at a time. They take turns keeping watch over us in six-hour shifts. So, if we manage to disarm a new shift, gag their mouths and tie them up, 6 hours will lapse until a new shift discovers that we've run away.

Thoma: I don't agree with you, Ushba. So many unforeseen things might happen if we follow your plan, we simply can't anticipate and consider everything. I have a different plan; if it appeals to you all... But first I want to ask you if you have ever rolled downhill with haystacks. I'm not asking Ushba and Beso, I know for sure that they have, but what about others?

Jango: I used to do this in summer, Thoma.

Gigi: I have done it, not so many times, but still I know how to roll downhill with a haystack.

Thoma: And what about you Dachi?

Dachi: So, do you think I grew up in Tbilisi? My mother is from Gudamakari, and I grew up there. So, I do know how to do this.

Thoma: That's great, guys! What a relief. So, the only person who hasn't done it is Batsi, but it's not going to be a big problem. Batsi and I will roll down together. You don't have to be scared, Batsi. You simply must close your eyes and that's all… I'll take care of the rest. So, we must switch to a new strategy. We must go on mowing in the direction of the slope and we must mow the grass to the edge of it. Then we'll have to build seven haystacks at the edge of the slope. I will convince the Germans that it's easier to build haystacks of freshly cut grass; that they'll dry up until we finish mowing and it will be easier to take them out. They'll believe me, I'm sure. I'm going to tell them that we follow Georgian traditions. I've noticed them watching us with interest and they'll find our offer interesting. When we finish building haystacks, we'll need some ropes. But I'll try to get them. Ushba and I will tie the haystacks and prepare them. In the evening, when we'll have finished mowing, I'll tell them we are ready to take out those haystacks. That's why I plan to build seven of them, to make them believe that there a haystack per person. The rest is up to us. We'll have to stand on the edge of the slope and take a couple of steps to roll down. But we must do it simultaneously. As Batsi and I are to roll down together, I'll give you a signal. We don't have to be scared. Everything is going to happen in the blink of an eye. The Germans will take a long time to realize what has happened. They'll be really disarmed as they can't roll down that slope and even if they fire their weapons the bullets can't reach us, as we'll be protected by huge haystacks. It'll take us a minute or even less to reach the woods. And let them chase us there. That's all I wanted to say. If you have any questions, we should discuss them right now.

Batsi: Everything's clear, but can you tell me what I should do? I don't want to stand in your way there; so, if you don't explain to me how I should behave there, I might be of some help to you.

Thoma: Ok, Batsi, let me explain to you. Have you ridden on a sled in winter in your childhood?

Batsi: Of course, I have.

Thoma: So, you must imagine that you're riding on a sled, you must take the same position as on a sled: sit in front of me and stretch your legs forward. That's it. Don't be scared, we'll have to entrust the rest to the haystack and the slope. We've got time. So, I'll explain everything in detail to you later. You know what matters most is that now we have the goal and life has become meaningful.

Jango: You're right. But do you know what I was thinking about right now? Just imagine what might have happened if one of the Germans standing outside had understood our language. Wouldn't it have been a world-wide trick?

We hear the young men laughing again. We are outside and see the buildings standing on a small meadow disappearing in the darkness of the Alps, together with the young men full of life and joy, imprisoned in one of these buildings.

***

It's afternoon. Seven haystacks are standing side by side built by the Georgians. The hay seems quite dry. We see the seven of them mowing grass quite far of the haystacks. One of the German gunners standing nearby whistles loudly. The prisoners stop mowing and look at him. The German is waving his hand and shouting:

The German gunner: Dinner!

The young men walk towards an improvised dining place. They help each-other wash their hands by pouring water from a water-cask standing nearby, some of them pour water on their heads as well and they gather round the place where the cook is distributing their dinner. The young men are having their moderate dinner in silence. It consists of mainly dry food: some bread, sausages, fat pieces of pork and overgrown big cucumbers. Jango chooses the biggest cucumber, takes it in his hand and says:

Jango: Should I be eating this staff here? We grow such cucumbers in our kitchen garden that if Hitler ever happened to taste it, He would give up the war and start growing cucumbers.

Dachi: Jango, I think we should be grateful for what we are having right now. I do agree with you that they taste awful but at least we are having cucumbers.

Dachi takes one of the cucumbers, breaks it into two pieces with his hands and gives one piece to Thoma. Thoma takes the piece of cucumber and turns to one of the Germans currying his gun.

Thoma: If you provide some ropes, we can tie the haystacks today and take them out, after we finish mowing. We'll take all seven of them to the road in the evening.

He says and takes a bite out of the cucumber in a relaxed manner.

The German gunner: Ropes won't be a problem. I'll tell Lieutenant. But are you going to carry such huge haystacks on you back?

Thoma: Yes, we are. Those haystacks are already dry, and they are not very heavy.

The German gunner: It's very interesting. I would love to see it. My shift finishes at 3 p.m., but I won't go anywhere; I'll stay and watch you. Where else will I be able to see such a thing?

Thoma: I agree with you. It's quite entertaining. The people carrying haystacks are not visible and you get the impression that the haystacks move by themselves. It's a spectacular scene to watch.

While Thoma is explaining this to the German gunner, Jango and Ushba have already started arguing.

Jango: Believe me, it's Italy, I'm 100% sure.

Ushba: You must be either pulling my leg or you're a bit stupid! You can't be sure. It's not Italy there but... what's its name?...

Jango: You call me stupid? Then go and tell me... Why are you looking at me? Tell me which country is there!

Ushba: Which country? It's Svanetia!

Having heard Ushba's answer the young men start laughing hysterically. Dachi even drops the piece of cucumber he has been holding. Everything seems natural. Ushba looks at the guys for a while, then starts laughing himself and says:

Ushba: It'll be good if you don't die of laughter! I meant it looks very much like Svanetia.

The German guards don't understand anything, but they smile and one of them asks Thoma:

The German guard: It seems he has said something very fanny. What are you laughing at?

Thoma can't stop laughing but manages to answer:

Thoma: That short man with a dark complexion says that there is Italy beyond those mountains... and this big guy tries to prove that t's not Italy, but Svanetia... Let me explain to you... The point is that Svanetia is a region in our country, Georgia... It's in the Caucasus. It's at least five thousand kilometers away from here... That's why we are laughing.

The German guard: Is he stupid?

Thoma: No, he added that it looks very much like Svanetia... He lives in Svanetia, in the mountains... and...

The German guard: Ok, now I understand, He must feel homesick.

Thoma: You're right.

The German guard: What can be done about it? I miss my home too, but I am here with you. Besides, my home is a lot nearer than his one. It's just beyond those mountains. As for that side, they have argued about. It's neither Italy nor… how do you call it?

Thoma: Svanetia.

The German guard: Yes, nor that one. It's Switzerland there. It's across just several mountain ranges.

The expression on the young men's faces change. This all makes the situation seem a bit strained. Thoma notices it and to improve the situation he stands up and says in German:

Thoma: Well guys, let's stop discussing Geography and get our work done. (Then he continues in Georgian) We must thank him for being such a good guide.

The young men all leave their seats. Some of them haven't finished their dinner and are eating something on their way towards the field. The German guards seem not to be watching the prisoners as closely as they did before.

Beso: So, it's for sure now, isn't it?

Thoma: It's for sure! But they must bring ropes first.

Ushba: It's for sure and let it be! If you would like we can even go on trekking till we reach Svanetia. They can't catch us in the mountains.

The young men hear the German guard calling:

The German guard: What length of ropes do you need? We must cut them.

Thoma turns around and shows them his five fingers and says loudly:

Thoma: Five meters each (Then he adds in Georgian) Now it's decided for sure… We're off. And the time is perfect. They won't manage to chase us till morning. So, we'll be a whole night's time ahead of them.

Batsi: Do you think we'll find it easy to walk in the dark?

Thoma: It isn't going to be dark, Batsi. We've considered that as well. We have the full moon these nights and we can see quite well. I think everything works in our favor… May God have his mercy on us…

Thoma crosses himself and the young men answer:

- Amen! Amen!

Then they take their scythes and start mowing with the same enthusiasm they have shown before.

***

A German soldier is striding along the path carrying his gun and some ropes on his shoulder. He is whistling a simple tune. He suddenly stops, stops whistling and stares at something. A bird of prey is sitting on a rocky ledge nearby and is looking down the ravine. The solder breaks a small piece of rock off the cliff with his hand, but the bird stretches lifts its wings, shakes them a few times and flies down to the ravine. The German soldier throws the piece of rock carelessly he seems disappointed, and then he starts whistling again and continues his way. He approaches the grassland, comes up to a piece of board serving as a table and throws the ropes on the ground. He turns to another German soldier sitting nearby.

German soldier I: Aren't you going to go and have a rest? Your shift has finished, hasn't it?

German soldier II: It has, but I want to watch them carrying those haystacks. Look, aren't they huge? I can't imagine how they are going to carry them with these five-meter long ropes. I don't want to miss that. I'll see if they really manage to take the haystacks to the road all by themselves and then I'll go back with them. I'll manage to have a good sleep till 12 a.m.

German soldier I: I agree with you. I think we'll be entertained a lot if those Georgians aren't planning to play a trick on us.

German soldier II: What might they be planning? We haven't ordered them to do that; it was their initiative. You know what? Let's tell them to stop mowing a bit earlier today. Carrying those haystacks is a part of their work, isn't it?

German soldier I: That's right! (He looks at his watch) They must finish in 40 minutes anyway. I'll go and tell them… and I'll give them these ropes… Come on, let's go to the haystacks and watch them.

Both soldiers walk towards the haystacks. Then one of them shouts to other guards who are standing near the prisoners:

German soldier I: That's enough for today. Bring them all to the haystacks.

The young men stop mowing and walk to the haystacks accompanied by the guards. We hear Thoma speaking to his friends, smiling as he speaks.

Thoma: Keep calm, guys. We must pretend that nothing special is going to happen. They shouldn't smell a rat.

The young men come to the haystacks and Thoma points to the ropes and addresses one of the soldiers standing there.

Thoma: May I take these ropes?

The soldier throws the ropes at his feet. Thoma takes all the ropes together and coils them around his arm in a quick and skillful manner and says:

Thoma: Stay here. Ushba and I will tie the haystacks, get them ready and call you.

Ushba and Thoma go to the haystacks. We see them tying the haystacks. They finish tying all seven of them and Thoma calls the others standing nearby to come. First, he says for the Germans to hear him:

Thoma: We've prepared all seven of them.

Then he continues in Georgian, but the Germans can guess what he is saying through the gestures he uses.

Thoma: Jango, the first haystack is yours.

He points to the first haystack with his hand. Jango goes to the first haystack, gets hold of the rope to examine it and he pulls it so strongly that the haystack is shaken.

Thoma: Dachi, the second one is yours.

Thoma points to the second haystack.

Thoma: Gigi, the third haystack.

Thoma: Ushba, yours is the fourth.

The German soldiers smile and nod their heads in satisfaction as they see that the fourth haystack stands out among the rest with its size, just as Ushba stands out among his friends.

Thoma: Beso, the fifth haystack is yours.

Beso goes and takes his place by the fifth haystack.

Thoma turns to Batsi looks into his eyes and says:

Thoma: Come on, Batsi. We must take out the sixth and seventh haystacks.

Thoma and Batsi walk towards the last two haystacks. When they walk past each of their friends, Thoma encourages them one by one. He gives some of them a pat on their shoulders, and some of them a tap on their stomachs and says:

Thoma: Never say die, brothers!

When he reaches the sixth haystack, he stands to cover Batsi with his body from the sight of the German soldiers and shouts to the rest of them:

Thoma: Hey, Georgians, are you ready?

We hear the young men shouting is the response:

- We are ready, Thoma!

Jango: Go, Thoma, count to three… and let's go!

Thoma: Come on, Batsi, sit here! One! Two! Three! Go…

The young men take two steps towards the slope and almost simultaneously throw themselves down into the ravine with their haystacks. The German soldiers can't realize what has happened; they stand motionless with their mouths open and look down at the haystacks becoming smaller and smaller as they roll downhill at a high speed. We hear echoes of the Georgians crying: Hey… hey… hey…

Then suddenly silence prevails. The German soldiers are still standing and looking down and we see the six small haystacks lying against the trees standing at the entrance to the woods. The Georgians seem to have disappeared.

We see the face of the German soldier who stayed to see the job done by the Georgians and we hear him saying:

German soldier II: My God! Did it really happen or am I daydreaming?

***

It's night. The Germans are gathered in the building standing in the middle of the small meadow. The lieutenant is furious. He walks up and down the aisle between the beds and speaks non-stop, loudly and emotionally.

The lieutenant: No, this is incredible. There were seven soldiers armed with machine guns. That means an armed German soldier per a weak and unarmed prisoner of war and they managed to run away... and not one or two of them, but all of them at once. I have been listening to you, but I still cannot understand how they might have managed to do that, in front of you. I must phone and inform them about what happened! What shall I tell them?! That we stood and looked at how they were running away from us! You might at least have shot... I do not understand why you didn't shoot. There was nothing that could have stopped you!

German soldier I: Who should we have to shoot at, sir? The only things we saw were the haystacks. Besides everything happened so quickly; it was so amazing… a real miracle. If you had been there, Lieutenant, you too wouldn't have done anything but look at the scene. I have never ever seen or met such daredevils. They might even not be alive. Anyway, we saw the haystacks crashing against the trees. We must go down the ravine tomorrow morning and search for the surroundings.

The lieutenant: Tomorrow morning, you say? What are we supposed to be doing till morning, sit here and talk with each other? We'll find it difficult to catch them if we give them a night to advance. We don't even know which direction they will head. I wish we had some dogs here... Now maybe you can recall something that you didn't pay attention then but might prove to be important now. Think and try to recall...

German soldier II: What might we have noticed? They spoke their language all the time. We couldn't understand what they were talking about. Only one of them spoke German and he appears to have been very cautious. We didn't hear him mentioning anything like this.

German soldier I: Wait, wait, Ian! Do you remember today... after dinner...? My God, they were choosing a route... That's for sure. Lieutenant, I bet they are going to Switzerland.

The lieutenant: I don't understand what does dinner has to do with a route? Can you explain more clearly?

German soldier I: Of course, Lieutenant. Today, when they were having dinner two of them quarreled about which country is located beyond the mountains. The first was saying it was Italy and the other didn't agree with him.

The lieutenant: Then?

German soldier I: Then the one who spoke German asked us which of them was right. Ian said that there was Switzerland, not Italy. When they heard it, all of them were conspicuously silent for a while. Then they stood up and went to work in the field. Now I understand that they have played a trick on us, but I couldn't think of this then.

The lieutenant: Now I understand. So, you said Switzerland, didn't you?

German soldier I: I'm almost sure, Lieutenant.

The lieutenant: I'm afraid they won't find it difficult to reach Switzerland as they managed to escape so handily from here. The only way to catch them is to start chasing after them tonight. If what we suspect is right, we must catch them tomorrow. They'll stop somewhere to have a rest or sleep. They can't trek the mountains 24 hours a day non-stop; besides they must be weak because of hunger and hard work they've been through. But… in case we fail to catch them, I'll be responsible for not having reported on the case. I must make a phone call and report to Sturmbannführer… immediately.

He goes to a small table and takes up a telephone receiver in his hand.

***

Moonlight shines on the Georgians walking in a line like mountain climbers in the woods. The group is led by Thoma and Ushba is walking at the end of the line. They are currying the ropes they have used to tie the haystacks; some of them are carrying them on their shoulders, some have them wrapped around their waists like belts. They are heading uphill. They've already crossed one mountain and are now on their way to cross the second one.

We return to the room where the Germans are gathered. The lieutenant is standing at attention, straightened upholding the receiver against his ear and is listening to someone shouting. He occasionally manages to say a single short phrase:

The lieutenant: Everything is clear, Herr Sturmbannführer!

The lieutenant: Everything is clear, Herr Sturmbannführer!

At last, the person at the other end of the line stops shouting and the lieutenant seems relieved. He puts the telephone receiver back in its cradle and stands in silence his face all red. All the people in the room are staring at him, awaiting explanations.

The lieutenant: Well, they say catching them is the matter of life and death and of our dignity. And it's true. If they manage to cross the border of Switzerland, the case will become known to the whole world through the press… Sturmbannführer says that such a reckless escape is a shameful stain on us. He was furious when I told him that they had run away and had taken haystacks with them. I'm sure you heard how angry he was. He says we must catch them and bring them to the camp. He says he will attend their shooting. So... take your torches and let's go… all of you.

***

We see the same scene and hear the same dialogues given at the beginning of the first part.

There is a small field among the trees of the forest, where we can see seven young men. Five of them are sitting on the ground leaning against tree trunks. One of the young men is standing his back pressed against a tree trunk and one of them is sitting on a dead tree branch.

Gigi: If only I could find a dry leaf somewhere…

Dachi: why do you need a dry leaf, Gigi? I'd understand if you wished to find dried fruit…

Gigi: Why? I would crumble it and wrap it in a paper, like tobacco. I tried doing this with needles, but it tasted awful… bitter… pah!

Thoma: My dad was fond of cutting tobacco leaves. Though, to tell you the truth, I don't quite know whether he loved doing this or not. I know that he used to cut tobacco leaves; I loved watching him doing this. First, he whetted a knife; rubbing it earnestly against a whetstone, slowly… like this… he would put tobacco leaves twisted together… on a plank placed on his lap… and go… The knife was so sharp… a Georgian knife, with crosses engraved on the bone handle. And the odor around... I have never smoked tobacco, but I'm crazy about its odor. I could smell it for hours. Dad kept the tobacco in a wooden box in the attic. All I wanted was to take the lid off the box and stick my nose in the pile of tobacco leaves, but I would not dare, I was afraid ... I was afraid of being caught by Dad; he would think I smoked ... and I was afraid. Though, Friday was a market day. There was a separate row for tobacco. So, I used to go there, I could stand there all day and smell tobacco.

Batsi: For God's sake, stop talking about tobacco! We've already devoured all the snacks we had. The evening is not a problem and we'll manage to survive till tomorrow morning, but what shall we do after that?!

Thoma: Don't panic. We aren't going to be starved to death. We are in the woods after all… we might find a bird's nest or berries. There are thousands of things we can think of. If only the Germans stopped chasing us, and then I know what I'll do.

Batsi: What will you do? Will you heap up charcoal and let us have a barbeque? (Laughing)

Ushba: Come on… where's barbeque? But Thoma is right… we should search for birds' nests.

Thoma: yeah, birds… You see they remind me of my dad…

Jango: Why? Did he finish cutting tobacco and switched to birds' nests?

Thoma: Let me finish, Jango, tobacco has nothing to do with it! My dad met a German archeologist in Guria; he was staying at someone's house in Ozurgeti. Dad knew German well, he taught me to speak the language.

Batsi: Where did he learn German, in Guria?

Thoma: Where? He was a prisoner of war in Germany, just like us, but it was during the first war, the war that was before this one. It was there that he learned German.

Jango: Ok, go on, you were talking about birds…

Thoma: Well, do you remember the toy I gave to Maria? … for her son… With the image of a cage on one side and the image of a bluebird on the other… A German man gave this toy to my dad… for me. It was the only toy I had in my childhood… I loved it… You know… I used to carry it with me everywhere… in my pocket… until I gave it to Maria.

Beso: It was a really great thing. A cage was on one side, a bluebird - on the other, and when you spun it, you would see the bluebird in the cage. I've got no idea why we saw it this way! Weren't the images on different sides?

Jango: Before a Rachian understands why it happens so, the bluebird will pierce the cardboard with its beak and really enter the cage.

Young people start laughing. Jango continues.

Jango: But why did you recall that bird and the cage, Thoma? It seems to me that you wanted to say something, didn't you? We all do remember that toy; we used to play with it when Beso went to sleep. But why now…

Thoma: Why? I don't know… Maybe our life is like that of the bluebird…

Dachi: Will it fly away like a bird?

Thoma: No, I wanted to say that our life is an illusion like that toy. You live in peace and quiet, then, someone like Hitler comes up with some insane ideas, grabs hold of the strings of your life and spins them so rapidly… that you find yourself in a cage right away. He spins and spins them and bam! You're in a cage! He spins again and bams! Cage… we are 5 thousand kilometers away from our homes… What the hell are we doing here?! Did anybody ask us whether we wanted to be here or not? What are we after? What are we looking for?

Jango: We are looking for birds' nests, right now; we'll see what we are going to look for next…

Thoma: Even now, we are planning something, and the cage might be waiting for us nearby.

Jango: Bam! And Cage? Do you say?

Young people laugh again.

Thoma: Thank God, we can all find reasons to laugh… OK, let's do something: I'll go up the hill. I have noticed a tall tree. I'll try to climb the tree and see if I can find something in the surroundings, some building maybe. I'll be back soon. Try to have a nap. We have been walking all night…

Dachi: If you want to conquer a height, you don't have to go far. You can climb Ushba…

Young people start laughing again.

Ushba: Don't you want me to go with you, Thoma? Maybe you need my help when climbing the tree.

Thoma: No, I don't, Ushba, you need a rest. I'll be back soon. Don't worry; everything's going to be all right.

Thoma starts walking towards the trees and disappears behind them. The boys fall asleep.

Thoma walks down the hill between the trees. He seems full of vim and vigor with a hopeful expression on his face. When he approaches the field, where he left his friends, suddenly, he stops dead in his tracks and we can see his big sad eyes out on stalks. We can hear music, Thoma tries to hide behind a tree trunk, but we can still see his eyes wide-opened.

We see German gunners quietly coming out from behind the trees like ghosts and approaching the sleeping young men. Thoma, who has hidden behind the trees, is watching the scene. A gunman stands by each sleeping young man pointing their machine guns at them. The lieutenant looks carefully at them one by one, chooses Ushba, leans down to reach his face and pats him on the cheek, satisfaction and a mocking smile are mixed on the lieutenant's face.

The lieutenant: Peek-a-boo, my boy. It's time to wake up…

Ushba opens his eyes; but at first, he thinks he sees the uniformed German in his dream and stares at him without any reaction. Then he looks around to see other German soldiers and bites his lips to hide his despair.

The lieutenant straightens his back and shouts very loudly and is a very strict tone:

The lieutenant: Get up on your feet right now, all of you! Hands up and come and stand here, in the middle. Quickly, quickly!

The young men jump on their feet, but they are confused and do not know what to do. They don't understand the commands the lieutenant is giving. The lieutenant takes one of them by his hand and drags him in the middle of the small field. The German gunners push the others and make them move to the center of the field. The young men are standing in the center of the field surrounded by the German gunners. The lieutenant counts them aloud one by one.

The lieutenant: One, two, three, four, five, six… (Then shouts very loudly) Seventh? Where is the seventh?

The young men are standing still and say nothing. They seem to be still underestimating the gravity of the situation.

Batsi: It seems to me that we are doomed, but they might be looking for the seventh one… Thoma.

Ushba: We should let him know what's going on and tell him not to come here.

Jango: How can we let him know?

Ushba: I know, how. They are asking us where he is shouting… I'll shout as well as if I'm calling him… (He starts shouting very loudly) Thoma! Don't come here… Do you hear me? Run… We've been caught here… Run!

The lieutenant snatches the automatic rifle out of one of the gunner's hand and hits Ushba in the stomach with the rifle. So violent is the blow that Ushba drops down, wincing in pain.

Thoma comes out from behind the tree looking very pale.

Thoma: Why did you hit him, Lieutenant? He was calling me…

The lieutenant turns promptly as soon as he hears Thoma's voice. Points the rifle at him and shouts:

The lieutenant: Hands up!

Thoma raises his hands up and joins his friends. He helps Ushba to get on his feet. Ushba still winces in pain.

The German gunners snatch the ropes from the young men, tie their hands behind their backs with these ropes and push them to make them move forward.

***

It's evening. German gunners are leading the young men with their hands tied behind their backs in the territory of a concentration camp that looks different from the one the young men had been accommodated before they were sent to work in the Alps. They are in a different concentration camp. The seven of them are made to stand in line in the center of a special site for ceremonies. The German gunners remain with the prisoners and the lieutenant goes to the headquarters building. The young men watch several German militaries running out of the building and towards the barracks; a few seconds later they come out of the barracks leading a lot of skinny prisoners who are then arranged in five rows around the Georgian prisoners. The Georgians are standing in the middle surrounded by the prisoners from every side.

Sturmbannführer escorted by several officers comes out of the headquarters building and goes to the place where the prisoners are standing. When he comes closer he starts walking down the row where the seven Georgians are standing very slowly, stopping by each of them and looking into their faces. He obviously intends to impress them and to break them down psychologically. When he finishes this ritual, he walks up the row and looks at Dachi's face again. He stares at him for a while and eventually asks:

Sturmbannführer: Judah?

Dachi: Thoma, what does he want from me? Has he called me Judah?

Until Thoma manages to say something, Sturmbannführer's interpreter says in Russian:

Interpreter: Sturmbannführer asks whether you are a Jew.

Thoma answers in German instead of Dachi.

Thoma: No, we are Georgian.

Sturmbannführer looks at Thoma but says nothing to him. Then he turns to a German soldier standing nearby points to Dachi and says:

Sturmbannführer: Untie his hands!

This soldier fulfills Sturmbannführer's order and immediately unties Dachi's hands. Dachi looks confused; he is standing and rubbing his wrists.

Sturmbannführer turns to the interpreter and says something in German. The interpreter translates his words in Russian:

Interpreter: Sturmbannführer wants you to pull off your pants and stand naked from your waist down.

Dachi asks in a desperate voice:

Dachi: Thoma, have you got an idea of what these bastards intend to do with me?

Thoma: Dachi, don't be scared, man! I think they want to see whether you've your foreskin removed or not. Have you heard about the ritual the Jews practice? It's called Circumcision. Show it to them and they'll leave you alone.

Sturmbannführer looks very angry. He comes up to Thoma and shouts at him:

Sturmbannführer: Did I give you permission to speak? Answer now! Did I give you permission to speak?!

Thoma: No, you didn't… I'm sorry. But I have explained to him what you wanted him to do.

Sturmbannführer: Then? If it's so, what is he waiting for?

Thoma: Dachi, they are waiting… do it until they get nervous.

Dachi seems to have lost his temper and suddenly he says in an angry voice:

Dachi: To hell with them… I'm not going to pull down my pants. Tell him to bring his wife here and I'll show it to his wife and she'll tell him what it is like…

Despite their situation, a slight smile lightens up their faces for a very moment when they hear Dachi's words. Sturmbannführer's keen eyes notice this and he asks the interpreter in a very strict tone:

Sturmbannführer: What did he say?

Interpreter: (shrugging his shoulders says) I don't know Herr Sturmbannführer. They speak their own language. I can understand only Russian.

Sturmbannführer looks at Thoma and says to him:

Sturmbannführer: Now I give you permission to speak. I saw you hardly kept yourself from smiling when you heard his words. Translate what he said word by word… or I'll…

Thoma: He said… he said that… his wife always helps him to take off his trousers…

Sturmbannführer first looks at Thoma inquisitively right into his eyes. Then he turns to Dachi again, produces a parabellum from the gun holster on his belt puts it against Dachi's forehead and squeezes the trigger. He maintains this position for a while.

Dachi thinks Sturmbannführer has done so to make him do what he wants. So, he stands there with a parabellum against his forehead and smiles. A shot is heard. A bullet tears the back of Dachi's head. Dachi's head is thrown backward and he falls on the ground.

A short deep heart-rending groan is heard uttered by Dachi's friends standing there. We see Jango taking his fist to his mouth and biting it so that his chin is immediately covered in blood. Thoma's face darkens and tears start rolling down his cheeks.

Sturmbannführer puts his parabellum back into its holster and turns to the same soldier who had untied Dachi's hands a minute ago:

Sturmbannführer: Go; pull down his trousers and check. Let everyone see that he was lying.

The soldier kneels by Dachi's dead body and does what Sturmbannführer has ordered. There is a dead silence there. Everyone is waiting for what he has to say. The soldier raises his head very soon; he looks astonished and says to Sturmbannführer:

The soldier: He was not lying, Herr Sturmbannführer. He is not a Jew.

Now Sturmbannführer looks astonished but he tries hard to cover his feeling, but he couldn't cover his embarrassment and says:

Sturmbannführer: Maybe he was not a Jew, but he was stupid, that's for sure. Take the rest of them and place them in a separate cell till morning. Shoot them all in the morning for everyone to see.

Sturmbannführer turns and takes several steps towards the headquarters building. His escort is ready to follow him, but he stops suddenly, looks at the military men escorting him and says:

Sturmbannführer: I can't see the doctor. Where is he?

One of the men: He's in his room, Herr Sturmbannführer!

Sturmbannführer turns to an adjutant.

Sturmbannführer: Ok. He must examine all of them before they are shot. Do you hear what I say?

The adjutant: (nodding his head) I do, Herr Sturmbannführer!

***

The young men are sitting right on the floor in a semi-dark place resembling a room. We see their faces one by one. Then we hear one of them groaning and saying:

- Well, I think this is the end… It's hard to believe.

We see that the one speaking is Jango.

Batsi: What do you find hard to believe?

Jango: That they are really going to kill us!

Batsi: Oh, you are so naïve, Jango. Didn't you see what they did with Dachi?

Gigi: I wish he would have pulled his trousers… and shown to them…

Beso: You don't say so! I almost believed he was a Jew.

Thoma: would it justify killing him, you mean?

Beso: No, I don't mean that. Damn… He put his gun so calmly against his forehead! And Dachi was smiling… He was smiling when he fell. If only I hadn't looked at him!

Ushba: He proved that he was courageous, a real man. I wouldn't have pulled my trousers either. It makes no difference whether I'm killed today or tomorrow. Dachi was the first to go. Tomorrow we'll be together again…

A German interpreter opens the door, looks at the young men; then he fixes his gaze on Batsi and says:

Interpreter: Stand up! You must come with us!

Batsi stands up and walks through the door. The young men see that besides the interpreter there are two more armed soldiers waiting for Batsi at the door.

After Batsi leaves the room, the young men sit in silence. We see their faces again. Each of them is engulfed in their own thoughts. Beso breaks the silence.

Beso: They may change their minds… Miracles happen … sometimes.

Jango tries to joke and says with a bitter smile on his face:

Jango: Let's ask Ushba what his heart is telling him.

Ushba: You may as well make fun of me, but my heart is telling me that we aren't doomed to die…

Jango: No, Ushba, I'm not making fun of you, on the contrary, I want to thank you for encouraging us. But our hearts sometimes deceive us, don't they? What shall we do about it? When we ran away, you said your heart was telling you that they would never catch us.

Ushba: What should I have said, Jango? Should I have said that they would catch us, and we would end up in stalemate? Should I have said this and killed your spirit and hope? Hope should die last…

The door opens and Batsi is pushed into the room. Now they take Jango with them.

Beso: What did the doctor tell you, Batsi?

Batsi: Nothing. He didn't say a word. He looked up and down me, made me open my mouth and let me go. Only the interpreter asked me my age, I don't know why. I told them, and that doctor wrote it down. I think we're doomed...

There is silence once again and we see Thoma's face. He seems to be far away sunk in his own thoughts.

We see the scene from Part 1. The dream Thoma's father – Theopile Darchia used to have. An old pomegranate tree on a hill and a picturesque view from above on the background of the same beautiful melody: a valley, a village road leading to the yard, the yard and a wooden house; a river with a bond bridge. Thoma sees the same image Theopile used to see, but there aren't Attila and Ocean in his dream. Thoma doesn't see the bulls.

From time to time, against the background of beautiful music, Thoma hears the noise of the door being opened, words said in not so good Russian – "Now it's your turn", then the noise of steps and the noise of the door being closed. The noises from reality enter Thoma's dream. They take the young men one by one who then are brought back.

Thoma startles at a noise of the door being opened and returns to reality. Now it's his turn. He stands up and follows the German soldiers. Batsi says to him to hear in a desperate voice:

Batsi: Thoma, you're the only one among us who speaks German and maybe you'll find out what awaits us? Are we really going to die like sacrificial lambs?

A middle-aged doctor is sitting at the desk in his room. We can recognize Tobias Koch, the archeologist from Part I. Thoma's father – Theopile Darchia met him in Ozurgeti nine or ten years ago. Now he is dressed in an official uniform and is knocking monotonously with his fingers on the arms of the armchair he is sitting in.

Thoma enters the room. The doctor looks at him indifferently and asks the interpreter:

The doctor: I think he is the last one, is it so?

Interpreter: Yes, Doctor Koch.

The doctor: Thank God! I feel so sleepy. It's my fault. I should have shunned all the formalities by going there where they are jailed and examining all of them altogether. Sturmbannführer is eager to establish fare rules, and I must spend sleepless nights... Ok, ok, anyway he's the last. Ask him his age and let's call it a day.

The doctor moves his armchair closer to the desk, takes a pen in his hand and looks at a sheet of paper in front of him, ready to write on it. Thoma says in German:

Thoma: We can talk without an interpreter.

The doctor: (looking surprised) Do you speak German? And you want to say that you understood everything I spoke about?

Thoma: Yes, I'm afraid!

The doctor: Why didn't you tell me that from the beginning? You had to. It's not fair!

Thoma: I would have told you if you had asked.

The doctor: Ok, ok. It makes no difference. Tomorrow morning you'll be... So, tell me about your age.

Thoma: My age? I am very old, Doctor. I am 3 500 years old.

The doctor first looks at the interpreter and then again at Thoma.

The doctor: Surely, you're joking, but do you think the situation you're in allows you to joke?

Thoma: No, I'm not joking. Anyway, I don't understand why you need to know my age to kill me! Do you choose bullets according to a prisoner's age?

The doctor: Bravo! You must be a master of sarcasm, but we don't need to know your age to choose a bullet for you. We need it for statistics.

Thoma: Then I was right when I told you that number 3 500. It should be reflected in statistics that it's more than 3 500 years I've been persecuted and put to death. First, it was the East, then the South, then the North decided to exterminate me, and now, you see, the West has found time to care about me. Don't you think that this is important data for statistics? It's already 3 500 years we're put to death and nobody tells us what for! Neither me, nor the guys you've examined so "attentively", whose hearts still retain a glimmer of hope, we have never ever held a gun in our hands, neither have we shot a bullet. But who cares? For example, do you care? Until you go to bed, would you be so kind as to tell me why we must be executed? What have we done wrong? Can you answer my question? We – Georgians have been waiting for 3 500 years to find someone who has an answer to this question, but in vain. We've been fighting for survival for 3 500 years.

The doctor seems to be a little confused but asks Thoma with a kind of embarrassment in his voice:

The Doctor: You identify yourself with your homeland, don't you?!

Thoma: No, I don't. What I wanted to say is that if a man is morally stainless, his fate is closely linked to the fate of his homeland. But, you'll find it difficult to understand my point.

The doctor: Why are you so confident? I know a lot about you. I mean your homeland – Georgia. I might even know more about it than you do. I've been to Georgia. So, to your chagrin, quite a lot is familiar to me from what you're saying. For example, I understand where your philosophy comes from.

Thoma: And where do you think it comes from?

The doctor: It comes from fear, my friend, from the fear of impending death. The very fear of impending death makes one think philosophically. Don't you agree with me?

Thoma: I don't even know what to answer. You might be right. But I think it's more a question of injustice than impending death. As for the fear of impending death... I don't remember the name of the Holy Father who said that the fear of death comes from the mind's weaknesses. I remember how I liked these words when I read them. But then I couldn't have imagined that one day I would have to experience them in my own life. It's not the death itself that one fears, Doctor, but impending death... just as the state of impending pain is unbearable, and the pain itself can be bearable. Not to go too far, Doctor, what we have recently witnessed here is a kind of proof of it. My friend was standing there with the barrel of a parabellum pressed against his forehead and he was smiling. Why? One will ask. Was he so brave? No, of course, he wasn't; he was not expecting death and that's why he was smiling.

Thoma's voice becomes hoarse; we see tears running down his cheeks. But he tries to suppress his emotions and continues:

Thoma: He was shot! He received a bullet right in his forehead… I say it with my own eyes; I saw the bullet blasting through the back of his head. He was lying there dead and smiling. He's much luckier than we are. He passed away knowing nothing of the fear of expecting death. That's exactly what tortures us, who are not among dead yet. That Holy Father meant this very feeling. The human mind, in the majority of cases, is unable to overcome the fear of impending death. I'm trying hard to do exactly that right now; maybe that's why I speak so much, but I see, I fail to make much progress in this regard…

Thoma's voice trembles as he talks. The doctor's facial expression changes gradually; he seems to be engaged in Thoma's discourse and seems to be thinking about it. His face shows not only compassion but occasional sings of the sense of guilt as well. He turns his head aside and staring off into the middle distance somewhere says:

The doctor: I can't find words to console you… The only words that come to my mind form a well-known French phrase - "C'est la vie"[66].

Thoma says nothing and the doctor continues:

---

66 That's life.

The doctor: I have dreamed of great archaeological discoveries throughout my life but... you see well, what I've eventually achieved. I work at this smelly camp as a doctor. If only I were treating patients here. I sit in this room and my sole obligation is to approve and sign death orders for my "patients". A strange twist of fate: I used to think my mission in this life was to excavate masterpieces and artifacts created by human beings from the ground and instead I send people there under the ground. (He bursts out laughing but manages to pull himself together soon and continues) That was the reason why I traveled to your country. I went there in search of Golden Fleece as Jason once did by his Argo. Have you ever heard of the myth about Argonauts?

Thoma: Of course, I have.

The doctor: So, I followed in their tracks and that's how I found myself in Georgia. Though your secret police you so-called Chekists cut the wings of my dream shortly after my arrival there.

At this point, Thoma understands who he is speaking to and his face expresses surprise. The doctor naturally can't realize anything yet and goes on calmly:

The doctor: Not only did they cut the wings of my dream, but they also planned to kill me. And they would eventually have killed me if not a local Georgian. He spoke German as fluently as you do. I dare say that man saved my life. He saved my life but endangered his own. I even remember asking him why he was behaving that way, why he was endangering his life for my sake. His answer was a bit strange. He answered he was obliged to do so. But he didn't say why he was obliged; he said we didn't have time to discuss this...

The doctor stops, looks aside and says to himself:

The doctor: I wonder if he is still alive…

Thoma looks thoughtful for a while on hearing the doctor's words and then says suddenly:

Thoma: No, he's not alive. He was killed by Chekists the day after you left the country.

We see the doctor's face who looks very surprised.

The doctor: You don't say. How do you know that?

Thoma: I do. The man who saved your life was my father.

Thoma casts down his eyes. The doctor, on the contrary, can't take his eyes off Thoma and we see him breathing heavily from excitement. He starts speaking using short phrases:

The doctor: It's increasable… You're his son… Though, nothing is impossible… You know what?... Just to make sure… A simple detail… Wait! Wait! I've got it… Your father… if he really was your father… wrote something on a sheet of paper and gave it to me. If everything is as you say, you might know what he had written on that sheet of paper.

Thoma: No, I'm afraid I don't. This is the first time I hear about it. Dad had never told me anything about it. But as you are eager to make sure that what I am saying is true. I can give you proof. Do you remember giving that man a toy for his son? A cardboard toy with a bluebird on one side and a cage on the other… That boy the toy was intended for was I.

The doctor: My God! My God! That's true! Everything was exactly as you say.

The doctor stands up and starts walking in the room. Then he stops and turns to the interpreter who has been standing there leaned against the wall all this time.

The doctor: I've made you stay here for so long... You may go. I'll take care of this man.

Interpreter: Thank you, Doctor Koch.

The interpreter leaves the room. Tobias takes a chair, moves it near his desk and says:

The doctor: Sit down. We have a lot to talk about.

***

We see the faces of the young men sitting in the same semi-dark room. No one speaks but their faces show that they are impatiently waiting for Thoma to be brought back. They are in a mode of anticipation of a glimmer of hope that Thoma's return might bring forth. But Thoma is nowhere to be seen. And the very fact that he's so late ignites the small glimmer of hope inside his friends. Beso can't wait any longer and he is the first to break the silence.

Beso: He's very late.

Jango: Let him be late; he may as well come in the morning. They won't be holding him there so long for nothing. I think something's going on there.

Gigi: May God hear your words, Jango. Do you remember two previous cases when he was late just like now? He came back with good news in either case. We might be lucky this time as well.

Batsi: You're lucky anyway as you haven't lost your hope…

Jango: Ushba, why don't you say anything? Isn't your golden heart telling you what will happen to us?

Ushba doesn't answer.

Jango: Ushba, I'm speaking to you. Are you asleep?

Ushba: No, Jango, I'm not. My sleep died before me. I think even in case we survive, I won't be able to go to sleep throughout my life. Simply I've got nothing to tell you. Leave me alone.

There is silence again. We return to the doctor's room.

***

The doctor: In sort, this is not the most important point now, but I would like you to know that I fulfilled your father's wish as soon as I returned to Germany. I found the grave and brought some flowers there. Now, as for what matters most… Unfortunately, I can't save the lives of all of you, though I wish I could. But saving your life, to quote your father's words is my direct obligation. At this stage the only thing I can do is to transfer you to another camp, which provides better conditions. Then time will show us what might be done. The most important thing now is to save your life.

Thoma listens to the doctor attentively and understands absolutely everything but we see his face expressing even greater sorrow instead of happiness. He starts speaking slowly and deliberately with frequent pauses:

Thoma: All I can do is to thank you… for being so kind… but… only me… how… Jango… Ushba… Batsi and Beso… Gigi… Dachi is no longer among us… They'll be all shot, and I'll be the only one alive?! Say, you saved my life but what shall I do now? I must go and join them now… How can I look into their eyes…? How am I supposed to do that? No. Doctor, I can't…

The doctor looks even more surprised. He even seems to have little understanding of what Thoma is saying.

The doctor: You say you can't… I don't quite understand. If I heard, you aright you said you can't. Does that mean that you voluntarily choose to die? Would you please explain it more clearly?

Thoma: It's anything but easy, Doctor. I understand you're giving me a chance to live. But… you recalled my dad's words a minute ago, the words he said to you, that he was obliged to do so… I've been raised with these principles… Dad used to teach me that when he was alive. He would teach me that one should not allow even impending death to make him forget about obligations. That's what he did. That's what I experience right now.

I remember once, in my childhood, some guys from my village had taken their cattle to pastures in the mountains. There had been three of them all from the same village. One of them had gone down to the river when the remaining two were attacked by some rustlers. When the first man was returning to the place where he had left his friend He saw his friends engaged in an unfair fight with the rustlers. He watched them killing one of the rustlers, but there were a lot of them there, they killed the two friends and took the cattle with them. This boy escaped his death by hiding in the bushes nearby. When he came back he told everyone what had happened to those poor boys. My dad asked him what he was doing in those bushes when his friends were being killed by the rustlers and why hadn't he gone to their rescue. The boy replied that they could have killed him as well if he had appeared there. And do you know what my dad said? He asked the boy: Do you think you're alive now? He looked at him in silent contempt and walked away.

My situation is very much like that of that boy. If I don't go to them and don't share in their fate, do you think I'll be alive? No, I can't.

The doctor looks at Thoma and seems to be amazed. We see his eyes welled up with tears on hearing Thoma's last words. Thoma notices this and casts his eyes down. He tries his best to hide his emotions and he hears the doctor saying:

The doctor: Ok, let's assume I've understood your decision, but... Do you think they would do the same? I mean your friends. We can even carry out an experiment. I'll call the interpreter and tell him to bring all of them here one by one. I can offer each the same as I've offered you. Do you think any of them would sacrifice their life for your sake? Will you take my offer then?

Thoma: No need, Doctor! I'm sure anyway that not all of them will be able to do that... because it's anything but simple. Though it doesn't really matter, because what I am sure is that they'll all, without exception, have a desire to behave as I do. Whether they'll be able to put it in practice is just the other side of coin. As I've said before it's not easy. I don't find it easy myself, that's why I mentioned mind's weakness. So, I'll leave you now, if you allow me to die...

The doctor looks at Thoma and this time starts crying with tears.

***

The young men in the cell hear the noise of footsteps and we see that they are all strained. Thoma enters the cell and the door is locked securely behind him. The young men look at Thoma who is standing at the door, but nobody dares to ask him anything.

Jango is the first to speak, but his voice sounds as if someone else is speaking.

Jango: What's up Thoma? Were you made to confess on behalf of all of us?

Thoma: I've got no other good news, guys, but the one that we have the whole night ahead to think about death. I follow in my father's footsteps. He was shot, but not here but in Georgia, by Chekists.

Jango: You've never mentioned this before… was he a Menshevik?

Thoma: Menshevik? No, he was an ordinary farmer, hard-working, honest and diligent, ready to lay down his life for his family, neighbors, and friends, who was in love with life, an ordinary man… but he was shot to death.

Ushba: I wonder what a man is doing just before he's shot. Does he cry or lose consciousness? Does he recall his childhood? I wonder what I'll be doing tomorrow morning when we are taken there… They say some even wet their pants from fear. Is it so?

Thoma: Dad had sung!

Ushba: What did you say Thoma? Your dad had sung?

Thoma: Exactly, Dad had sung before he was shot to death. He had turned his back to them… to the Chekists… looked up into the sky and started singing. Do you remember the song I taught you while we stayed at Maria's house? Voisa… Dad sang that song. But he sang it alone. That's why I learned that song… because of my dad.

Jango: You don't say, Thoma! Did he really sing there? And then, don't tell us that they shot a singing man…

Thoma: They did, Jango. There were two of them. One of them couldn't shoot saying he couldn't kill a singing man, but the other did; he shot him in the back of his head.

Jango: Is it possible? Those goddamn bastards…

Thoma: Since I learned about this, I have often wondered how he could do that. So, it seems that I've overdone and now life is testing me whether I'll be able to die with the same dignity as my dad did.

Thoma stops speaking and the young men sit in silence for a while. Then we hear Thoma start singing in a very low voice:

- Voisaaaa…

He goes on singing high his voice combining singing with crying. Someone joins him singing the same high. And we hear a loud knock on the wall that is followed by someone's words speaking Russian:

- Да заткнитесь вы там! Ну блядь, эти грузины... Утром расстрелять должны, ночью концерт устроили.[67]

Then there is silence. The young men's faces gradually disappear in the darkness and after a short period of time, I hear somebody sobbing in the absolute darkness.

***

---

[67] Oh, shut up, you there! Damn, these Georgians. They are to be shot in the morning, and they've organized a concert at night.

It's gloomy misty morning; it's not raining; some invisible negative forces add to unpleasant expectations.

Officers can be seen marching out of the headquarters building. Sturmbannführer is marching ahead and his escort is following him as usual. This time the doctor can be seen among them. They reach the inner yard of the concentration camp overcrowded with prisoners. Thousands of prisoners have been arranged in a military manner and are ready to watch an execution ceremony.

One of the Unter-officers makes several military steps to meet the senior officers and after a traditional greeting, reports:

The Unter-officer: Herr Sturmbannführer, everything is ready for the ceremony.

Sturmbannführer: You may start, we are ready.

The Unter-officer: That's right, Herr Sturmbannführer.

The Unter-officer leads a squad of gunners; they march to a building with a locked door. They open the door and the Unter-officer shouts:

The Unter-officer: Come out, one by one and stand in a line.

We see the young men coming through the door one by one. Ushba comes out first, then Jango, followed by Batsi, Beso, and Gigi. The last person to come through the door is Thoma; he stops at the doorstep, looks up in the sky and joins his friends. Several German militaries come to the young men and tie their hands behind their backs. After that they lead them to the place, make them march in front of the officers and prisoners and make the six of them stand at the wall of a dull building. Then two Germans walk up to them and blindfold them with black pieces of cloth.

The Unter-officer looks at Sturmbannführer expecting his order and soon he gets it.

Sturmbannführer: Start!

Sturmbannführer waves his hand giving the signal to start the ceremony.

After the signal received from the Unter-officer, the squad of gunners is arranged in front of the blindfolded young men and stand still expecting the order.

The order is heard and the ten of them simultaneously point their guns at the prisoners. The young men hear the noise of 10 guns being simultaneously loaded.

A pause follows. The Unter-officer looks at the camp commandant, but he seems not to be in a hurry to order shooting. He's obviously enjoying the process; he says to the officers standing next to him:

The commandant: I think we must take our time; I want them to feel the intensity of expectation, those who are to be executed as well as those whose turn may come tomorrow.

He has hardly finished these words that he hears someone singing. The commandant looks in the direction of the place from where the voice is coming. We follow him and see Thoma; he has his head cast backward as if looking up into the sky blindfolded and sings with a very sorrowful but extremely beautiful voice. He sings Voisa, alone, slowly, far more slowly than the song requires. He seems to have run away from the reality and be walking his homeland all alone, far away from this place, singing solo in the face of multiple problems he is supposed to be solving on his own. He sings solo for quite a long time. The others seem to find it hard to decide on joining him. Then suddenly, we see Ushba leaving his place in the row, moving to the place where Thoma is standing, slowly making his way through the other young men standing there by touching them with his shoulders as he walks blindfolded. He finds Thoma, stands by him, smiles a very strange smile and lets out a very brave bass from within his lungs. Gigi is standing next to Thoma and as they sing one verse of the song to the end and move to the other he joins in with his higher.

We see Beso's face with his lips pressed together very tight. Tears can be seen running down his face from the black blindfold. He is standing still, listening to his friends and when Thoma finishes the verse, he starts with a very strong voice. Tears don't stop running down his face. He is singing and crying simultaneously. Batsi joins him with his higher and Jango with his bass. Their singing gradually gains strength, is mainstreamed and reaches the heights of perfection.

The voices full of despair and sorrow disappear and we see 6 young men blindfolded, standing with their hands tied behind their backs and singing farewell to this ungrateful world.

We see the faces of German militaries and then the faces of the prisoners. Sturmbannführer with the military men accompanying him, the doctor, the Unter-officer, and the soldiers standing with their guns pointed at the prisoners, all the people gathered there without exception are listening to the Georgian prisoners and we can judge through their faces how they appreciate what they hear and how they are moved.

The Georgians' ecstasy is gradually transformed into bliss. They seem to be in the grip of the demon of songs. They seem to have forgotten the death itself. They are no longer in the position to perceive reality. They go on singing and now they are singing the last part of the song.

Suddenly, a single shot can be heard, and the young men stop singing abruptly. Silence reigns for a while in the crowded yard. Nobody knows who shot the gun. All of them have only heard the shooting that stopped the song.

The young men come closer to one another standing with their shoulders touching those of another. The whole place is immersed in silence.

And suddenly and as unexpectedly as the shooting a minute ago, a single, rhythmic clap of hands can be heard. We see that the person applauding is Sturmbannführer, who smiles and claps his hands. First, the officers standing next to him join him and start applauding and, as if having received a signal, all the people standing in the yard, thousands of prisoners start shouting and yelling; the place resembles a stadium after a favorite team scoring a long-wished-for goal.

We see the young men as well. Now tears are rolling down from not only Beso's black blindfold, but all of them are also crying with tears. They are standing and trembling. Then we hear the ovation at the background and Jango's words pronounced in a half crying manner:

Jango: Thoma, can you tell me what's going on?

Thoma: I don't quite know what to say, Jango, I don't fully understand but I think my dad from the other world has just saved our lives.

***

It's evening. Two black cars stop at the entrance to the camp. A German officer – Ober-lieutenant - gets out of the first car. Two other men get out of the second car. One is wearing civil clothes and the other is dressed in a black Chokha with Officer's shoulder-straps. The one donned in Chokha is tall and well-built he is also wearing a not very high Papakha[68], a silver dagger and a belt around his waists. His Chokha is decorated by an order.

Soldiers standing at the boom barrier give them a military salute. We see them from a distance. The one dressed in Chokha asks something to solder and the solder points to the headquarters building. The three of them enter the yard and walk to the headquarters building.

Tobias Koch is sitting at his table in his room. The young men, who have escaped their death sentence, are sitting in front of the doctor. The doctor is working on psychological rehabilitation. There is a tray full of sandwiches and a half-empty bottle of cognac on the table.

There is a knock on the door. The doctor stands up, walks to the door and opens it. The three men, who entered the camp yard recently, are standing behind the door. The one who is not wearing a uniform (Mikhail Kedia) says:

Mikhail Kedia: We came to see the singers and we were told that we could find them here. May we come in?

---

[68] A wool hat worn by men throughout the Caucasus

Tobias Koch: (smiling) Come in, please.

The young men stand up and look at the men entering the doctor's room. Traces of the stress they experienced in the morning are still clearly visible on their faces. The same man addresses them in Georgian:

Mikhail Kedia: Good evening, Georgians!

Tears well up in Ushba's and Jango's eyes and the expression on their faces show their emotional struggle, when they hear him speaking Georgian. The man continues.

Mikhail Kedia: Let's Get Introduced! This is Mr. Givi Gabliani, a doctor, ober-lieutenant. This man in black Chokha is Mr. Shalva Maglakelidze, a genuine warrior a founder and a commander of Georgian Legion. Very soon he will be a Major General of the Wehrmacht. And I'm sure we'll celebrate this event together. As for me, I am Mikhail Kedia, from Zugdidi. And I am delighted to meet you. Come here, my boys, I want to give all of you a big hug. Your tears are so precious. Do you realize what you have done? The whole Germany is talking about you.

He comes closer to the young men and hugs them one by one. Givi Gabliani and Shalva Maglakelidze shake hands with each of them. Mikhail Kedia turns to the doctor.

Mikhail Kedia: (In German) Are we bothering you with our emotions? I apologize, we'll be leaving soon.

The doctor: I'm not bothered at all. On the contrary, I have just realized that I've been missing the Georgian language so long. I traveled to your country and spent about two months there ... that was 9 years ago.

Mikhail Kedia: Really? Then you won't be surprised at our noisy manner of meeting each other; especially on the occasion like this. (He switches from German to Georgian again and says) Have you heard about Friedrich-Werner Graf von der Schulenburg?! He served as the German ambassador to Moscow before the war. On the morning of June 22, it was he who told Molotov that Germany had declared war on the Soviet Union. He called me and told me about your song. He had been informed about it by Erich Engelhaup - the head of SS Department of Caucasus, who in his turn had received a phone call from SS Chief Himmler's deputy - Obergruppenführer Krueger - the person who had been informed by the camp commandant. Can you see what's going on?! What have you done?! What your song has done?! I immediately told Givi and Shalva about you and the three of us hurried here to see you.

You were lucky as the camp commandant's lecturer of the theory of music, when he studied at Berlin University before the war, was Professor Pere, who provided his students with the opportunity to listen to some Georgian songs he had recorded during the first war; the records of the songs sung by Georgian prisoners of war. He says he was amazed when he listened to you. He even applauded you, didn't he? I wonder what you sang. But we'll have time to discuss this. We'll leave this place; we'll go together. It's over, guys; your nightmare is over. How did you do that? It's incredible. Even now I find it hard to believe. A man, who is about to be shot, starts singing... unimaginable.

Tears well up in his eyes; he walks up and down in front of the young men, looks into their faces and see his own face and tears running down his cheeks. Givi and Shalva are looking at him and smile. Mickael Kedia swallows his tears and continues:

Michael Kedia: I say, no one of you will ever be made to suffer anymore. It's over. You're going to start a new life today. We will live to return to a new independent Georgia.

After a short pause, he turns at his companions looking a bit humble and says:

Michael Kedia: Givi, Shalva, don't you want to say anything? I'm so excited that if you don't stop me, I'll go on speaking forever. Maybe you would like to add something...

Givi Gabliani: I have a lot to say and plenty of questions to ask, Mr. Kedia. As you say, whole Nazi Germany knows about these young men, but we don't even know their names.

The young men's faces lighten up a little and they take the turn to humbly tell them their names.

Jango: I'm Kakhaber Jangirashvili, from Telavi. The guys call me Jango.

Ushba: I'm Odishar Ratiani. I'm Svanetian. They say I'm tall and that's why they call me Ushba.

Batsi: I'm Batsi Zeragia, from Tbilisi.

Thoma: Thoma Darchia, from Guria.

Beso: Besarion Togonadze, Beso, I'm from Racha.

Gigi : Gigi Demetrashvili, from Imereti.

Thoma: There were seven of us when we were brought here. Dachi Duduchava was shot yesterday...

There is silence for a while. Nobody can speak. Then Michael Kedia speaks again:

Michael Kedia: We know that. The camp commandant told us; he says he's sorry and that he was almost sure that he was a Jew. As if a Jew is not God's creation. Well, let's decide what we're going to do next. Shalva and I will go to that very commandant as we must sign some documents; you may say good-bye to the doctor and go outside and wait for us in the cars. We'll soon come there too.

Shalva Maglakelidze and Michael Kedia walk out of the room. Thoma and his friends turn to the doctor:

Thoma: We'll go now, Doctor. Thank you so much for everything... for listening to and talking with me last night and for the way you treated us today. It was nice to know you.

The young men all bow their heads to the doctor and are about to leave the room when the doctor starts talking and all of them stop and listen to him:

The doctor: I would like you to know that I'll never forget what you have done. I would also like you to know that last night when your friend (He points to Thoma) left this room, I couldn't go to sleep for a long time, I prayed; I implored God to save your lives. My prayers were heard, and I am happy! Farewell! I'll always remember you.

The young men bow their heads once again and walk out of the doctor's room one by one.

***

Two black cars are driving along a road in WW II[69] period Germany. They approach us and pass by. We see that the driver in the first car is Michael Kedia and the second car is driven by Givi Gabliani.

We are in the car driven by Givi Gabliani. Givi adjusts the cabin's rear-view mirror so that he can see the young men sitting in the back of the car. Kakhaber Jangirashvili is sitting next to the driver. Gigi, Beso, and Ushba are sitting in the back of the car. Givi looks at Ushba through the rear-view mirror and says:

Givi Gabliani: Your surname is Ratiani, isn't it? You should be from Ushguli…

Ushba: That's right. I'm from Ushguli…

Givi Gabliani: Now I understand why you look like a Svanetian tower. (Givi smiles).

Ushba: I don't know. They call me Ushba, as I have told you.

Givi Gabliani: A good nickname. Shall I as well call you Ushba?

---

[69] World War II, also known as the Second World War, was a global war that lasted from 1939 to 1945. The vast majority of the world's countries—including all the great powers—eventually formed two opposing military alliances: the Allies and the Axis

Ushba: Of course. No problem.

Givi Gabliani: Was it your idea to run away using haystacks? The commandant said he was furious because of that very intrepid escape. So, who was the initiator? Was it you?

Ushba: No not me. That was Thoma's idea.

Givi Gabliani: Would you remind me which one of you is Thoma?

Ushba: He is sitting in the car driving ahead of us... Thoma and Batsi.

Givi Gabliani: This was quite something! How did he think of it?

***

Shalva Maglakelidze is sitting next to Michael Kedia in the cabin of the second car. Thoma, and Batsi are sitting in the back of the car.

Michael Kedia: We are now driving to a small town. Luckenwalde. The main camp for our countrymen rescued from concentration camps is in Luckenwalde. We have a few more camps as well. There are so many people, that it is impossible to accommodate all of them in a single camp. We have saved the lives of over 30 thousand people. They would have died of hunger and cold if we hadn't come to their rescue. You might not know about the fact that 250 thousand Caucasians were taken captive in the first year of the war and the majority of them were Georgians. Winter began and 70% of these 250 thousand died from cold. It's a horrible statistic. I know I shouldn't mention this word when I speak about people's lives, but I got used to it here in Europe. Germans treat the prisoners taken from the Russian front with cruelty; and it's not surprising, because Stalin refused to take care of his people when he officially declared: "There are no Soviet prisoners of war, only traitors." This unscrupulous man condemned millions of people to death with this single statement. Almost 5 million militaries surrendered to Germans soon after the war broke out. So, as I've just told you, most of them died during the winter. Now the situation has changed a little. General Vlasov's Army has saved a lot of Russians. Vlasov is going to make a triumphant entry into Moscow with his army. May God be with him, but what can we Georgians get from it? Vlasov's view of Georgia does not differ from that of any other Russian. He as well is obsessed with imperial bigotry. For us – Georgians - it doesn't make any difference who is a top dog Vlasov or Stalin. The latter can at least speak Georgian. Have you heard "better the devil you know than the one you don't"? That's the case with us… So, we – Georgians - have to walk our own road like Shalva and I do.

***

We return to Givi Gabliani's car.

Givi Gabliani: You must be sleepy, guys. If so, you may go to sleep, don't pay attention to me.

Beso: We didn't get a wink of sleep last night, though I don't feel sleepy... that's probably because of exhaustion... I have experienced it before, but nothing can compare with what we went through last night... It was the most terrible night of all.

Givi Gabliani: I guess... especially if the exhaustion has emotional grounds. The human nervous system is totally out of order currently. As a doctor, I can assure you that what you have experienced is worse than death. That's something I wouldn't wish on my worst enemy... But don't worry; everything is going to be all right. What matters is that we found you alive. We'll arrive at the camp and in a week's time, you'll forget about that hell. A young organism doesn't take long to restore the original state and regain vitality. By the way, Germans are reputed to be a musical nation. They love music and that was what saved your lives. Did commandant really applaud you?

Ushba: He did! We all were blindfolded and couldn't see anything, but we heard a single man clapping his hands and we guessed it was him.

Gigi: You should have seen what happened next! The whole camp was shouting and yelling; they met our song with ovation. We were standing there blindfolded and crying; we didn't know that they were no longer going to shoot us... eh, only Dachi is not among us... I wish he had taken off those goddamned trousers. He would have been here with us now. They had thought he was a Jew. In the end, they discovered they were wrong, but Dachi had died before that...

Givi Gabliani: I wish we had come earlier to find him alive. We would have saved his life, even if had been a Jew. Michael Kedia, the person who drives the other car is an expert in this area. He has already saved the lives of thousands of Jews. He doesn't talk about this; he thinks it's his obligation. But I can tell you about him and about Shalva Maglakelidze ... I would like you, guys, to know that both are great figures. One of them saved the lives of tens of thousands of Georgians and Caucasians, in all, and the other saved the lives of additional thousands of Georgian Jews. If it were down to my discretion, I would build monuments to commemorate them both in their lifetime.

***

We return to the first car to see Shalva Maglakelidze's face. He seems to be immersed in thoughts. Michael Kedia is speaking again.

Michael Kedia: I would like you to know that Michael Kedia has never been a person obsessed with illusions. I could see your faces in the mirror when I mentioned the name of Stalin and I noticed you got a bit strained, especially the guy sitting on the left. Batsi is your name if I'm not mistaken.

Batsi: You're right, I am Batsi.

Michael Kedia: I understand well, that stereotypic thinking is resistant to change in general, especially for persons born and brought up in the Soviet reality strongly impregnated with Communist doctrines; I would like you to know that this is not our goal at this stage. What matters is your life and Shalva's and my goal at this stage was to save your lives, your lives and the lives of thousands of others like you. And we are successful in achieving our goal. You'll gradually learn through your own experience that Communist Russia is our enemy. Then it's up to you to decide which side of the barricades you would like to stand on. Until then we must show ostentatious support to Nazis. And that should be done for the sake of your own lives and not for the sake of Shalva Maglakelidze or Michael Kedia. We must outlive this damn war. Our homeland, whether independent or, God forbid, in the grip of the Communist regime, needs you… It needs you to be sound and safe. And this is the primary goal and a case where, to quote Machiavelli, the end justifies the means. To tell you the truth, this is politics, guys. You can't call a politician a person who alienates himself from a given reality. You're a Nazi! You are an aggressor! So, I do not want to talk to you… teasing Germans and giving them the silent treatment?! This approach is not clear to me. Politics doesn't bear the silent treatment! On the contrary, you should spare no effort to talk with aggressors and oppressors to mitigate that very aggression and violence if you're unable to completely avoid it. An aggressor is an aggressor and whether you talk with him or not, they'll go on doing things the way they think they should be done, isn't it so?! You must manage, or at least to try to fish in troubled waters. You should forget about hatred, you should draw near, and, by any means, by offering something, by begging or beseeching or by even imploring their mercy try to get some goodness. The only thing you shouldn't compromise is your dignity. A man devoid of dignity is abhorred even by his enemies. Many in the Georgian diaspora mistrust us – Shalva and me. They say we shouldn't cooperate with the Nazis that this equals to high treason. But when you see 170 thousand out of 250 thousand of Caucasian prisoners dying from hunger and cold, what are we supposed to be doing? Give the Nazis the silence treatment or try to save the lives of those who are so badly in need of our help? Tell me in which case we will be true to ourselves, when we give the Nazis the silence treatment and condemn them explicitly and implicitly or when we wheedle them in saving the lives of some? Nothing is easier than to condemn others or stop speaking to them. You don't need to be wise or prudent to behave so, all you need is to unleash your tongue and speak whatever comes to your mind. Just look at Shalva, he practically says nothing, but he has saved the lives of tens of thousands of young Georgians. This is what matters. Let them call you whatever they want, that's something you can endure. What I hate most of all in this world is lying, but when I felt I needed it I kept on telling lies to Nazis. I think Heavenly Father will forgive me because not hundreds but thousands of lives depend on each of these lies. That's why we are on guard 24 hours a day... Shalva and I and Givi, who is driving behind us now. There are some others as well who think just like us. Germans will put an end to Stalin's regime without our help, but what then?! Will they give us independent Georgia as a present?! We must fight for our homeland. We are preparing the youth for this. Have you heard a famous saying, "the enemy of my enemy is my friend?" This is just the case with us. By the way, when they accuse us – Shalva and me and others - of cooperating with Nazis, aren't America and England doing just the same? They are acting exactly according to this formula - the enemy of my enemy is my friend. That's why they support Stalin's regime. Neither of them cares about the USSR, but they formed an alliance with the USSR against the Nazis. The USA and Great Britain behave just like Shalva and I do, but their behavior is branded as politics and ours as treason.

Michael Kedia looks at the young men in the back of the car through the rear-view mirror to see them fallen into a deep sleep, smiles and says to Shalva in a very low voice:

Michael Kedia: It appears I was speaking to myself; they are asleep - both.

Shalva Maglakelidze looks back, smiles and says:

Shalva Maglakelidze: No, not to yourself, I have been listening to you…

***

All the passengers in the cabin of the second car are awake. Givi Gabliani is speaking again.

Givi Gabliani: I guess what you mean, Ushba. There's nothing offensive about it. So, you ask why I - a man from Svanetia – am wearing German military uniform; because I was taken captive just like you. When the war began, there was such a panic and disorder around; nobody knew where to go and what to do. I am a doctor and I was not directly involved in this war. When I was captured what helped me to stay alive was my profession. I speak German and soon I found a job as a surgeon at a hospital. Then I got in touch with Georgian emigrants, honorable people: Kalistrate Salia, Mikhako Tsereteli, Victor Nozadze, Grigol Robakidze… They are all great people committed to their homeland and they can't go a day without thinking about it. As for Michael Kedia and Shalva Maglakelidze, I have already told you about them. I was taken captive and they fled the Communist regime. I've told you before, that if it were down to my discretion, I would build monuments to commemorate them both in their lifetime. I am sure that someday the time will come when their contribution will be recognized and rewarded. Do you remember I mentioned Georgian Jews? Let me tell you what Michael Kedia planned to save their lives. He managed to make the Nazis believe that Georgian Jews are simply Mosaic confessors, and specimens of Georgian "race" - pure-blooded Georgians, that is Aryans, and made them pass a special law on Georgian Jews. Then he got in touch with Joseph Eligulashvili, the president of the Community of Mosaic Georgians in France, together with him he compiled a list of the household members of the community and the Occupation Authorities in France put on it their seal of approval that these families wouldn't be subjected to any measures administered against the Jewish community. Nowadays, every department of the Gestapo in France is provided with a copy of this list and if it happens so that a Georgian Jew is arrested, all of them know their own family numbers on this list, they tell them and are immediately released. The scheme was initiated and carried out by Michael Kedia, owing to which he saved the lives of the members of 100 families. When other communities of Jews learned about this they found Michael Kedia and asked him to help them as well. So, he compiled a new list of Persian and Turkestan Jews so-called Juguti and claimed that they were Georgian Jews and saved the lives of the members of 99 more families, risking his own life. Doesn't it sound incredible? A single person managed to do all these. Owing to his charm he made a lot of friends among Germans, not among bigoted Nazis but honorable Germans like Friedrich-Werner Graf von der Schulenburg, the person who called us to inform about you. Professor Gerhard von Mendez – the head of the political department at the Reich Ministry for the Occupied Eastern Territory; Professor von Oberländer – an expert on Russia; Professor Raupach etc. Thanks to the support provided by these people Michael Kedia and Shalva Maglakelidze are able to do the greatest job. Both of them are great. Only Michael is always anxious, unlike Shalva.

***

We see the faces of Michael Kedia and Shalva Maglakelidze in the cabin of the first car. They are both silent looking at the road in a strained manner. It's getting dark but roadside houses and neat yards are still clearly visible. Thoma and Batsi are fast asleep again.

We look at Thoma's face for a while. Then we take a look at the road and we see a church silhouette from a distance. Soon the car passes by the house and yard, which have previously seen and where a long time ago Thoma took his first steps. Then we enter the churchyard to see Thoma's mother's grave with some withered flowers on it. Then we return in the car again to see Thoma fast asleep sitting in the back of the car.

***

Givi Gabliani: It's getting dark, but we are already near… I remember a puzzle from my student years at Tbilisi Medical Institute. Presume you were given a task to build a house having all the windows with a view to the South, what would you do? Where and how would you build it?

Beso: All the windows with a view to the South? I should ask my dad if I ever return to Racha. My dad is a builder.

Gigi: Is that possible at all?

Givi Gabliani: It is, but only theoretically possible. You should build the house on the North Pole and you'll certainly have all the windows with a view of the South. But let me tell you why I recalled this puzzle: Michael Kedia has been living in France since he was 21, but he has a view of Georgia not Paris from every single window of his house.

We see a fork in the road ahead with a road sign in German language indicating that Berlin is on the right. The cars take the left road.

***

A military camp of the Georgian Legion... It's evening. Some young men, naked waist up, are playing Lakhti[70] on the green grass. A lot of people are attending the game. Michael Kedia, Givi Gabliani, Shalva Maghlakelidze and a handsome man dressed in civilian clothes are sitting together on a long sawn log and are watching the game. Not far away some blood-horses grazing on grass can be seen.

Givi Gabliani: It's fun watching these guys playing Lakhti, but I'll go and check, the boys might have woken up.

Michael Kedia: It's high time. I calculated that they have been asleep for 18 consecutive hours now.

Givi Gabliani: That's the result of the stress they've been through. A strong stress sometimes causes a long sleep. But that's not a big problem, they'll be fine soon.

Givi Gabliani stands up and is about to leave. The man wearing civilian clothes (Datashka Kavsadze) stands up and says:

Datashka Kavsadze: Shall I go with you? I can't wait to see them. And I want to know which song they sang. I might not know that song...

Givi Gabliani: Is there a song that you might not know?

---

[70] a traditional Georgian sport game

Datashka Kavsadze: Who knows... There are so many songs people sing in Georgia; life is too short to learn all of them.

***

A simple room. The young men are lying in the beds. Some of them are sleeping, some are waking up and stretching themselves; Thoma is awake, sitting up in the bed and looking through the window. There is a knock on the door. Thoma turns his face to the door and says:

Thoma: Come in, please.

The door opens and Givi Gabliani enters the room smiling. He is accompanied by Datashka Kavsadze. Gigi jumps out of his bed dressed only in his pants; he looks to be very happy, cries –"Teacher", runs towards him and gives him a hug, then almost immediately steps back and as he realizes that Datashka Kavsadze can't recognize him, he looks in the direction where young men are lying in their beds to find Thoma who is the only person sitting up and says with an excited voice and expression:

Gigi: Thoma, this man is my teacher; he's Datashka Kavsadze. He used to teach me singing when I lived in Tkibuli[71].

Datashka Kavsadze: Let me have a look at you... You must be Gigi, Gigi Demetrashvili...

---

[71] A town in west-central Georgia

Gigi: So, you remember me, don't you? Teacher… I'm Gigi! Why are you here?… Is that because of the war?

Datashka Kavsadze: The war, Gigi, this damn war! I and my brother Gigusha, do you remember him? We both fought in the Crimea, Gigusha died there, I was captured by Germans. Givi brought me out of the camp. We've been here since then. We are now looking for young men among the Georgian Legion to form a male voice choir; the initiative to establish the choir belongs to Mr. Michael kediasa and Shalva Maghlakelidze. So, the six of you happen to be in the right place at the right time. Aren't you going to introduce your friends to me?

Gigi: With great pleasure; this is Thoma, our chief, he taught us the song that saved our lives. I'll introduce the rest of them to you when they wake up.

Givi Gabliani: Datashka, let's go and wait for them outside. Let them get up and get ready… We'll be waiting for you outside, guys; get ready and let's have supper together. You've been sleeping for 16 long hours. I already started to miss you.

Givi Gabliani smiles and both men leave the room. The young men seem to be reluctant to get up but they still get up. All of them are a bit disorganized due to the dramatic change in the situation.

***

A mess hall … Dinner is over. Shalva Maghlakelidze, Givi Gabliani, Datashka Kavsadze, and the young men are sitting at the end of a long dinner table and are talking. Michael Kedia comes in the mess hall; we see him walking at his usual quick and energetic pace; he comes to the table and says:

Michael Kedia: That's all, congratulations to all! All the concentration camps commandants throughout Europe have already been warned; they are waiting for us. We have to collect all the Georgians from the camps. They expressed a light objection first, saying we were collecting too many people for a single choir, but I said that all of them would need intensive rehabilitation and that they should be recovered prior to their auditions. I managed to persuade them that it can't be done right on-site. We have to start tomorrow. Givi, you'll be there as an officer and the one who can speak good German; Datashka, you'll be there as a coryphaeus. I would recommend you take Thoma with you, if he wants to go and unless he's very tired. He speaks German and will be of great help to you. Would you like to go with them, Thoma?

Thoma: I'll do as you say. But I don't quite understand what I'm supposed to be doing there.

Michael Kedia: Ok, let me explain it to you. The three of you will have to visit concentration camps, one by one. The prisoners of war will be arranged in groups at each of these camps. Then you have to march in front of each group of prisoners and say in Georgian for all of them to hear: those who understand our language take a step forward. Datashka's going to say that. So, you can take with you all of them who understand our command and takes a step forward. It doesn't matter who they are or where they are from Georgians, Armenians, Kurds, Hebrews or even Russians; if they understand your command you'll take them with you. We have to save the lives of as many of them as possible. The point is that we have to help them out of that hell, then we'll help some of them, others will find their own ways. What do you think, Thoma? Will you go there?

Thoma: Certainly, I will, Mr. Kedia.

Michael Kedia: Very well. Shalva, what's there in the bottle? Is that the one I love? Why are you smiling? Pour me a glass, my throat got dry after talking so much and I'm sure it'll help.

***

Several similar scenes of visiting prisoners of war camps: the name of the camp; the camp yard and prisoners arranged in groups in the yard: miserable prisoners of war - skinny, looking like living skeletons with blank, distant, emotionless eyes.

Givi Gabliani dressed in the uniform of ober-lieutenant, Datashka Kavsadze, Thoma and one or two German officers – representatives of the local administration march in front of each group of prisoners. Datashka Kavsadze addresses each group saying in Georgian:

Datashka Kavsadze: Those who understand the language I speak take a step forward!

Dozens of prisoners step forward not from all the groups of them but from every single camp. Givi Gabliani interviews them one by one, asking them their names and where they are from. Not all of the prisoners that step forward are Georgians, Armenians, Azeris, Ossetians, Kurds, Assyrians, Kists[72], Greeks and others are among them. They are all taken out of the camps notwithstanding their different nationalities.

---

[72] Different ethnic Groups

Two most memorable episodes:

Episode I: During the visit to a POW camp. Datashka Kavsadze, standing in front of a group of prisoners says in Georgian:

Datashka Kavsadze: Those who understand the language I speak take a step forward!

A prisoner of Slavic appearance steps forward. Afterward during the interview, he doesn't answer the questions asked by Givi Gabliani. Givi asks the same question twice but the prisoner doesn't answer. He is standing with his eyes cast down and looks very nervous, drops of sweat can be seen running down his face. Thoma looks at him attentively and says to him:

Thoma: Listen, I've got the impression that you understand everything we say but you can't speak Georgian; is it so? If it's the case, simply nod your head, don't be nervous.

The prisoner raises his eyes to look at Thoma; his face expresses supplication; he nods his head. Givi Gabliani asks him in, Russian:

Givi Gabliani: Calm down. You may answer in Russian. Who are you and where are you from?

The prisoner: I am Major Shiriaev. I served in Tbilisi for 6 years before the war. It's my fault, I failed to learn to speak the Georgian language, but ... I beg you ... Do not leave me here...

We can tell from Datashka's and Thoma's faces that they feel sorry for the man, but they wait for Givi Gabliani to comment on the prisoner's words. Givi Gabliany tries to comfort him.

Givi Gabliani: I've already told you, there is nothing to be so nervous about. Calm down, everything's going to be all right! Don't you want to smoke a cigarette? Here you are… wait I'll help you to light it up…

Givi Gabliani holds out a pack of cigarettes. The prisoner first stares at the pack greedily; then he takes two cigarettes with his trembling hands and puts them whole into his mouth. The three Georgians and a German officer are looking at him in amazement as he chews the cigarettes in frenzy and finally swallows them. Givi Gabliani, still holding the match ready to light up his cigarette in his hands, says:

Givi Gabliani: Let's take him with us. Though I think he's going to die soon, unfortunately. He's going to have some spasms soon. Let's see ...

Episode II:

After Datashka Kavsadze's address to a group of prisoners at one of the concentration camps, three prisoners step forward. Givi Gabliani interviews them in turn; he asks one of them:

Givi Gabliani: Tell us what your family name is and where you are from.

Prisoner I: I am from Didi Jikhaishi, Amiran Nozadze.

Datashka Kavsadze: Can you sing, Amiran?

Prisoner I: Sing? I can when I am sitting at the laid table and if I am a little drunk... if you can call it singing.

Datashka Kavsadze: Ok, we'll see...

Givi Gabliani: (addresses the second prisoner) And you? What's your name?

Prisoner II: I'm Givi Gamrekeli from Tbilisi.

Givi Gabliani: You're my namesake. I suppose you can sing.

Prisoner II: No, unfortunately, I can't. I have never tried... I can't tell you a lie.

Givi Gabliani: That's Ok, don't worry about it. (He turns to the third prisoner who looks really worried) What can you say about yourself?

The prisoner startles and says:

Prisoner III: Me?

Givi Gabliani: (smiling) No one else is left here besides you.

Prisoner III: I... I can sing...

Givi Gabliani smiles again. Datashka Kavsadze and Thoma smile too. Only the German officer stands there without reaction.

Givi Gabliani: That's good that you can sing, but have you forgotten your name or what?

Suddenly the prisoner's facial expression changes, wrinkles appear on his face and his eyes well up with tears, but he tries his best not to cry and says with his eyes cast down:

Prisoner III: The fourth man is German, isn't he?

Givi Gabliani: He is, but what's the problem?

Prisoner III: The problem is that... But please, don't tell him. You'll understand what I mean, but don't tell him I implore you… I'm Abraham Krikheli from Sukhumi.

Givi Gabliani: Aha! Now I understand. You don't have to be ashamed of your name. You must be proud of it. Don't be afraid, brother, we'll take you out of here and everything will be all right. Georgians and Jews are brothers, it has been the case for so long and it's going to continue forever.

On hearing these words Abraham is no longer able to hold back the tears and he starts crying. Thoma goes close to him, puts his arm around his shoulders and tries to comfort him.

***

The same military camp of the Georgian Legion in Luckenwalde. It is winter, and it is snowing. From a distance, we hear someone singing: ზამთარიოოო...[73] We follow the beautiful voice and enter into a mess hall. Young men are sitting at the empty wooden tables there and are singing. The only person standing is Datashka Kavsadze. He is listening to the soloists with his eyes closed. One of the soloists is Jango, the other the Jew from Sukhumi – Abraham Krakheli. They sing beautifully. Thoma, Batsi, Beso, Gigi, and Ushba are all sitting as a group and singing bass. Datashka Kavsadze stops the soloists and says to Abraham:

Datashka Kavsadze: Listen, Abraham. Wouldn't it be better if this part was sung this way?

Datashka Kavsadze starts singing: ზამთარი ვარდსა დააჭკნობს, ფურცელიიი ჩამოსცვივაო...[74] Then he stops and repeats the last tune a couple of times - ფურცელიიი ჩამოსცვივაო...[75]

Datashka Kavsadze: Do you understand?

Abraham Krakheli: Yes, I do. Shall I try it now?

Datashka Kavsadze: No, wait, I have to tell the guys something.

Datashka Kavsadze turns to Thoma and says:

---

[73] A traditional Georgian feast song "Zamtari" ("Winter"), which is about the transient nature of life and is sung to commemorate ancestors.

[74] Roses wither in winter, their petals fall on the ground

[75] their petals fall on the ground

Datashka Kavsadze: Thoma, haven't I told you and your friends to stop singing bass? You have to practice the song that you have to sing...

The door opens and Michael Kedia enters the mess hall. The young men stand up to greet him.

Michael Kedia: Don't... don't stand up, please, I've asked you not to do this. I had some good news for you and now I changed my mind I won't tell it to you.

The young men smile and sit down. Michael Kedia walks closer to Datashka Kavsadze and says:

Michael Kedia: I have two pieces of good news for you, Datashka, and for the guys. The first is that Joseph Eligulashvili, the president of the Community of Mosaic Georgians in France called me and told me that the Chokhas for our young men were ready and if we could send someone to take them... The second piece of good news is that we don't need to bring those Chokhas here, we have to travel to where the Chokhas are, as my friend Field Marshal General Gerd von Rundstedt, who oversees German forces in the West, personally invited us to organize a concert in Paris; so we have to travel to Paris. The concert is to be held on 26th of May - Independence Day of Georgia.

On hearing the news the young men leave their places and we hear their whoops of joy. We see Michael Kedia's happy face brightened up with a smile of happiness.

***

Paris during World War II… It's spring… 26th of May. We see the sights of occupied Paris and hear the music of that time. After a while we have a close look at a large announcement banner hanging from the roof of one of the buildings, which shows a picture of a choir of men all dressed in Georgian national clothes with a relevant caption and on the foreground, we see the photo of the coryphaeus – Datashka Kavsadze dressed in a black Chokha.

We enter the hall, and everything around indicates that the place is being prepared to host a concert. Some personnel is sweeping carpet flooring of hall aisles; others are cleaning seats; something is being hung up on the stage, but we can't see what it is; some stands are being brought from the wings and are being installed; in the foyer a barman behind the bar is busy cleaning the glasses. There are oval staircases on both sides of the foyer leading to the upper balcony. A large Nazi flag with a swastika symbol is hanging from the balcony. Similar but smaller flags can be seen here and there.

We walk to the backstage. The young men are gathered in a large room. All seem to be anxious. We see some Chochas hanging from a long horizontal bar.

Datashka Kavsadze: Michael Kedia says the occupation authorities are coming in full strength. Needless to say, all of the Georgian emigrants will be here. Michael also said that too many people wanted to come and see you, Noe Jordania in the first place, but he said he had managed to convince everybody that it wasn't a good idea to bother you before the concert. Eligulashvili and Georgian Jews have booked upper seats. They are coming together with their families... In short, the concert has gained great publicity and it's natural that there is a high interest in it. I can't tell you that you don't have to be nervous, as you see that this is how I feel myself right now. (He smiles and continues) But believe me the stress will disappear as soon as we start singing. Now go and get dressed! May God bless you!

Datashka Kavsadze crosses the young men. The young men reply to his last phrase: Amen! Amen! Amen! They stand up and take the Chokhas to get dressed.

Datashka Kavsadze: I'll leave you now. I'll go to my room to get ready. Wish you luck.

Datashka Kavsadze leaves the room. We are in the hall again. We see the curtains were closed and several men who were busy preparing the stage are no longer seen. People start gathering in the foyer. All are dressed festively, and high-ranking military men are accompanied by charming ladies in evening dresses. Some girls wearing uniforms and holding trays in their hands are serving drinks to guests.

Some families of the Georgian Jews are coming into the hall. They stand out by their modest behavior and unlike others, are obviously more reserved and they hurry to their seats upstairs on the balcony as soon as they enter the hall. We have a close look at one of them (Pinas Beberashvili): a middle-aged man holding a 5 or 6-year-old boy's hand, he's going upstairs and simultaneously watching people coming through the entrance door. He seems to be waiting for someone's arrival. People around him greet him, and he responds but he doesn't take his eyes off the entrance. Then we see from his facial expression that the person he was waiting for enters the hall. He hurries downstairs together with the child. We follow him to see Michael Kedia with a pleasant-looking woman and a man. The man with the child approaches them, stops at a proper distance and addresses the man accompanying Michael Kedia:

Pinas Beberashvili: Joseph, could I have a word with you?

Joseph: O, Pinas! It's so nice to see you here! (He turns to Michael Kedia) I have to leave you for a brief moment, Mr. Kedia.

Joseph smiles and takes some steps to greet Pinas Beberashvili. After a friendly handshake, they start talking about something and soon we see Joseph, Pinas Beberashvili and the child walking to the place where Michael Kedia is standing.

Joseph: Mr. and Mrs. Kedia, let me introduce to you Mr. Pinas Beberashvili, An old friend of mine. He's come from Lyon together with his son to attend the concert and he has a strong desire to get acquainted with you.

Michael Kedia: No problem. I am delighted to meet you! My pleasure little gentleman! What's your name?

The boy casts his eyes down shyly and his father answers instead of him:

Pinas Beberashvili: Albert, his name is Albert; he's very shy. Mr. Kedia. My desire to attend the concert was great, but the desire to see you was even greater! I knew I would meet you here and I came here from Lyon to express my gratitude towards you; and I brought my son with me; He is still small, but I wanted him to see you with his own eyes and to remember your face, to physically touch the kindness you've done to my family. But for you, we most probably won't be alive.

Pinas Beberashvili is very excited; then he turns to his son and says in French:

Pinas Beberashvili: Look at this person, my son and try to remember him. This very person saved your father's life and your life. No matter where you are and how long it has passed since this day, you should always remember him. You should remember that we owe our lives to Georgians.

Michael Kedia seems a bit confused and answers in French:

Michael Kedia: You don't have to, my friend. Even if I managed to do something for you, that was my obligation and you don't have to thank me for that. Thank you so much for coming here from Lyon.

Pinas Beberashvili: Well, Mr. Kedia, I am not going to bother you (He switches to Georgian language) We'll go now. We, Georgian Jews are sitting on the upper balcony… Goodbye Joseph.

He makes several steps backward and says to himself:

Pinas Beberashvili: I wish this war would end soon and then I know what I'll do.

Michael Kedia, his wife Nino and Joseph enter a half-full pit parterre. Joseph stops at the entrance and says:

Joseph: I have to leave you, Mr. Kedia. I have to join my family upstairs.

Michael Kedia: Ok, Joseph, I'll be waiting for you after the concert.

Michael Kedia leads his wife to the front seats. Then he helps his wife to take her seat and says:

Michael Kedia: I have to go now Nino, I'll be back soon. I should see the guys. I think you'll be all right in my absence. Givi and Shalva will appear in a minute.

We see Givi Gabliani and Shalva Maglakelidze in the foyer. The former is wearing a full-dress uniform of ober-lieutenant; the latter is dressed in a black Chokha with officer's shoulder straps and is wearing papakha. Michael Kedia walks out of the pit parterre, catches a glimpse of them and raises his hand and calls:

Michael Kedia: Givi, Shalva! This way…

They meet each-other and Michael Kedia says:

Michael Kedia: I want to see the guys. Stay here; they might get even more nervous when they see all of us together. Nino is alone in the pit parterre… join her.

Shalva Maglakelidze: I wanted to see them before the concert, but let it be as you say. I'll see them after the concert and give each of them a big hug.

The young men are again in the dressing room but this time all of them are wearing Chokhas. Some of them are wearing white kabalakhis round their necks. Datashka Kavsadze is dressed in a black Chokha with a black akhalukhi[76] and black masrebi[77]; the outfit suits him a lot; he's tall and slim.

Michael Kedia enters the room.

Michael Kedia: What's up, guys? Are you ready to conquer Paris?

The young men answer: - Yes, we are! – Certainly; - We're ready.

Then Michael Kedia walks up to Datashka Kavsadze and says:

---

[76] a shirt worn underneath the Chokha - a garment of the Chokha outfit

[77] the bullets put into breast pockets - a garment of the Chokha outfit

Michael Kedia: Datashka, this is the most special day for me and I have no doubt for you too. Not only because it's May 26 the Independence Day of Georgia; unless Georgia is free again and until it is in the grip of the Russian Bolshevism, in principle, we have nothing to celebrate. I came here to tell you something entirely different. Our life is like an open sea, my sons; sometimes it's stormy and sometimes it's tranquil and peaceful; we are all struggling with and crashing heads on into its gigantic waves to reach a safe coast. I would like all of you to be aware of the fact that your song today is going to be one more step taken in the direction of this desired coast. Diplomats take years to accomplish what might be accomplished today by you with your songs - win the favor for the sake of our small country. I am confident that you will accomplish this mission with dignity and virtue and that's why I would like to express my gratitude towards you in advance, to applaud to you in advance and I would like you to know that I love you all very much!

Michael Kedia turns and hurries to leave the room.

***

The hall is practically full. Only a few people who are a bit late are looking for their seats. Michael Kedia takes the seat next to his wife. Shalva Maghlakelidze and Givi Gabliani are sitting next to them. The hall is full of representatives of Georgian Diaspora, French communities and, of course, the occupation authorities.

The Balcony has been occupied by Georgian Jews. The audience is buzzing with pleasant anticipation. At last the curtains open and on the background of a wild applaud we see a huge poster hanging from the catwalk over the stage; the poster shows a panoramic image of the Caucasus Mountains partially covered with a bright red panel; there is the image of an eagle with its wings spread holding a white circle in its claws with a black swastika inside. There is a caption in Russian on the poster: кавказ будет свободным![78]

In front of the poster a choir made up entirely of the Georgian prisoners dressed in black Chokhas is standing. Datashka Kavsadze appears on the stage; applauds become stronger. He bows deeply to the audience, turns around and sings a tune for the choir of the young men; then he waves his hand in the dead silence and the powerful resounding polyphony of a Georgian song immediately fills the hall. The concert has started but we can't see Thoma, Ushba, Jango, Beso, Gogi or Batsi on the stage.

---

[78] The Caucasus will be free!

The concert is proceeding normally: a song after a song, a soloist taking the stage after a soloist. We alternately have a look at the stage and at the audience; we see the faces of the people attending the concert, of the Georgian Jews sitting on the balcony. Then we hear and see the choir singing the song they have been rehearsing - "Winter"; but this time Abraham Krikheli's strong voice is accompanied by Datashka Kavsadze's voice instead of Jango's. This song ends, and a pleasant-looking woman appears on the stage. She is smiling and addresses the audience in French:

The MC: Many of you in this hall might have heard the extraordinary story, which I have to tell you, a story about the six Georgians, who were sentenced to death for their attempt to escape from the Alps using incredible means. Early in the morning the six of them standing against the wall, blindfolded, with their hands tied behind their backs and waiting for their death sentence to be executed, all of a sudden, started singing a song. This very song saved their lives and now they will appear before you and perform this song.

A half of the audience, apparently a French part of it, applauds. Then the MC repeats the same in German and leaves the stage in the middle of enthusiastic applause. The choir standing on the stage leaves the stage as well. They divide in half and the groups head towards the wings in opposite directions.

The stage darkens. Then the poster hanging from above slowly goes up and we see the six young men in the limelight. An unseen audience groans at the sight of the scene because the young men are standing there exactly the way they stood awaiting execution before the firing squad. They are wearing the same clothes; their eyes blindfolded with black pieces of cloth and we can't see whether they have their hands tied but they are holding their hands behind their backs. They are in the limelight so that they make an impression of not standing on the floor but of hovering in the air.

Thoma starts singing solo. And everything we have seen before is being repeated but after the young men have sung a couple of verses a bit strange but the appropriate melody is intruding, which gradually becomes louder and finally covers the voices. On the background of the music we see the most dreadful scenes from the film:

The First World War! Gas! Blood-stained handkerchief! Theophile's face covered in blood! Nobles being executed! Blood flowing from the carriage! Oboladze's and Lazare's throats being cut! Train being bombed! The lieutenant's torn hand! Dachi's execution! Miserable prisoners of war! The Russian prisoner eating cigarettes! Abraham Krikheli crying, etc. From time to time we hear the young men singing the song. Their song resembles attempts of a drowning man fighting against the waves and trying to reach the surface. A dramatic climax follows, and everything stops all of a sudden; the stage darkens, and the screen goes blank.

***

In sharp contrast to the previous episode, we see a single storied white and blue house standing by a lake in the mountains. Peace and quiet reigns around. The only thing we hear is that of beautifully singing birds coming from afar. There are some sheets of paper on the white woven table in the yard. Michael Kedia and Thoma are sitting at the table in the woven armchairs.

A caption on the screen reads: Austria – 1945.

Michael Kedia looks weary. His appearance seems to have changed a lot for the last three years. He is sitting in the armchair looking somewhere in the distance. Then he starts speaking.

Michael Kedia: I'm so pleased you decided to come to see me before your departure. Though, I think you shouldn't be leaving. However, who knows... Datashka has already gone, He said he had done nothing wrong and didn't have to be afraid to return to his homeland. You are saying the same! It should be the way you say, according to all the rules and laws, I agree with you, but life is like a roulette wheel, Thoma, the ball may fall into the number you've placed your bet on or it may miss your number. Givi, Shalva, I, and multiple of others, even your friends were not fortunate, as you can see. Givi in going to move to America, Shalva has disappeared as well as your friends after being enlisted in the "Edelweiss" Elite Infantry Division and sent to the Caucasus. They disappeared somewhere on the outskirts of Georgia, we don't even know whether they died or are alive. So, let's see, maybe the ball hits the number you and Batsi have bet on. I hope to God! For me, it's all over. Look at me, I found shelter in my friend's cottage for a time being, until I move to Switzerland. I'm not allowed to enter the territory of France and the Red Cross managed to obtain a visa for Switzerland for me. I have no idea what I will be doing there. A hopeless emptiness is awaiting me...

What's left here for me is to live in my past. I've been through so much in my life that I can't attune myself to peace and quiet. Life makes sense only when you live for an idea; and when that idea dies you die with it. You may still exist, but this is the end of your life... It's even worse than death itself... you're alive and there is nothing that makes you feel alive. As for you, regardless of what you've been through, you're happy because you live for your idea... the idea of returning to your homeland.

Do you remember, Thoma, the words I told you in Paris, before the concert? That we're all in the stormy sea of our lives and we have to struggle to reach the desired coast. I've spent all my life striving to reach my destination, my desired coast... but in vein. Life loves playing tricks on us. It tricks us, then steps aside and sniggers.

God save you, Thoma, but not to go too far, isn't my example enough to prove that? I have literary saved more than 30 thousand Georgians and non-Georgians from the clutches of imminent death. Nevertheless, I am condemned and persecuted in my own homeland and denounced as an enemy of my own people. The Red Cross is granting me a visa for Switzerland for my contributions. The Swiss Government agrees to shelter me, but they warned me beforehand that they would put me under house arrest at Stalin's request...

My closest friend Werner Graf von der Schulenburg, a real medieval knight, was charged with high treason for an attempt on Hitler's life and hanged at Plötzensee Prison. And I am considered to be not a friend of his but a friend of Hitler's.

They've deprived me of the right to live in France with my family and I receive a two-page letter from the Association of Israelites in the same France expressing gratitude for saving the lives of Georgian Jews. You may even have a look at it, it's on the table, here you are... France's chief rabbi is sending me a separate letter of gratitude. I have forgotten his name.

Michael Kedia takes a sheet of paper in his hand, looks in it and reads:

Michael Kedia: Chief Rabbi of Paris Julius Weiss...

He puts the sheet of paperback on the table and continues looking very thoughtful and sad.

Michael Kedia: It's a good thing, Thoma that people recognize and appreciate worthy deeds done by others. It is a bit strange, but very often expressing appreciation is even more exciting than the deeds themselves that deserve it. Expressing gratitude is a laudable and virtuous feeling. There have been times when I had a desire to express my gratitude on behalf of my country to someone, but to whom, Thoma?! We, Georgians, have never ever been given an opportunity to express our gratitude, as all around us have always wished for invading our country. Some have been destroying it explicitly; some – implicitly, but their aim remained unchanged – to crack us.

But it should be mentioned that we appeared to be too tough to be cracked. So many times, we've been offended, attacked and destroyed but… we still exist. (Michael Kedia thinks for a while and then continues) As I see it, it's unlikely that we will ever be given an opportunity to express our gratitude to someone. There will always be the ones who will have an unquenchable thirst for cracking us… So, Thoma, if I were to write my own obituary, I would most probably find it difficult to properly summarize my own life. I would certainly write the truth about myself but no wonder some would suspect me of lying. That's the truth of life, Thoma, for some you are a hero and for some a villain. The most important point is that you mustn't ask yourself why it happens so, and what for… You have to avoid asking yourself that question, Thoma, as no one will ever be able to answer that question and if you think a lot about it, eventually you'll do what I intend to do…

Thoma: What do you intend to do. Mr. Kedia?

Michael Kedia: You'll learn it soon. (He stands up and says) Well, let me at least embrace you and say goodbye. You might be tired of listening to my long speech. Life really plays tricks on us otherwise we wouldn't be saying good-bye to each-other somewhere in the mountains of Austria... Not to mention my case, look, you are so young, not 25 yet and life has dragged you as if you were tied to the tail of a wild horse. It has shown to you not only trouble but death as well. When you were blindfolded and standing against the wall to be shot, you looked into the eyes of death, didn't you?... Come, let me give you a big hug...

Michael Kedia and Thoma embrace each-other.

***

Bosporus Strait... Constantinople... Hagia Sophia and the Blue Mosque... music mixed with Oriental tunes... a narrow street with retailers on both sides of it, selling various items. The place is crowded enough. People sitting and drinking coffee at small tables standing here and there in the streets ...

Thoma and Batsi are walking down the street. They are walking slowly looking around. We hear them talking.

Batsi: Thoma, when are you going to fulfill your promise? We are already in Istanbul...

Thoma: My promise?

Batsi: Yes, your promise. Aha, I knew you would forget... Didn't you say you would tell me why you wanted to return to Georgia via Turkey when we were in Istanbul? Look around we're already in Istanbul...

Thoma: I've told you, you would learn it without me telling you. But a promise is a promise! My brothers live here, Batsi, my elder brothers have been living here in Turkey for 13 years. They left Georgia 13 years ago.

Batsi: Really? But why did they leave Georgia?

Thoma: Because... they were made to; why else might they live here... I didn't mention this before. But now I've got nothing to hide from you. You are like my brother. You might not have heard of Oboladze.

Batsi: Wait, who do you mean? A famous Chekist who was murdered in Guria?

Thoma: Yes, I mean that Chekist. But actually, he was not a Chekist he was an executioner. He killed my dad for nothing. He liked our bulls and killed my dad. He could have taken them as if he couldn't. But his perfidy cost him his life. My brothers cut his throat in his own bed. Then they fled to Turkey and sent me to Tbilisi; since then I lived there, with a family of a Georgian Jew - Moshe Megrelishvili. You may even have heard of him; he was a well-known watch-maker. I can't wait to see him as well. First, I'll visit my mother in Guria and then I'll go to Tbilisi to visit Moshe. What's the matter with you, Batsi, why are you looking at me like this? According to the information I had long ago, they should be living in this street # 23, if they haven't moved... My heart feels like it is going to explode. I haven't seen them for 13 long years. What might they feel when they see me, I wonder...

Thoma and Batsi walk up to a small two-storied house. There is a number 23 written on the wall. Thoma breathing heavily goes close to the door and knocks on it lightly. He knocks once… twice. Two Turks are sitting nearby, playing backgammon. Both of them look at Thoma and one of them says something in Turkish.

Thoma: (answers in Georgian) I don't understand what you're saying. I don't speak Turkish.

The same man asks immediately: Gurji?[79]

Thoma: Gurji! Gurji!

At the end of the street a boy has a carpet spread on the pavement and is washing it with enthusiasm. The man playing backgammon looks in the direction where the boy is standing and cries something in Turkish. The boy straightens himself up, throws a long-handled brash he is holding on the carpet and walks towards Thoma with a smile on his face. The boy has blue eyes and blond hair. He has his trousers rolled up to his knees and is naked from the waist up.

When he comes close to Thoma and Batsi he asks:

The boy: Are you really from Gurjistan?[80]

Thoma: Yes, we are!

The boy stretches his wrist instead of his hand to Thoma and Batsi and shakes it with them saying:

---

[79] Georgian?

[80] Georgia

The boy: I'm Tornike!

Thoma: Are you Georgian, Tornike?

Tornike: I'm Laz! My mother taught me the Georgian language. Are you looking for anyone here?

Thoma: Yes, we are. I'm looking for my brothers. They must be living in this house.

Tornike: I see, you're looking for Gurji Manuchar and his brother Sisona, aren't you? They moved to Trabzon. As soon as the war started they left for Trabzon. If you want to see them, you have to go to Trabzon.

Thoma: We can go to Trabzon. Our route runs through it anyway. But Trabzon is not a village, how can I find them there? Does anyone know their address?

Tornike: You don't need their address. You have to go to the bazaar to the row where tobacco is sold and ask about Gurji Sisona, anyone can tell you how to find him. There are plenty of our countrymen there in Trabzon. Manuchar and Sisona had sold everything that had belonged to them here and bought some land near Trabzon; they grow tobacco in that land and sell it. Everyone there knows them.

Thoma: Thank you, Tornike. We have to go now.

Tornike: No, you can't go like this. Come to my house. Mom will be glad to see Gurjis. You can have a rest there; we can offer you some tea; Mom will make dinner for you. Stay the night with us and you can go to Trabzon early in the morning. Mom says God sends us guests... She'll be very happy.

Thoma: Thank you so much, Tornike, but I can't. I haven't seen my brothers for 13 years. I can't wait to meet them. Please, send our regards to your mother and tell her that Gurgis wish her all the best. We'll go now. And thank these men on our behalf.

Thoma points to the men playing backgammon. Thoma and Batsi turn around and walk up the street. Tornike and the men, who were playing backgammon, watch them walking away.

***

It is afternoon and it is very hot. Trabzon bazaar hums and buzzes as typical to an Oriental bazaar. We see Thoma and Batsi among the crowd. Just as he used to do in his childhood, Thoma stops, closes his eyes, inflates his nostrils and inhales air deeply and powerfully with his head slightly raised. Batsi looks at him performing this ritual and smiles. Then Thoma opens his eyes and turns his head to the side, where he can smell the sweet odor, saying:

Thoma: This way…

They come to an open place and see a long row of tobacco, with wooden counters piled high with finely-chopped tobacco leaves, whole dried leaves are hanging up at stalls.

Thoma and Batsi go close to a counter and ask something to a man behind the counter. We see from a distance that the man comes from behind the counter and points to a single-storied building standing nearby. Thoma and Batsi walk in the direction of the building. The building is a big store with something written in Turkish on the signboard outside.

Thoma enters the store. Batsi stays outside. Inside the store along the whole length of the back wall, there are white sacks with the trademarks of the same design. This serves as a background of a man sitting by the counter and looking down at something. We can't see his face yet, but he is well-built and seems to be strong.

On hearing someone entering the store he raises his head with a smile ready for a customer and stays still in this position for a while. Then he narrows his eyes and says in a very low voice:

Sisona: My God, is that you Thoma?

Thoma: Yes, Sisona, it's me… Thoma

Thoma answers in the same low voice and he seems unable to continue speaking because of tears that filled his eyes and he feels that he has a lump in his throat. Sisona jumps to his feet breaks himself through the counter and says this time in a loud voice:

Sisona: Brother!

Sisona embraces Thoma and holds him tight. Now Thoma hears his words near his ear.

Sisona: What have you done to us, Thoma! It's the luckiest day for Manuchar and me! He'll be on cloud nine… He keeps your name on his lips, day and night. Now, I'll close this store and we'll go home. Manuchar is at home… He'll be over the moon.

Sisona lets his brother go, turns to the counter, then back to Thoma, tries to say something, throws up his hand and goes to the counter. He seems to be so excited that he can't decide what to do. Thoma looks at him and smiles. Then Sisona says:

Sisona: Let me be first to go into the house. I'll tell Manuchar… He'll be surprised to see me there so early… so I'll tell him that someone has arrived from Georgia and wants to see him. He'll ask where that man is and you'll enter at that moment. I wonder whether he'll be able to recognize you… I'll close this shop now… Though, I can't wait… let's go now; I'll leave it open… No one will touch anything here… Even if they do, I don't care, it's all the same to me now as I have seen you again…

Thoma: Ok, Sisona, let's go, but I'm not alone. I'm here with my friend; he's waiting outside… You see, he's not just a friend but a very close friend, he's like my brother. We've been together for five years and God knows what we have been through together… I'll tell you everything later.

Sisona: You say a friend? What's the problem? You might as well bring here a hundred of them… Let's go out and you'll introduce him to me.

They leave the store together. Sisona closes the door behind him; then he walks close to Batsi and shakes hands with him. Sisona looks in his face for a while and then embraces him, saying:

Sisona: Thoma told me you were like brothers… Thoma's brother is my brother as well, isn't it so? What's your name?

Batsi: I'm Batsi, Batsi Zeragia. Thoma's right. We are like brothers. We've been together through thick and thin. So our relationship has definitely grown to resemble that of brothers'.

Then the three of them start walking and we hear their conversation:

Sisona: Manuchar and I heard that you were sent to Lithuania after graduating from the institute. Moshe let us know about this. We could somehow get in touch with him before the war started. But then the person, who used to provide us with information about the developments there in Georgia, was arrested and shot by Chekists. That's why we couldn't learn anything about you since you left for Lithuania. All our attempts to learn where you were or how you were doing were in vain. We have heard absolutely nothing about you for the last five years. So, Manuchar is going to be more than surprised when he sees you. You tell me that Batsi and you are like brothers; that's why I speak so openly, otherwise I wouldn't even have mention Moshe's name.

Thoma: Batsi already knows everything. He knows about Moshe and Oboladze as well. So, you don't have to be afraid of anything.

Sisona: Here we are. Look, that's Manuchar's house. He lives here together with his family. You'll see his sons soon. They are great guys. His elder son's name is Theophile. You'll soon meet at Theopile Darchia. He's so manly, just like his grandpa. Manuchar's married to a local woman. She used to be a Muslim, but she converted to Christianity because of her love for her husband.

Thoma: And what about you?

Sisona: I'm fine. If you're asking about my family life, I am not married yet. I'm single. Though I have my own house, Manuchar doesn't allow me to move there and live alone. He says he'll let me go only when I get married. Thus, I'm obliged to get married. We've come. So, as we agreed, you and Batsi are to stay here, I'll go in and tell him that someone wants to see him. Then I'll lead you in. I wonder whether he'll recognize you after all these years.

Sisona enters the house. Thoma and Batsi stay outside. Thoma says:

Thoma: Sisona hasn't changed at all. He is exactly the same he was 13 years ago. I remember when we were saying good-bye to one another… Manuchar, Sisona, and I… it was a late-night and we sang a song together. I remember it as if it were yesterday.

Thoma stops as he sees Sisona rushing through the door and calling them:

Sisona: Let's go in. Manuchar is waiting for us.

They enter the house; pass through a small hall to find themselves in a big bright room. Manuchar is standing and waiting for the guests to come in. He looks first at Batsi, then at Thoma... He can't take his eyes off him; he looks at him for a while and suddenly we see that his facial expression changes, wrinkles appear on his face, he turns back, and we see his shoulders trembling as he cries.

There is silence for a while. Then Sisona says:

Sisona: Is that all, Manuchar that you can do? Turning your back on your brother who you haven't seen for 13 years?

On hearing these words Manuchar turns around, he tries to smile but he fails. He starts walking towards Thoma wiping tears off his face with the back of his hands; it comes very close to him and as soon as he hugs him he starts crying and sobbing. Sisona looks at them and we see tears welling up in his eyes.

***

It's evening. A small table is laid on a terrace. Far away down a blanket of white foam covers the Black Sea coastline. Further away in the open sea glowing light on a silhouette of a small fishing boat is perceived from a distance like a glowing firefly. Manuchar, Sisona, Batsi, Thoma and Manuchar's sons are sitting at the table. Sisona is sitting between his nephews and he is hugging, petting and kissing them one after the other. The boys are both well-built and healthy-looking. Manuchar's wife brings some dish and puts it in the middle of the table. The men continue their conversation.

Manuchar: You know better, Thoma, but I think it's not a good idea to go back there… at least for a time being. Let's wait for the situation there to improve a little and then you'll have no problem. I understand that you miss Melita a lot… you said you couldn't wait to see her… I do understand it as we feel the same! But you should be mindful of and consider some likely consequences as well. What if, God forbid, something unpleasant happened to you there, can you think how would she feel? We can inform her that you're here, with us, safe and sound… She might feel better knowing that you're far away but safe and sound; in this case, she won't have to worry about you. You know I don't intend to make you do as I think is right. But still maybe you will think it over again. You can live in Sisona's house until you find a place of your own. You can live there together with your friends. We'll see then, depending on how things will go, we can either all move to Georgia or take Mom here. Communists can't carry on like this… in isolation.

Thoma: I understand everything well enough, Manuchar. But even if I do as you say… what about Batsi… He could have directly traveled from Berlin to Georgia together with others, but he didn't want me to travel alone, that's why he followed me and he's nowhere with me. I can't just tell him: "You know, thank you for accompanying me; now you may go alone as I'm staying here!" how can I do this?

Sisona: Yes, Thoma, but Manuchar told you that you could both stay at my house…

Thoma: Well, we have to ask him whether he wants to stay here or not. So, let's not waste our time. It's already been decided, we're returning to Georgia. Besides, I've told you that Batsi and I have done nothing wrong to provoke their interest. It can't be considered as our fault that we are alive! After all, we couldn't even manage to become soldiers.

Manuchar: But for Chekists, it makes no difference whether it's your fault or not... You're alive, that means you're guilty... You might not know them well enough... F...k them all! What makes me feel relieved a little is bearing in mind that Sisona and I have cut the throats of at least two of them!

We see that Batsi's facial expression changes as he hears the last words said by Manuchar. He seems not to like what he has just heard, but we can't yet guess why.

Manuchar: Well, Thoma, let it be as you say. But you have to follow one of the pieces of my advice. You shouldn't cross the border officially... just to be on the safe side. Sisona and I will arrange that. We have a few people ready to help us. We can show you the route that will lead you right to our house. And if we start early in the morning you'll be there until it gets dark. I'm sure you remember the Rukhumela gorge, so that route leads to the gorge and then you have to go straight ahead. It's the best option believe me. You'll get home and be safe there. They might even not notice your arrival. There so many of them there who return from war. Batsi will have to stay in our house night and leave to Tbilisi the next day. You may go there together; you said you wanted to visit Moshe, didn't you? As for money you don't have to worry about it. We'll give you enough Russian Rubles to keep you both going for quite a long period of time.

Thoma: I have nothing against it but let's ask Batsi opinion.

Batsi: As far as you guarantee that we cross the border without any troubles, I have nothing against it either.

Sisona: That's fine. Everything's going to be all right... Manuchar, wouldn't you like to give a toast?

Manuchar raises a glass full of wine and says:

Manuchar: Let's drink this toast to our guest, to Batsi. Thoma told us that he is like his brother, but today he's our guest... and that's why I want to propose a toast to Batsi and to bless him. May you never ever in your life experience the troubles that you've been through together with my brother and may our Heavenly Father have mercy on you and pave the way for you to stride along it safely and firmly, from now until the end of your days. May your friendship last forever and never ever be clouded by even thought of betraying each-other. As for you, Thoma, I wish you found a real friend in the person of Batsi, who'll be able to stand by you when we are so far away. I wish you all the best! Amen!

We hear the reply: Amen! Amen! And they empty their glasses.

***

The dense woods in the mountains... It's a foggy day. Manuchar, Sisona, Thoma, Batsi and a man, who seems to be their guide, are making their way through the trees. After a while the guide stops and says:

The guide: That's it, Manuchar-Effendi. We can't go any further. The guys have to go down and they'll find a small river. They have to cross that river and they'll find themselves in Gurjistan. They don't have to be afraid of anything, Manuchar-Effendi, they won't meet anyone there. When they have crossed that small river, they have to go uphill and then downhill again and there is the Rukhumela gorge there. You told me they knew how to find their way from that gorge to their home…

Manuchar: That's right, they do. I have explained it to them a thousand times. By the way, Thoma, you'll pass by the place where Dad was killed. There is an old ash-tree there. Do you remember the pitch-dark night we went to find Dad there, Sisona?

Sisona: Please, don't remind me of that terrible night!

The guide: Well, it's time to say good-bye. (He looks up in the sky and continues) It's going to rain. The river they have to cross is small, but it can swell all of a sudden, so they have to hurry.

Thoma: Do you remember calling on me at midnight, 13 years ago, when I was staying at Ivliane Vashalomidze?

Manuchar: Certainly, we do. What made you recall that night?

Thoma: And do you remember the way we said good-bye to one another?

Sisona: (smiles) I understand what you mean, Thoma, So, what are you waiting for? Start… It was you who started then…

Thoma starts singing the same song, but this time his voice no longer sounds childish. The brothers join him, they walk close to each-other singing, put their arms around one another's shoulders and go on singing for a while. The guide and Batsi watch them singing beautifully and smile.

***

It's evening. Thoma and Batsi are in the center of Thoma's village. It's raining, and the young men are standing under a huge lime-tree; they are wet from head to toes. Thoma is looking around. We see that almost nothing has changed there. We see Kallisto's snack bar and the entrance to the marketplace... everything is as it was before.

Thoma: I have the feeling that I'm in a dream, Batsi. I was a child when I left this place and what I feel it as if it were yesterday. Nothing has changed, what I see... Oh, yea, maybe except that building - it's a post-office; it wasn't there when I left this place. There was a post-office, of course, but not there.

Batsi: I wonder if they have a telephone in that post-office. I'll go and see, wait for me here, Thoma, I'll be back soon; I'll try to phone my family in Tbilisi. I don't want to make a surprise appearance as you did, I don't want them to be shocked.

Thoma: Ok, go... I'll be waiting for you here... But, please, don't be late... I can't wait to see Mom...

Batsi runs across a small square and into the post-office. There is no one either in the street or inside the building except for an elderly woman half-asleep behind a screen. She raises her head on hearing Batsi's footsteps and gives him a curious look. Batsi approaches the screen, with an unusual strict expression on his face, chooses a blank form from the sheets of paper lying in a disorderly heap there and makes a gesture indicating that he needs a pencil. The woman gives him one. Batsi writes a number on it, slips the paper under the screen together with the pencil and says sternly:

Batsi: I'll enter that box now, and you have to immediately connect me to this number. Look at it; I think you understand what it means!

The woman looks scared; she looks at the paper and promptly nods her head.

Batsi: Well, do it quickly and when I start speaking, don't forget to close your ears. Understood?

The woman nods her head again. Batsi enters the box. We see Thoma sitting on a wet tree root, with his eyes closed and his forehead exposed to the drops dripping off the tree leaves. Then he looks in the direction of the light coming from the window of the post-office, but he can see nothing inside as the window glass is covered in the rain.

We are in the post-office again. The woman is sitting. She has not only cupped her hands over her ears, but she has her eyes closed as well. We hear Batsi speaking inside the box.

Batsi: At 9 o'clock sharp! Neither a second early nor a second late! It's a strict requirement! Don't forget the performance. You have to treat me exactly as you treat him... That's all. I have to go now. See you tomorrow morning.

He hangs up, looks at the woman, smiles and says:

Batsi: It's over; you may open your eyes and uncover your ears, but... (He puts his finger to his lips and then continues) Understood? You mustn't tell anyone...

Batsi walks out of the building and towards the place where Thoma is waiting for him.

Thoma: Were you lucky?

Batsi: Don't ask me… I would have to wait till morning… Not a big problem. I'll call them from a street phone box when I am in Tbilisi… Let's go now. Where is your house… How long are we going to stand here in the rain?

Thoma: Let's go. I wonder if the bridge is there where it used to be. Do you hear the rumbling of the river? I have never seen it so swollen. God forbid but who happen to fall into it, will be doomed to drown.

They come from under the lime-tree and walk in the direction from where the rumbling of the river is heard. It's already dark.

***

We see Melita's face against the light coming from a kerosene lamp. Her hair is grey now, but her face is as beautiful as before. She is standing in front of the icon of the Virgin Mary as before, is looking at the icon with beseeching eyes and praying.

Melita: O, Ever-Virgin Mary, Holy Immaculate Mother of Our Lord who has been raised to Heaven, I humbly beseech Thee, Thou who radiate innocence and shine upon everything. I, the one who has sinned and fallen many times dare beseech Thee, as Thou are the Mother and I am a mother. Jesus Christ Our Lord was conceived in Thy womb and born as a man, but he, who I pray for, was not conceived in my womb, but, long time ago, he called me the divine word, the one that is life-giving for all women; he called me Mom, Virgin Mary, and that is why I pray for him to Thee.

I earnestly plead with Thee, protect and defend my Thoma, have your mercy upon him. And have mercy upon me - a sinner - grant me the strength and serenity to endure the pain of the time spent apart with him, as, if Thou hear the voice of my supplication and if Thou will is to return him safe and sound, do not deprive him of the joy of meeting his mom. Grant me the strength to live to once again hear the life-giving word – Mom!

Thoma: Mom!

Melita starts at hearing the call and listens attentively. She thinks she heard the call because she wanted to and then she hears again.

Thoma: Mom!

Melita jumps to her feet, breaks through the door leading to the hall and stops. Thoma is there smiling and saying in a calm voice:

Thoma: It's me, Mom, Thoma.

Thoma comes close to Melita and embraces her and kisses her grey hair. Melita is crying and Thoma tries to calm her down.

Thoma: Calm down Mom… It's over; it's all over; it's in the past. Everything is going to be all right from now on. What matters is that we are together again, you and me, Mom.

Batsi is standing at the door leading to the balcony and is watching the scene. He seems to be a little excited and we see some signs of regret crossing his features.

***

It's morning. A rooster flies up on the fence and crows very loudly. Then it turns it head towards the balcony and we see there Thoma standing and looking around; he gives everything a loving look. Then he stretches himself and enters the room. Batsi is dressed and is sitting on the bed. He looks at Thoma, who has just entered the room, first, and then at an old-fashioned clock hanging on the wall. The clock shows 8:30.

Thoma: What's up, Batsi? Just look at yourself! Is it because you didn't sleep well?

Batsi doesn't pay attention to his words and asks a question in response.

Batsi: Listen, does the clock show the correct time?

Thoma looks at the clock.

Thoma: Why are you asking me? Are you in a hurry? Melita will bring us warm milk in a couple of minutes. I've been missing its taste for 13 years.

Batsi doesn't react on these words either and asks again.

Batsi: Didn't you hear what I asked? Does this clock show the correct time?

Thoma: What's the matter with you, Batsi. Why do you keep repeating "clock" "clock". Yes, it shows the correct time. It's twenty-five to nine. My dad and I brought it from Germany. It always shows the correct time. If you like it so much, let it be, I can give it to you as a present.

Batsi: Listen Thoma. I don't have enough time to explain everything to you. Simply, you must do as I will tell you now.

Thoma: What MUST I do? What are you talking about? What's the matter with you! Just look at your face! Isn't it too early to play tricks on me?

Basti: No tricks, Thoma. You must run! Now! Your yard will be crowded by Chekists in twenty minutes. If you don't run now, then it will be late. You won't be able to escape them. You have to go back to Turkey. I hope you remember the route. Don't look at me like this. I warn you we don't have time for explanations. Run. I'll explain everything to your mother.

Thoma: What are you going to explain to her? Why should those Chekists be coming here? Did they see in their dreams that Thoma's returned? What are you talking about?

Batsi: You're really naïve, Thoma. Do you think that they would have sent seven young men to the borders of Germany just on the brink of war without one of them being a Cheka agent? I am that agent! Do you understand it now?! They didn't see you in their dreams. I informed them about you yesterday evening when I went to the post office… Run! I say run! 15 minutes are left and they'll be here. I will tell them that you've suspected something and run away. Hurry up! I'll send them in the opposite direction. But hurry up, man! Don't stand there like a statue. Don't look at me like this. I already know what you might be thinking of me right now, and I agree with you, agree to absolutely everything. But Go!

Thoma is shocked and confused. His facial expression has changed dramatically. He seems to find it difficult to believe what Batsi is saying. He goes to the window, draws the curtain and looks in the direction of the bond bridge. He sees Chekists coming. They are walking arranged in a line down a wet hill towards the bond bridge. He moves away from the window and sits down on the bed, with his head cast down, his elbows placed on his knees and holding his head in his hands. Batsi stands up, goes close to Thoma gets hold of his shoulders and starts shaking him.

Batsi: Don't you hear me? I've told you, we don't have time. Come on, stand up and run!

Thoma removes his hands from his head and looks up at Batsi giving him an empty look, stands up, takes two wandering steps towards the door leading to the balcony, then stops, turns around and looks into Batsi's eyes. We have a close look at Thoma with incredible frustration spread across his face. We guess he isn't going to run. Tears of sorrow well up in his eyes; all of a sudden, he throws his right hand up and punches Batsi right in the face.

Batsi loses balance stumbles over a chair and falls on the floor with a bang. He lies on the floor with his lip bleeding. He feels his lip with his palm, looks at the blood on it, then looks up at Thoma and says:

Batsi: Run!

Thoma doesn't move. He is standing still with a desperate and frustrated look on his face. Now we see Batsi's face and the expression on his face changes. He instantly jumps to his feet, grabs Thoma's arm and says:

Batsi: It's not too late. Let's go. Let's run together. I'm coming with you. They will never catch us and they won't shoot as I'll be with you. Ok, Thoma, Let's go!

Thoma: (hesitates and utters a single word) Melita?

Batsi: We don't have time for that. When she sees them, she'll guess what's going on and will feel relieved to know that we've run.

Chekists are crossing the bond bridge one by one. This time the door on the balcony opens and Thoma and Batsi run through it. They jump over the guardrail into the yard, and then they jump over the fence and run in the opposite direction from where the Chekists are coming. They start running uphill. The Chekists, who have already crossed the bond bridge, see them and immediately chase after them. Approximately a dozen of them are chasing after Thoma and Batsi. They find it difficult to run uphill with their heavy boots on the wet ground. But Thoma and Batsi have to stop all of a sudden as they find themselves standing on the edge of a cliff. Down there is a rushing river, behind them there are Chekists. Thoma and Batsi even hear them talking.

Chekist: Don't you dare shoot. If a bullet accidentally hits that one, we will be all doomed… Anyway, that can't run away… They are both ours.

Batsi and Thoma are standing on the edge of the cliff. Then Batsi looks at Thoma, smiles at him and says:

Batsi: What do you think, Chief, shall we do as before?

Thoma smiles back and says in a very low voice:

Thoma: Go! I'm with you.

Batsi, as once in the Alps, jumps off the cliff and plummets down to the river with a loud cry. Almost simultaneously Thoma throws himself off the cliff and their voices merge resounding in the air. And we leave the two friends here, flying down to the roaring and rumbling river.

***

Maria's yard and her house in Lithuania... Maria is sitting in the room knitting something. The door opens and a 4-or-5-year old child walks into the room. He looks like small Thoma. He is holding a toy with a bluebird and a cage in his hand. He is accompanied by another a bit older boy. Maria looks at both of them and says in Lithuanian:

Maria: Come in, Thomas! Who's that boy? Aren't you going to introduce him to me?

Thomas: Mom, this is Mindaugas. He arrived yesterday and is going to stay in the house next to ours for two weeks. Would you let us listen to Dad's song?

Maria: Of course, Thomas. Wait a minute; I'll turn on the tape recorder.

Maria puts the ball of yarn and knitting needles aside, stands up and goes to the tape recorder we have seen before. She turns it on and we hear the voices of Thoma and his friend on the recording once made during a rehearsal. We listen to the song together with Thomas and his friend Mindaugas.

We hear someone coughing and Thoma's voice singing "Voisa". Gigi joins him but his voice cracks as he tries to sing higher. Then we hear laughter followed by Ushba asking "What are you laughing at?" Than we hear Thom's voice saying: "Maria don't stop recording. We'll start from the beginning." And they start from the beginning and sing. Thomas keeps commenting on what we hear:

Thomas: It's my dad coughing... Dad starts singing... Dad laughing...

Then Thomas stops commenting and listens to the song with a serious expression on his face. Then he says:

Thomas: I'll go to Georgia when I grow up. I have to learn Dad's song.

Mindaugas: Why do you need to learn that silly song?

Thomas: Why? Because I am Georgian!

We see Maria's face, giving her son a loving look.

Then on the background of the song and relevant reverberation we once again see the picturesque view from a hill where the old pomegranate tree is standing. The image Theopile and Thoma used to see, but this time we also see Thomas' eyes full of light as a background on the screen.

The End

www.ingramcontent.com/pod-product-compliance
Lightning Source LLC
LaVergne TN
LVHW041055080826
845145LV00007B/1585

* 9 7 8 1 7 3 3 9 5 8 2 0 2 *